DUBLIN'S SUBURBAN TOWNS, 1834–1930

Maynooth Historical Studies

GENERAL EDITOR, RAYMOND GILLESPIE

Over the last three generations the study of Irish history has been transformed almost out of recognition. The work of scholars such as J.C. Beckett, R. Dudley Edwards, R.B. McDowell, T.W. Moody and D.B. Quinn established scholarly standards within which the study of Irish history could proceed and, with their students, demonstrated in their writing how those standards could be applied. In the main these writings concentrated on the traditional historical themes, dealing with the political and constitutional problems which Ireland encountered in the past. More recently a new generation of scholars have built on these insights but have also looked again at the traditional canon of Irish history. Some have re-examined older problems in the light of fresh evidence or new conceptual models. Others have broadened the range of the debate on the Irish past by insisting on the importance of economic, social, local or cultural factors in shaping the Irish historical experience.

The result of this expansion in historical research has been a dramatic growth in publications dealing with the whole range of Irish history and hence a series of lively debates on the nature of the study of the Irish past. Maynooth Historical Studies is part of that new phenomenon. The series contributes to the debate on the interpretation of the Irish past by presenting the results of new research which either looks again at old problems or casts light into hitherto dark corners of the historical landscape. Both the individual volumes, and the series as a whole, reflect the complexity of understanding the evolution of Irish society and in so doing presents the study of Irish history as the vibrant and challenging discipline that it is.

IN THIS SERIES

Dublin's suburban towns
1834–1930

*Governing Clontarf, Drumcondra, Dalkey, Killiney,
Kilmainham, Pembroke, Kingstown, Blackrock,
Rathmines and Rathgar*

SÉAMAS Ó MAITIÚ

FOUR COURTS PRESS

Typeset in 11 pt on 12.5 pt Ehrhardt by
FOUR COURTS PRESS LTD
7 Malpas Street, Dublin 8, Ireland
e-mail: info@four-courts-press.ie
http://www.four-courts-press.ie
and in North America
FOUR COURTS PRESS
c/o ISBS, 920 N.E. 58th Street, Suite 300, Portland, OR 97213.

A catalogue record for this title is available
from the British Library.

ISBN 1-85182-722-6 hbk
ISBN 1-85182-723-4 pbk

SPECIAL ACKNOWLEDGMENT

This publication was grant-aided by the Heritage Council of Ireland
under the 2003 Publication Grant Scheme.

AN
CHOMHAIRLE
OIDHREACHTA

THE
HERITAGE
COUNCIL

Printed in Great Britain
by MPG Books, Bodmin, Cornwall.

Contents

Abbreviations

CSORP	Chief Secretary's Office Registered Papers
DB	Dublin Builder
DCA	Dublin City Archives
DLRCCA	Dún Laoghaire-Rathdown County Council Archives
DTC	Dublin Tramways' Company
FJ	Freeman's Journal
HC	House of Commons
IB	Irish Builder
IFS	Irish Free State
IT	Irish Times
NAI	National Archives of Ireland
NLI	National Library of Ireland
RFP	Rathmines Free Press
RNDL	Rathmines News & Dublin Lantern
SDC	South Dublin Chronicle
SN	Saunder's Newsletter
UDC	Urban District Council

Illustrations

PLATE CREDITS

Author's collection: 5, 10, 11, 13, 14, 18, 19; Dublin Civic Museum: 7; Dún Laoghaire/Rathdown county council: 12; Irish Picture Library: 1, 2, 6, 15, 16, 21; Kearns postcard collection: 3, 17; National Library of Ireland: 8; Rathmines Senior College: 9; Brian Siggins: 20.

Acknowledgments

I would like to thank Professor Vincent Comerford of the department of modern history, National University of Ireland, Maynooth for the opportunity to pursue a PhD in history and my supervisor, Dr Jacqueline Hill, for her consistent advice and encouragement from the start. I would also like to thank Dr Jacinta Prunty (NUI Maynooth) and Dr Maura Cronin (Mary Immaculate College, Limerick) for their helpful suggestions on reading the thesis on which this book is based. The editorial expertise of Dr Raymond Gillespie is deeply appreciated.

Thanks are also due to individuals and staffs of the various archives and libraries which have helped me in my researches. These include: the director and staff of the National Library of Ireland; the staffs of the John Paul II Library Maynooth, and of the Berkeley Library, Trinity College Dublin; the staff of the National Archives, Dublin and Paul Ferguson of the Map Library, Trinity College, Dublin. Special thanks to Mary Clark and her assistants in the Dublin City Archives, Máire Kennedy and staff of the Gilbert Library, Dublin, Tina Hynes in the Fingal County Archive, and Martin Allen of Dún Laoghaire/Rathdown County Council for access to its extensive collection of Kingstown, Blackrock, Dalkey and Killiney archives. The staffs of the Irish Architectural Archive and the Architectural Library, University College Dublin, Richview proved very helpful also.

The members of Rathmines, Ranelagh and Rathgar Historical Society, especially Noel Healy, Tom Harris, Angela O'Connell of Rathmines Public Library, and the late Deirdre Kelly were particularly helpful with their knowledge of the area. Brian Siggins and Jim Cooke were of assistance in queries relating to the Pembroke township and the history of vocational education in Dublin. Peter Walsh was very helpful in providing material in helping me to trace the boundary of the Meath estate, and Stephen Hannon of the map library, Department of Geography, UCD, helped me in the preparation of others. I would like to thank Michael Adams and his staff at Four Courts Press, especially Martin Fanning, for their patience, professional help and guidance.

The trustees of the National Library of Ireland are acknowledged for permission to reproduce illustrations from the Frederick Stokes album; also Séamus Kearns and David Davison for material from their extensive collections.

Tá buíochas ar leith tuillte ag Gráinne, Aoife agus Connla as m'airese orthu a roinnt leis an saothar seo leis na blianta. Mo bheannacht leat, a scríbhinn!

In the centre of Fedora, that grey stone metropolis stands a metal building with a crystal globe in every room. Looking into each globe, you see a blue city, the model of a different Fedora. These are the forms the city could have taken if, for one reason or another, it had not become what we see today. In every age someone, looking at Fedora as it was, imagined a way of making it the ideal city, but while he constructed his miniature model, Fedora was no longer the same as before, and what had until yesterday a possible future became only a toy in a glass globe.

Italo Calvino, *Invisible cities*

Introduction

I grew up in the shadow of Rathmines Town Hall, and so was aware from an early age that Rathmines must have been a town, and so it was. It and eight other suburban areas in Dublin were legally constituted towns, each with its own town hall, administration and staff. Apart from the presence of a number of town halls, these entities have largely been forgotten, buried under what has now become sprawling suburbs. Even in their heyday in the nineteenth century, these areas were suburban in character, marking them out from all other areas designated as towns in Ireland. For that reason the title 'township', found in no other Irish context, was more commonly applied to them, and this is the title mostly used in this book. I also became aware of the name 'township' as a child when I upturned a vase full of household bric-a-brac and out fell a shiny brass button inscribed 'Rathmines Township' which had belonged to my firefighter grandfather. This further aroused my curiosity about the history of the area, culminating, many decades later, in the present work. While the nine towns were designated 'urban districts' under the 1898 local government act, the name 'township' continued to be generally used when referring to them, and this is the practice followed here.

Mary Daly, in her plea for a more balanced view of Irish history, says that 'growing tolerance and the cooling of nationalist passions permits the realisation that Irish history was made, not just in the countryside, but also in the towns, and that the Victorian architecture of Rathmines and Monkstown is part of the Irish heritage, as much as the thatched cottages or round towers'.[1] While things have begun to change in the decade and a half since those words were written, there is no doubt that urban history has been greatly neglected in Ireland. Indeed, urban history does not have a long pedigree as a recognized academic subject in these islands. James Dyos, who became professor of urban history at Leicester University, was the driving force behind the establishment of the Urban History Group which was set up in the university in 1963. Subsequently the *Urban History Yearbook*, which later became *Urban History*, was inaugurated. For the first time, the city was being directly addressed and not just tangentially as had been the case until then. With the publication of *The study of urban history*, the proceedings of a seminar on the subject held at Leicester in 1966, the subject had well and truly arrived as a serious academic discipline in its own right.

Dyos' abiding interest was the Victorian city, and the two-volume work, *The Victorian city: images and realities*, which he co-edited, displayed the multifaceted approach to the subject matter then in vogue. Dyos made a particular study of the development of suburbs and his seminal work on the process of suburbanization in a particular area, *Victorian suburb: a study of the growth of Camberwell*, was published in 1961.[2]

This interest in the suburbs by the key figure in the new sub-discipline put it at the heart of urban studies from the start, and within ten years, a number of studies of other suburban areas had been undertaken; a distillation of some of the best was published under the title of *The rise of suburbia* in 1982.[3] Urban history as established by Dyos was very much an interdisciplinary subject, with an input from historians, geographers, planners, sociologists and economists. The Leicester-based urban history emerged from a particular milieu; the early sixties was a time when urban life was the focus of much debate arising from problems such as inner city blight, alienation of youth and violence. From the ensuing soul-searching arose a new interest in conservation, planning and the creation of a renewed built environment.

In Ireland, especially in Dublin, many of the same forces were at work. As much of the Georgian fabric was subjected to the demolition ball, and inner city communities were moved wholesale to the periphery, a renewed interest in what was being lost led to conservationists and academics coming together to fight such campaigns as that to save Wood Quay and whole terraces of Georgian squares. At the academic level, the outcome has been a renewed interest in Viking, medieval and Georgian Dublin. Much of the scholarly work produced so far by this movement has concerned itself with these periods.[4]

The nineteenth century was late in gaining recognition, largely one suspects, because, as Mary E. Daly points out, historians are not as much at ease portraying success as failure;[5] and the history of nineteenth-century Dublin has been perceived as a story of stagnation and deterioration, despite the creation of an impressive band of Victorian and Edwardian development enveloping the decaying core. However, in the 1980s things were beginning to change, especially with the publication of Mary E. Daly's own pioneering *Dublin: the deposed capital*, a work that recognized the part played by the suburbs in the overall development of the city. The thrust of Daly's work was essentially economic and social, but due regard was paid to the part played by urban politics and administration. This aspect of Dublin history has also been explored by J.V. O'Brien in *Dear dirty Dublin: a city in distress, 1899–1916*.[6] For the first time the social reality behind the much-written of city of Yeats, Synge, and Joyce was explored, with attention being focused on the administrative deficiencies which were seen as the cause of much of the social devastation faced by the citizens. In Daly's work in particular, the importance of the suburbs and their interaction with the core was recognized, but the main focus was on the city.

Comparative urban history began to receive sustained attention with the inauguration of the *Irish historic towns atlas*, under the auspices of the Royal Irish Academy and a series of Thomas Davis lectures on cities and towns now available in print.[7] Hitherto, however, Irish suburbs have not been the subject of sustained analysis. Suburban accretions to the city were looked at by various essayists, although not in any great depth, in *Victorian Dublin* (1980), and more recently the architecture of the suburbs has begun to be celebrated.[8] Two postgraduates have studied the development of two squares in the Rathmines area – Susan Roundtree in the case of Mountpleasant Square and Ann Lavin in that of Leinster Square and Prince Arthur Terrace.[9] The latter's work, in particular, has been valuable in revealing the manner in which speculative builders went about their business.

More recent published work by the late Deirdre Kelly on the Rathmines area and Peter Pearson on Kingstown/Dún Laoghaire,[10] while excellent in themselves, have also largely concentrated on the social and architectural aspects of those areas. As in the works of Roundtree and Lavin, the existence of an administrative authority overseeing development in the suburbs is acknowledged but is not the main focus. The volume on twentieth-century suburban housing by Ruth McManus in the making of Dublin city series is a welcome addition.[11]

K.T. Hoppen reminds us that Irish politics should not be perceived as revolving around great national issues alone, but that for voters politics was often seen as 'local, immediate and pragmatic'.[12] This preoccupation with the local was common, and was summed up well by Derek Fraser:

> Politics for Victorians, unlike ourselves, began not at Westminster but at their own front gates. Whether the pavement was drained and swept, whether the poor should be incarcerated in poorhouses ... depended upon the exercise of power and were issues of as much intrinsic political interest as great questions of national policy.[13]

Great and pressing questions faced 'big government' in Ireland in the last century and this has tended to squeeze out an appreciation of the achievements of local government. L.P. Curtis, Jr. has called the local government bill of 1892 an 'unwanted child' of political liaisons.[14] It could be stated, indeed, that local administration itself, was looked upon as such a liability and was subordinated to national aims. While the cliché that all politics is local is often trotted out, historical analysis of politics at that level has also been something of a neglected child. This has now begun to be redressed since the centenary of the 1898 local government act and the establishment of urban district councils and county councils in 1899. A number of excellent county council histories have been produced, allowing for the first time the contribution of local politics to national life in the twentieth century to be appreciated.[15]

In studies of the history of nineteenth and early twentieth century Dublin an overgloomy picture has been presented. While the city grew but slowly and unemployment and under-employment were widespread, the suburban expansion was dynamic. The leafy suburban avenues and squares and the city slums were two sides of the one coin. While the poor and their living conditions, and even the protestant working classes, have received some attention, the middle classes, both catholic and protestant, have not attracted much study. The achievement of these groups through their local government bodies was mainly in the provision of basic services which are taken so much for granted today. They have also left an architectural legacy in both domestic and municipal building which gives to the inner suburbs of Dublin so much of their character.

Much of the British research has dealt with patterns of landownership, estate management and the activities of building speculators. In Dublin the presence of a large number of self-governing townships, the biggest of which displayed a remarkable longevity, was of paramount importance in the development of both city and suburbs. The powers vested in these townships, albeit at times of a very limited nature, provided the framework within which the suburbs developed.

The urbanizing process put old institutions like the grand jury and Dublin corporation under severe strain in the early and mid-nineteenth century. The ineffectiveness of these authorities in the face of urgent and pressing infrastrucural needs created an administrative vacuum that was filled by a middle-class urban élite consisting of builders, businessmen and professionals. The privileges of membership of élite township boards tended to create cohesion, but strains along sectarian, partisan and class fault lines are evident.

The aim of this work is to examine how élite groups in the expanding middle-class suburbs of Dublin from the mid-nineteenth century attempted to solve the problem of the provision of basic services needed to allow civilized life to advance, and the impact the methods chosen to achieve these ends had on the development of the greater Dublin area. The weakness of the existing local government institutions led to the creation of townships to achieve these aims, and the forces behind the establishment of the townships are examined, their *modus operandi* and achievement, and their impact on the development of the city, explored.

While the attainments of the largest, wealthiest and most successful township, Rathmines, is taken as the major case study, the focus shifts to one or more of the other eight townships when their actions have a major impact on the general scene or their records throw light on the administration of all.

In attempting to disentangle the complex skein of local administration I hope to contribute in some way towards an understanding and appreciation of the largely forgotten entities of the Dublin townships and the men and women who served in their administration. While the individual and collective achievements of the townships can be celebrated, set in the context of the greater Dublin area they had their negative side. The underfunding of the corporation, partly owing to the flight of the middle classes to the suburbs, allowed the appalling slum conditions so tellingly analysed by Jacinta Prunty, to fester.[16] I hope that this study of the other side of the coin, albeit largely focused on the administrative rather than the social, will help complete the picture.

The rejection of the existing local government structures and, in particular, the antipathy of the founding fathers of the Rathmines and Pembroke townships towards Dublin corporation are examined here. This aversion ran deeper than a simple lack of confidence in the corporation's ability to fulfill suburban needs such as a water supply and sewerage. The suburbanites' attitude was coloured by a complex socio-religious gulf between city and suburbs. The flight from the city centre by the middle classes was a phenomenon common to cities throughout the United Kingdom in the nineteenth century. The social gulf between those left behind in the neglected city centre and the businessmen, officials and clerks moving to the suburbs in Dublin had a religious and political complexion. While it is often difficult to attach religious labels to particular groups involved in the establishment and operation of townships, the book attempts to discern political and religious undercurrents which had a bearing on developments in the suburbs.

The fragmentation of local government as a result of the establishment of townships and the lack of an integrated structure supplying services in the city and suburbs are examined, in particular the problem of funding a satisfactory level of services from a small number of ratepayers. The rational recommendations of the Exham commission are outlined and the tardy and inadequate response of the government examined. An attempt is made to trace the evolution of the townships as they were moulded by new legislation consisting of various acts of parliament relating to services, as well as larger innovations such as the establishment of the local government board in 1872, and the landmark local government act of 1898.

Despite penny-pinching and parsimony, especially in the early years, by the 1920s the range of services provided by the townships had blossomed into a sturdy plant of many branches. A local historian of Liverpool in 1907 described the 'from cradle to grave' nature of services provided by his municipal authority which can almost in its entirely be applied to the Dublin townships:

> It offers to see that the child is brought safely into the world. It provides him in infancy with suitable food. It gives him playgrounds to amuse himself in and baths to swim in. It takes him to school ... it trains him for his future trade. It sees that the citizen's house is properly built and sometimes even builds it for him. It brings into his rooms an unfailing supply of pure water from the remote hills. It guards his food and tries to secure that it is not dangerously adulterated. It sweeps the streets for him and disposes of the refuse of his house. It carries him swiftly to

and from his work. It gives him good books to read, pictures look at, music to listen to and lectures to stimulate his thought. If he is sick it nurses him; if he is penniless it houses him; and when he dies, if none other will, it buries him![17]

The political world in which the townships were created was transformed with the struggle for Irish independence and the founding of the Irish Free State. A section of the work is devoted to the reactions of the various townships to the changed political situation in which they found themselves in this transitionery period. While the concentration of scholarship has been on the polical and military aspects of the period 1916 to 1921, the activities of Dáil Éireann's department of local government has been examined to a limited extent.[18] The impact of the events at the local level has been neglected, with the notable exception of David Fitzpatrick's study of County Clare.[19] The response in the Dublin townships to events of the 1916 rising and the war of independence is outlined and the attitude of the new independent Irish government, which many activists in the townships helped create, to the existing local government structure in the Dublin area examined. This attitude would lead to the demise of the townships.

The book is divided into eight chapters. As in much historical writing a problem arose as to whether to follow a strict chronology or separate themes. The chronological approach is predominantly followed here. Chapter 1 examines the pre-existing state of the Dublin suburbs, their local government and chronicles the establishment of the townships. Chapter 2 analyses the composition of township boards and their *modus operandi*.

The provision of services can be divided roughly into early and late, the basic and infrastructural on the one hand and the cultural and recreational on the other. Basic services are reviewed in chapter 3 and the later and more cultural services in chapter 6. Chapter 4 considers the Exham commission and the influence of national legislation on the townships. Chapter 5 looks at important changes resulting form the 1898 local government act and subsequent legislation. Chapters 7 and 8 analyse the response of the local bodies to war, both international and national, and the creation of a new state which would lead to the eventual demise of the townships.

We are fortunate that of the nine Dublin townships, the records of six are extant. Rathmines & Rathgar, Pembroke, Blackrock, Kingstown/Dún Laoghaire, Dalkey and Killiney all survived as separate entities up to 1930, and the fact that they kept charge of their own records ensured that they escaped the destruction of the Public Record Office in 1922. The records of the townships abolished in 1900, Kilmainham, Drumcondra and Clontarf are missing. Dublin corporation was the natural inheritor of such material but no evidence of it being in the possession of the corporation has been found. While it is possible that the records had been transferred to the Public Record Office after 1900 and were destroyed in the destruction of the office, it is strange that Herbert Woods does not list them in his comprehensive catalogue of material deposited in the office before 1922.

The material for the other six townships is extensive. It includes an almost complete set of manuscript minutes for all board committee meetings for the entire period of their existence and many minutes of sub-committee meetings, roads' committees, finance committees etc. In the case of Kingstown, from the 1880s, as well as the manuscript version, printed minutes are extant together with a set of invaluable reports drawn up by various committees, township medical officers, surveyors and other officials. The records are distributed between two archives. The Rathmines and Pembroke material is found in the Dublin City Archives, situated in its magnificent premises in Pearse Street. Apart from a complete run of township board minutes, also deposited there are committee minutes, especially those relating to the Rathmines and Pembroke main drainage board, maps and other miscellaneous material. The records of Dublin corporation, a body that was central to the fortunes of the townships, are also preserved in the Dublin City Archives. Of most importance to the study of the townships have been the manuscript and printed minute books of the municipal council. The manuscript volumes, covering varying periods of time were consulted from 1840. Printed minutes, generally bound in annual volumes appeared from 1881, and these were consulted to 1930. The municipal corporation also printed annual reports from 1869 which have also proved useful.

An extensive collection of records of Blackrock, Kingstown/Dún Laoghaire, Dalkey and Killiney townships is deposited in the archives in the headquarters of Dún Laoghaire/Rathdown county council, Dún Laoghaire. These include a complete run of minutes of the township boards except that of Killiney. Killiney township was founded in 1866, but extant minute books commence in 1871. As well as the minutes of the township boards and of various committees, there are also records of the Blackrock main drainage board, and some deeds and plans relating to various townships. In the case of Kingstown a report book of the medical officer of health for the period 1922–9 also exists. As in the case of Rathmines and Pembroke very little correspondence survives relating to the four coastal townships.

The township minutes are limited as sources for the history of the bodies for which they were compiled. In general they tend to record resolutions put to the meetings and not much of the discussion leading up to them. Sometimes a summary of the argument is included and sometimes not. Because of this it is necessary to supplement and flesh out the meagre official accounts by reference to newspaper reports, when available. This is difficult for the early period, as many bodies, including Rathmines, did not allow the press access to board meetings for many years.

Another limiting factor is the fact that discussion often took place as a result of correspondence from central government, other bodies or indeed individual ratepayers, which does not survive. To add to the one-sidedness of the remaining material, voluminous correspondence with the Irish local government board from 1872 can be studied only on the township side because the records of the board, along with much other local government material, was destroyed in the Custom House fire in 1920.

CHAPTER ONE

Establishing townships

The emergence of suburbia, in the sense of an almost exclusively residential area on the outskirts of cities and towns, has been largely ascribed to the post-1815 period.[1] However, it has antecedents in the eighteenth century in the larger cities like Dublin, and in London in the late seventeenth century. In London, a city in which much of Dublin's architectural and cultural influences lie, Covent Garden and Bloomsbury were developed in the period leading up to 1700 as single-purpose residential districts in the West End as distinct from the City. By the standards of the Victorian period, the degree of social segregation achieved in these new areas was moderate. The necessary presence of outdoor servants and their families in the mews at the back of the fashionable houses to look after horses, carriages and equipage (important status symbols of the time) made total segregation impossible.

The Victorians went much further in the process. They were, in the words of Donald J. Olsen, speaking of London,

> in part consciously, transforming the metropolis into an environment designed to reinforce certain specific values, notably privacy for the individual and his family; specialization and segregation were important means to that end. They (the Victorians) gave London order and system, not – like the Paris of Baron Haussmann – essentially visual and spatial in nature; but rather functional, moral and social.[2]

The phenomenon of residential suburbs has been much decried by social scientists, architects and others, but its very ubiquity is a testament to its attractions for vast numbers of people. The process benefited landowners, developers, speculative builders and fulfilled for the occupants of the new suburbs complex psychological and sociological needs. Its effects on the urban core, however, were detrimental, and in the mechanism through which it was achieved in much of the Dublin suburbs in the Victorian era, had far-reaching consequences for the development of the greater Dublin area.

While the great cities had been growing by accretion for centuries, it was reckoned that by the mid-nineteenth century every town which reached a critical mass of around 50,000 inhabitants was capable of sustaining some form of suburb.

Early suburbs, areas outside medieval city walls, had an unsavoury reputation. They became the refuge of those outside the civic juristiction, criminals and those engaged in obnoxious or dangerous occupations. Cook Street, where the highly hazardous task of cooking with fire took place, just outside Dublin's remaining medieval gate, St Audeon's, is a vivid reminder today of this relegation of the dangerous to an early suburb.

As the city began to expand, extra-mural land was appropiated for residential as well as occupational purposes. Dublin's medieval liberties and the Viking district on the north bank of the Liffey were early suburbs. By the time of John Speed's well-known 1610 map, the urban area was spilling out out in all directions especially to the east where Trinity College had been established.

The population of Dublin experienced a continuous growth from the middle ages. The figure of around 60,000 in 1700 had trebled by the end of the century. This growth began to slow down after the union, with an increase from 182,000 in 1800 to 232,726 in 1841.

Residential suburbs in most European cities tended to be on their west side, as was the case in Paris and London. Such expansion was precluded in Dublin owing to barriers such as the Phoenix Park and undesirable industrial development in the Liberties area. From the beginning of the eighteenth century, fashionable expansion was to the north.[3] Planned suburbs were created when Luke Gardiner bought the Moore estate north of the Liffey in 1714 and expanded his holdings from there. In 1730 he began to build Henrietta Street and went on to develop Dorset Street and Sackville Street. His descendants continued the work, culminating in the development of Mountjoy Square in 1792 under Luke Gardiner II.[4]

Another area of fashion developed around the St Stephen's Green area south of the river and the Dawson Street and Molesworth Street area especially after the erection of Leinster House in 1745 by James Fitzgerald, the earl of Kildare, later the duke of Leinster. There was also a move east by merchants, especially after the building of Essex bridge prevented ships from docking at the old quays further upstream. This trend culminated with the building of the new Custom House (1791) far to the east. The old houses of the wealthy and the merchants became the living quarters of the artisans and workers especially in the labour-intensive textile industry.[5] The new suburbs were planned as residential, although the need for manual workers and retainers saw to it that the back lanes, courts and especially mews became the residences of whole families.

In the years after the union there was a switch back south with the Fitzwilliam estate (later known as the Pembroke estate), spilling out beyond the canals.[6] This shift was accelerated in 1848 when the Gardiner estate was sold and broken up leading to a rapid decline of that area of the north side.[7]

The exodus of merchants and traders from Dublin city is difficult to quantify before the Victorian period. Jacqueline Hill has pointed out that the Dublin

directories of the eighteenth and early nineteenth centuries do not include separate residences of city businessmen. The reason for this is that usually the residence and place of business were the same. However, by the 1790s this can be
no longer taken for granted, and by the 1830s the directories often list separate
places of abode.[8] From the early 1850s the Dublin directories began to include
the city suburbs in a full and consistent way. From *Thom's directory* it is possible to build up a picture of the extent of suburban expansion. Ribbon development along the main arteries to the city was the usual pattern of development,
with individual villa-type houses springing up, succeeded in time by semi-
detached and terraced dwellings. Roads were then built off the main thoroughfares to open up new land for houses; many of these roads eventually became
'cross roads' linking the main arteries. A process of infilling then began. This
new development took place in areas already possessing small scattered villages.
Ringsend, two miles to the east of the General Post Office in Sackville Street,
was once a fishing village and the embarkment point for ferries to England and
Wales. Its industries had included a glass and salt works. By the 1850s it was
poor and dilapidated, with a greatly depleted fishing fleet and a small boat-
building industry. *Thom's directory* of 1853 described it as consisting of several
streets of very indifferent and irregularly-built houses, chiefly poor, and many
dilapidated. Together with Irishtown it had a population of nearly three and a
half thousand. To the west of Ringsend, Ballsbridge, on the road to Kingstown
and Bray, had a population of 573 and boasted several villas. Booterstown, the
next village on the road, had a population of 535 living in 109 houses; however,
ribbon development had taken place to such an extent that it was said to be
almost continuous with Williamstown to the south and Merrion to the north.
Blackrock had a population of nearly 2,500. It was described as consisting of
one main and several minor streets and avenues containing 485 houses, 'well
but irregularly built'. It was described as standing 'in a diversified country, studded with numerous marine and other pleasing villas, embellished with tastefully
laid out grounds, commanding fine views of the sea and mountains'.[9] Kingstown
with a population of some 10,500, was the mail packet station of Dublin, and
was linked to the city by the Dublin and Kingstown railway. Its principal street,
George's Street, was some half a mile in length and off it were some 70 avenues,
terraces and parades. A mere fishing village before the erection of the harbour
in 1817, it had since experienced a huge growth.[10] Dalkey was a picturesque
village at the extremity of Dublin Bay, eight miles from the General Post Office
in Sackville Street. It had 40 houses and a population of 250. Killiney to the
south of Dalkey, was so underdeveloped, that it did not merit an inclusion in
the directories at this time.[11]

The Leeson Street/Donnybrook Road artery led to the Stillorgan area with
its large villas. Beyond the Grand Canal, Charlemont Street led to Ranelagh on
the road to Dundrum and Enniskerry. Ranelagh had 439 houses on one main

street and a number of avenues and one square, Mountpleasant Square, built by the Dolan family, who will feature prominently in our discussion of the Rathmines township. Ranelagh was almost contiguous to the village of Cullenswood a half a mile south. The area included a large nursery owned by Messrs Toole and Mackey. Rathmines was approached by Mount Pleasant Avenue, an old path to Milltown, and Rathmines Road. It had a population of over 3,000 and included over 450 houses. Portobello artillery and cavalry barracks dominated the ground between it and Harold's Cross. To the south of Rathmines lay Rathgar which had less than half the number of houses of Rathmines. According to the *Thom's directory* of 1853 Rathgar had only sprung up in the previous twenty years; it stated that in 1823 there were but two or three houses or cottages on the road there.[12]

Harold's Cross, dominated by its ancient green and the more recent Mount Jerome cemetery and convent of St Clare, was the only other suburban area, besides Ringsend, to boast of any industrial activity. In this case the industry was confined to one large concern, the Greenmount cotton factory of Messrs Pim to the right of the village as one crossed the Grand Canal. Steam and water capable of powering 100 looms and 6,000 spindles gave employment to a large number of hands. The area to the south-west of the city leading to Crumlin was largely unbuilt on. To the west lay the suburban village of Kilmainham, dominated by a number of large institutions, such as the Royal Hospital, with up to 250 veterans and officers, and Richmond barracks; the woollen mills of Messrs Willans provided employment in the area.[13]

Turning now to the north side of the Liffey, the Phoenix Park precluded development in the north-west. The three highways out of the city on the north side were Drumcondra Road, Ballybough Road and the North Strand. Development here was of a very limited nature compared to the south side. One reason had been the presence of a large number of toll roads in the vicinity. The village of Drumcondra had no terraces of houses linking it to the city as many areas of the southern suburbs had. It was, however, an area of large houses and villas, topped by Marino, the house of the earl of Charlemont. The Roman catholic college of All Hallows also occupied a prominent position. To the north of Ballybough Road some development had taken place in the Richmond and Marino Crescent district. Much of the area to the east of this however, on the approach road to Clontarf was slobland. Clontarf itself, three miles from the General Post Office had a population of 875, inhabiting 138 houses. Originally a fishing village, in 1853 it consisted of a street running from the seashore to the gate of Clontarf castle, owned by the Vernon family.[14]

The modest suburbanisation depicted here at mid-century greatly accelerated over the next 50 years. Those who had a long familiarity with Dublin saw the flight from the city by the upper and middle classes as the cause of many of the city's problems. T.W. Russell, MP for South Tyrone and secretary to the local government board in England, who had taken a keen interest in Dublin for thirty-six years and had resided for a number of years in Rathmines, stated that Dublin in 1900 was 'essentially a city of poor people, and, to a large extent, of very poor people'. The change in the circumstances of Dublin, which had been going on since the time of the union, if not before, was, he claimed one of the most remarkable things he knew of anywhere. He reported to a parliamentary inquiry in 1900:

> At the end of the last century it had been the home of the nobility and gentry of Ireland. Since then, owing to political changes, there had been a continuous stream of better-class people out of the city into the townships and suburbs ... the homes of the old nobility were (now) either warehouses, convents, or hospitals and the homes of the better classes who had gone into the suburbs, had been occupied by a class lower, and he could name streets, and especially on the north side of the city, occupied, when he went to Dublin, by mercantile and professional people, which were now poor lodging houses, and in many cases tenements.[15]

The only ground on which middle-class houses could be built was on the fringes of the city as the municipal area was almost entirely built up. The percentage of the metropolitan population living in the suburbs ringing the city boundary rose from 12.4 in 1831 to 29.6 in 1891.[16]

When the corporation of Dublin was reformed in 1840 its boundaries were set at the canals. The area of the city was 3,655 acres and the fact that these were largely built on and that many of the buildings were decrepit and quickly falling into decay posed many problems for the city. Saddled also, as it was, with many charitable institutions such as hospitals and poor houses, the city was being retarded by falling valuation and burdensome responsibilities. So, instead of developing Dublin city was constrained and thwarted in its growth and progress.

By the thirteenth century much of the land later covered by the Rathmines, Pembroke, Blackrock, Kingstown, Dalkey and Killiney townships and known as Cuala(nn), anglicized as Colyn or Colon, was owned by the archbishop of Dublin. The northern part of this land, stretching from the city south as far as Ranelagh and Rathmines was within the archbishop's manor of St Sepulchre.[17] By the 1840s, however, the manor had no administrative functions left to it and can be dismissed as not relevant to our study.

In the 1840s, Dublin, city and county, was under the control of three local government bodies, the municipal corporation, the grand jury of the county of the city of Dublin, and County Dublin grand jury. The grand jury system, arising as it did in response to the needs of a rural and land-owning élite, was totally unsuited to the very different suburban experience, and even in its native rural environment, was regarded as being inefficient and corrupt. The main criticism was that it was controlled by large landowners, was unrepresentative of cess-payers and that its *ad hoc* nature and lack of corporate existence led to gross mismanagement.

A number of attempts were made in the early nineteenth century to make the grand jury more representative. By an act of 1819 greater flexibility was introduced into the system. Presentment sessions could now be held at baronial level. This provided for work to be done and charged on the barony rather than on the county at large. From 1833 on, the baronial sessions included from five to twelve members chosen from a list of the 100 largest ratepayers in the county, and the county at large sessions were to include one cesspayer chosen by the baronial sessions.[18] Parish vestries still had some residual local government func-tions. The only function that impinged on the work of the townships was that of firefighting; this will be referred to when basic services will be discussed (Chapter 3). The poor law introduced new administrative units; south Dublin became a poor law union of which Rathmines and Donnybrook became a dis-trict electoral division, electing two guardians each.[19]

Shortly before the establishment of the poor law system the police district had been drawn up. This was an area from which revenue would be drawn to fund the Dublin Metropolitan Police. This was the one example of a uniformly rated area covering a wide swathe of the city and suburbs (see fig. 1). The dis-trict had been set up by legislation in 1837 and was later extended. By 1876 it included all the townships and part of the county. The existence of the police district, seen by Dublin corporation as a model of how the greater Dublin area could be rated for further services was greatly resented by the townships, Rathmines in particular.

The establishment of the police district went against the strong trend of frag-mentation common at this time. This trend encouraged residents of any area that was subject to a growth of population, especially if they were people of means who wished to improve their standards of living by the provision of ser-vices such as water supply, paving and lighting, to take the matter into their own hands. The trend was reflected in the increasing complexity of local gov-ernment in Britain and Ireland in the second quarter of the nineteenth century. A period of spreading responsibility rather than concentration, and of multi-plying local authorities began, resulting in new municipal corporations with increased powers, poor law unions, and improvement boards, all superimposed on the ancient grand jury system. The movement towards giving each function its own authority was carried further with paving boards, police taxes, rates restricted to certain streets and many more.[20]

A plethora of general and local acts of parliament provided the legal frame-work under which these decentralized and local authorities operated. The most important general measure of this type in Ireland was the 1828 towns' improve-ment act,[21] a means by which an area could improve its situation as regards

Figure 1: Dublin police district and townships 1880

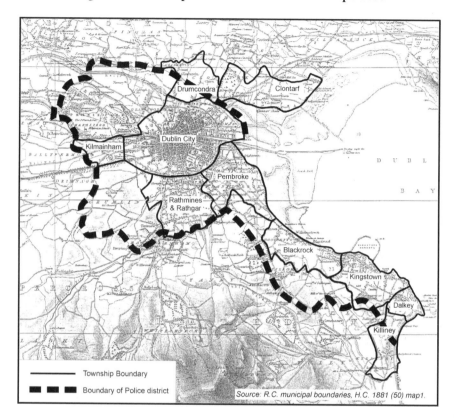

Township Boundary
Boundary of Police district

Source: R.C. municipal boundaries, H.C. 1881 (50) map1.

Source: Prepared from report of royal commission on boundaries and municipal areas of cities and towns in Ireland, H.C., (2827) pt. 1, map 1

lighting, paving, cleansing and watching by establishing a board of commissioners.[22] This act however did not remove an area from the jurisdiction of the local grand jury, as the responsibility for roads and bridges remained in its hands; many saw the new act as imposing double taxation. For a district to free itself from the control of the grand jury, private legislation was necessary and, as this was expensive, it was not often resorted to.

Kingstown was the first district in County Dublin to avail of the 1828 act. In 1834, on the opening of the first railway in Ireland, linking the town to Dublin, a number of its wealthy inhabitants adopted the act and established a township in order to develop and improve the area.[23]

On the city's boundary, the most promising area for the activities of speculative property developers was Rathmines and adjoining districts. Unlike Pembroke to its east, most of the land of Rathmines was in the hands of small

Plate 1: Kingstown, early 20th century: town hall seen on left

Town Hall, Pavilion and Harbour, Kingstown.

owners as the Meath estate and other landlords had leased property on very
long leases, sometimes up to 999 years, in the preceding century and a half. The
earliest registers in the Registry of Deeds in Dublin show that much of the land
in Rathmines was changing hands in small acreages in the early eighteenth century. Figure 2 shows the extent of the Meath estate in the Rathmines area in
the mid-nineteenth century. However, because the land was held by lessees on
such long leases, the interest of the Meath estate in the area was minimal. The
only remnant of an estate was that of Lord Palmerston in Upper Rathmines.
This absence of a large landowner controlling the supply of land made
Rathmines ideal for the speculative builder.[24]

The infrastructural deficiencies of the area owing to inadequate grand jury
management are evident in a letter of complaint published in the press by a resident there in the 1840s: Rathmines Road had been 'one mud pool' all winter,
and had only been repaired because the postmaster general had issued a certifi-
cate that the road was unfit for the mail. It was then repaired at the cost of an
expensive compulsory presentment for which the cess-payers of the district had
to pay dearly. The letter-writer believed that the improvement would not last
long and that another expensive repair would be carried out when it became
unavoidable, instead of the road being properly maintained. He also castigated
the owners of property in the area for recoiling at the thought of the introduction of lighting or water. As far as looking after their tenants was concerned, they
compared unfavourably with rural landlords.[25] The provision of the most basic
services fell on the residents themselves. Householders in the Rathmines and
Leeson Street area had to subscribe to obtain carts to provide a supply of water
for the area, especially to keep the dust down on the unpaved roads in summer.

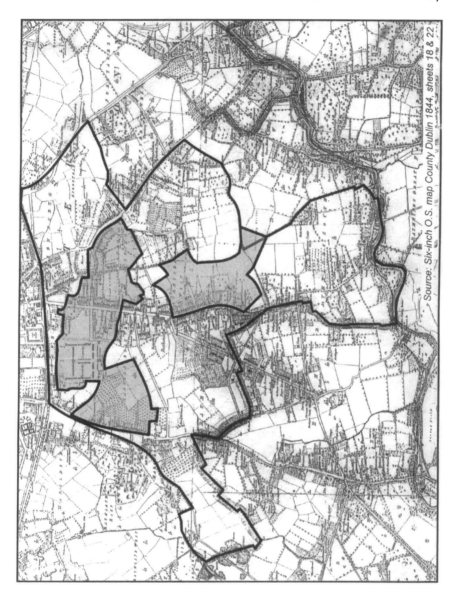

Figure 2: Township of Rathmines and Rathgar showing Meath estate, 1859 (Meath estate shaded). Based on map held by Meath estate, Kilruddery, Co. Wicklow

Plate 2: Rathmines Road, early 20th century

As the city began to expand beyond the canals, in the Rathmines area those spearheading the development, landowners, businessmen and builders, felt hindered by the inadequacy of the grand jury system. Prominent among them were Terence T. Dolan, Frederick Stokes and Frederick Jackson. Dolan was involved with one of the oldest developments in the area; this was what would become Mount Pleasant Square. Stokes was a businessman whose family resided in Upper Rathmines and was beginning a lucrative career in house building in the area. Jackson was a solicitor with a deep interest in local government.

Dolan and Stokes were very dissatisfied with the fiscal management of the grand jury. Stokes outlined to a government inquiry on the collection of rates in Dublin that 'before Rathmines was a township' Dolan had gone before the grand jury to complain about the amount of uncollected rates owed to that body. Both men appealed to the jury to make public the names of defaulters but ended up themselves posting such names outside chapels in the county. According to Stokes, this resulted in half the arrears being paid within a week.[26]

A number of house builders complained that they were not able to find suit-able tenants because of the state of the roads. The dilemma faced by developers was that, in the absence of the ability of the grand jury to provide the basic necessities more and more expected by Victorian urban dwellers, running water, lighting and drainage, either the services had to be provided by the builders or residents themselves or by the only other body capable of providing them, Dublin corporation.

The coterie that came together to found the Rathmines township had a strong aversion to coming under the control of the municipal corporation. The city rates were very high, and if they as property-owners paid them they would be a drain on their financial resources; if they had to be paid by tenants, the area would become less attractive to prospective householders. The greatest lubricant to the development of the business interests of developers would be low rates. Indeed, the Rathmines township secretary, John Evans, later loudly trumpeted the fact that he believed that the Rathmines rates were the lowest in Ireland.[27]

There was also a growing disenchantment among the larger businessmen in the city and suburbs with Dublin corporation. The government of the city by the municipal authority had been diminished in the eighteenth century by stripping it of important powers and assigning them to new bodies such as the wide street commission, set up in 1758 and the paving board of 1774. The writ of the city magistracy (the lord mayor was the chief magistrate) had never run in the ancient extra-mural liberties.[28]

The oligarchy of protestant merchants, traders and artisans that had controlled the corporation was broken by the Municipal corporations (Ireland) act of 1840. Even before this transformation the religious composition of the Dublin industrial and commercial class was undergoing a change. Up to the end of the Napoleonic wars the Roman catholic middle class was small. However, with the breakdown of guild control of the trades and emancipation, the Roman catholic political proportion was growing.[29] In the 1830s Daniel O'Connell's advocacy of repeal of the Union so soon after the granting of emancipation alienated much of the protestant support he had obtained for emancipation. Emancipation and parliamentary reform led to the formation of conservative parties in Britain and Ireland by politicized protestants. In Dublin the commercial classes, professionals and the clergy were active in this movement. O'Connell's alignment with the whigs tended to drive more and more protestants into the conservative ranks.[30] So, by the mid-1840s Dublin politics was broken down very much along the political/religious divide. The social composition of the dominant business élite in Dublin was also changing; the liberal and nationalist interest was in the ascendant since the reform of 1840, and was increasingly represented by small shopkeepers and publicans. The 1840s was seen as a decade in which performance and standards in Dublin corporation were regarded as being at a low ebb.[31] This change encouraged protestant migration to the suburbs. However, the corporation had little power and much of the effective running of the city was left in the hands of the boards, such as the paving board, which had existed under the old regime.[32]

The influx of a large number of highly politicised members onto the corporation allied to a lack of effective power led to much time of the corporation being devoted to politic debate and a concentration on matters of no great significance to the administration of the city.

Figure 3: Identified occupations of members of five township boards, 1879

Occupation	Rathmines	Pembroke	Blackrock	Kingstown	Dalkey
Builder/Contractor/Architect	4	4	1	1	3
Legal Profession	2	0	7	3	1
Merchant	8	2	4	2	1
Manufacturer	0	1	2	3	0
Grocer/Wine/					
Spirit Merchant	0	0	2	2	0
Management	3	1	1	0	0
Medical Profession	1	3	1	1	0
Army	0	0	2	0	0
Land/House Agent	0	1	0	2	0
Railway Personnel	0	1	0	0	0
Coachbuilder	0	0	0	0	1
Pawnbroker	0	0	0	1	0
Baths Proprietor	0	0	0	0	1

Source: Thom's Directory, 1879

An élite of builders, professionals and businessmen found an outlet for their civic-mindedness in the establishment and administration of townships. While it was in the professional interests of builders to become involved in the townships, and others also acted out of self-interset in ensuring that rates were kept low. Many other wealthy Victorian urban and suburban dwellers participated in local government for social reasons: 'to win praise and fame beyond their own firm, place of worship, political coterie and immediate social circle. Selection was particularly gratifying to the many who were upwardly mobile or thought themselves so; for the more established, membership provided a way to confirm and justify their respected places in local society.'[33]

The townships' élite was dominated by three professional groups (see fig. 3). First, those describing themselves as builders and contractors; architects are included in this group, as the profession was only beginning to emerge from the building trade at this time. The second group, the legal profession, including solicitors and barristers, was almost as well represented on township boards, followed by merchants, including large shopowners and drapers. When the composition of the inaugural Rathmines township board is discussed in Chapter 2 it will be seen that a deliberate attempt was made by the township's founding fathers to include both protestants and Roman catholic property-owners from the outset.

The key figure in the establishment of the Rathmines township and in its administration for thirty years was Frederick Stokes. Stokes was born in London in 1820, but had come to Dublin as a young man with his family.[34] His name begins to appear in the Dublin directories in 1844, living at various addresses in the southern suburbs of the city. He had numerous business interests; in 1847 he was listed as an agent for the Great Britain Mutual Life Assurance Company.[35] However, he very quickly established himself as a speculative builder, especially in the Portobello area of the city, and bought the defunct Portobello Gardens and built houses on it. His housebuilding gradually extended to the Rathmines area beyond the city boundary of the Grand Canal. Stokes involved himself in the work of the Dublin Artisans' Dwelling Company and in charity work for the Royal Hospital for the Incurables, Donnybrook. He became a governor of the hospital in 1860 and, as a member of the investment committee of the hospital from 1862, was largely responsible for a revival in the financial fortunes of the institution. His wife and daughter were deeply involved in fund-raising and visiting patients in the hospital. Stokes became chairman of the hospital board in 1866 and had a medical ward called after him. Stokes was a dominating influence on the hospital board, so much so that when he moved to England in 1878 because of declining health, the board unanimously decided that he remain as hospital chairman, a position he held until 1884.[36]

Stokes' views on Dublin corporation will be outlined when the Exham commission is examined in Chapter 4. However, Frederick Jackson, the solicitor for the Rathmines township bill and a founding township board member, gave his forthright opinions about the corporation in a letter to the authorities in Dublin Castle in 1848. He was promoting a bill for the improvement of Dublin city which would give extra municipal powers to a board of commissioners in opposition to a corporation bill giving itself similar powers. His views on the corporation more than likely reflect the feelings of his fellow Rathmines promoters and are echoed by Frederick Stokes at the Exham commission in 1879. Jackson claimed that the citizens of Dublin, whom he represented, believed that the corporation had misappropriated revenue from the pipe water rightly belonging to the citizens of the city. Under the management of the corporation, the pipe water was insufficient to fulfil the needs of the city and was not wholesome. He also claimed that the corporation did not truly represent 'the intelligence and property' of the city, and

as an avowed political body was not suited to manage increased revenue and powers. He charged the various committees of the corporation with neglect of duty
and claimed that the corporation had distributed patronage to avowed repealers
and that it was unlikely to act otherwise with increased revenues. He strongly dis-
agreed with the corporation's actions in this regard as he believed that repeal
would lead to the dismemberment of the empire.[37]

The origins of the foundation of the Rathmines township go back to 1844.
In that year Dublin corporation promoted a bill in parliament for compulsory
taxation for the provision of pipe water in the south suburbs. The corporation
claimed that a number of residents in the Rathmines area had requested it to
supply them with water. Dublin city was supplied with water piped from the
ancient city watercourse and from the Grand and Royal canals. The supply was
an important source of revenue for the corporation. By a seventeenth-century
act of parliament (28 George III, c. 50) the corporation had the power to lay
down pipes and supply water at any time to any street or lane in the manor of
St Sepulchre on a petition of two-thirds of the inhabitants.[38] Part of Rathmines
was in the liberty of St Sepulchre and so could be supplied with the pipe water
without further legislation. However, it would appear that the corporation was
seeking wider powers to supply the water over a greater area.

Alarmed at this encroachment by the corporation, a public meeting was called
for by a number of Rathmines developers including Terence Dolan and Frederick
Stokes. The meeting took place in the Portobello Hotel, adjacent to Rathmines,
on the city side of the Grand Canal. Among those present was Patrick O'Brien,
a member of the corporation who resided in Rathmines. O'Brien later gave a
report of the meeting to the corporation, when the matter of extending the pipe-
water to the Rathmines area was discussed. He disputed the fact, which Dolan
had publicized, that a large majority had voted against the provision of the water.
He claimed that there were very few present at the meeting, or at a subsequent
meeting called on the same matter. At the first meeting, the majority which Dolan
boasted about amounted to about eight or nine. At the second, which Dolan
promised to publicize more extensively, there was an attendance of only thirty-
nine. According to O'Brien, Dolan's claim that the meetings represented the feelings of an area containing 1,600 houses was clearly ridiculous. [39]

However, another member of the corporation, Daniel O'Connell, the 'Lib-
erator', confessed that he understood to a certain extent Dolan's point of view:
'the opposition of Mr Dolan is very natural,' he believed, 'but it is not very generous. He fears he will be charged with the pipe water money, and therefore
objects to it, though it will be a convenience to his own tenants.'[40] O'Connell
saw no reason why a clause could not be introduced into the act charging those
using the water, that is, the occupiers, rather than the owners.

Dolan and Stokes believed that the corporation was using the supply of water
as a pretext to gain a foothold in the Rathmines area, and bring them into the

corporation's rate net. They opposed the bill at their own expense, and presented a petition against it signed by 648 householders, then four-fifths of the
population of the Rathmines district. When the corporation applied to the government for support for the bill it was refused and it was finally thrown out
after costs of up to a £1,000 had been incurred. A permissive bill was passed
in its place, but it proved to be a dead letter and no water was subsequently
supplied to the suburbs under it.

An option for Stokes and Dolan was the adoption of the 1828 act. But this
was very limited in its provisions, as can be seen in its application to the provision of a water supply, the most vital issue in Rathmines. The powers granted
under the act limited commissioners to digging wells and erecting pumps.[41]
Wells and pumps were already present in Rathmines, but for the increased number of terraced houses being built a piped supply was necessary. The 1828 act
was more suited to a rural or small town situation, with a primitive infrastructure rather than to a rapidly growing city suburb.

Fortuitously, help was at hand for Stokes and Dolan. A general towns
improvement bill was introduced into parliament, incorporating many previous
acts regarding the improvement of roads, public lighting and other matters. This
general act was passed in 1847 and consequently any body representing a local
area could obtain a local act and adopt all or some of its provisions. Buoyed up
by their success in thwarting the corporation, this Stokes and Dolan proceeded
to do. Having a large stake in the development of the Rathmines area, they must
have felt that both the creaking grand jury system and the corporation were
major obstacles to the transformation of the suburb into a residential district.
In the absence of a local authority capable of dealing with the needs of the area,
new roads opened by developers had to be kept private and their maintenance
fell on their owners. However, if the developers could set up an authority under
their own control, they could charge rates and get all to contribute to maintenance and improvement.

A procedure existed for setting up a preliminary inquiry to see whether an
area should be given an improvement board, and a royal commission was set up
to look into the Rathmines case, directed by Abraham Hayward of the Inner
Temple, London and Charles Brassington of Dublin. The promoters of the bill
were instructed to appear before them in Rathmines with any maps, surveys, plans
and estimates relative to their project. Objectors were also invited to attend.[42]

The inquiry opened at 22, Rathmines Road in February 1847, and Terence
Dolan and Frederick Dixon, both described as solicitors for the bill, appeared
in support of it and Jonathan Sisson and Thomas McCreary, residents of the
area, opposed it. Much of the evidence concerned argument over the number
of signatures collected in favour or against the bill, with the promoters' side
appearing much more organised. A number of builders who claimed they had
each invested up to £4,000 in the area, including a John Butler who owned sixty

houses, spoke in favour of the bill. It was stated that up to sixty proprietors in the area had attended a public meeting about the bill and that there were only two or three against it.[43]

It was Stokes who provided the statistics to the inquiry. He claimed that there were over 1,400 cess-payers in the district and more than 600 had signed the petition in favour; more of them would have done so if they had more time. He contemptuously dismissed those who had not signed as mainly residing in cabins.[44] In Stokes' view it was the cess-payers, those with enough property to pay county rates, who should decide the fate of the area.

Giving some idea of the relative wealth of different parts of the district, Stokes outlined the average valuation of house property as follows: in Rathmines £31, Ranelagh £29 and Harold's Cross £16. The total valuation of the area was £39,338 10s., and comprised 1,438 houses distributed as follows: Harold's Cross 203, Rathmines 667, Ranelagh and Cullenswood 338, Milltown 123 and Upper Leeson Street 107. As an indication of how the area was rapidly developing, Stokes named some 15 new terraces and streets which had been built in the previous five years, adding up to 268 new houses. Eleven people to be named as the first commissioners were, he claimed, the largest holders of property in the area.

The county surveyor, himself a property-owner and resident of the district, lent his professional weight to the township case. Although he admitted that some sewers were in the course of construction in the district under the labour rate, the picture he painted was one of neglect. He informed the inquiry that, on a number of occasions, residents felt obliged to pay out of their own pockets to make up for the negligence of the grand jury, and that he himself had to make an extra payment of £14 for services which the grand jury should have been providing. In winter the roads were a river of mud and covered in dust in summer. The area was not represented on the grand jury and was not looked after by it. He himself was a developer in the area and had built twenty-five houses from which he accrued a substantial annual rental. He would prefer to have the roads in the area controlled by a turnpike trust, a body usually much disliked, despite the cost this would entail to all those using them, rather than allow them to be left to the neglect of the grand jury. In the past four years, he claimed, his houses had been less profitable, and he attributed that to the state of the roads.

A number of grievances against the grand jury were expressed to the royal commission. Rathmines was situated in the barony of Uppercross, and every year a list of work on roads and bridges was drawn up by the grand jury for that barony at the presentment session. However nobody from Rathmines had been on the grand jury list of those who made presentments for the barony in 1845 and 1846. It was stated that roads outside the district were looked after better than those within it. Dolan asserted that he had endeavoured to have a clause inserted in a recent grand jury act to have special sessions appointed for the benefit of householders, but landed property owners were too powerful; the selection process favoured them and the only way to ensure suburban roads were repaired was through agitation by residents.[45]

The township promoters were anxious to highlight the different character of Rathmines compared to its rural hinterland. Stokes pointed out that the barony of Uppercross comprised 13,140 acres and the Rathmines district of that covered only 1,400 acres, but was valued at £38,690 (almost 39 per cent) of the barony valuation of £99,900. Also, as far as population was concerned, the numbers living in Rathmines were equally out of proportion to the rest of the barony.

Referring again to the vexed question of water, the inquiry was told that the corporation scheme of 1845 to take water from the canal at Portobello basin for the Rathmines area was too expensive as a steam engine would have to be used to raise it to the higher levels of the district. The whole operation would cost the corporation £12,500, which would be too great an expense on the ratepayers. The promoters informed the inquiry that they intended to make a reservoir on the Dodder and use the city watercourse to bring water to the Rathmines district. They pointed out that they paid 1s. 4d. grand jury rate and had very little to show for it, while they themselves proposed to provide all the services outlined in the bill for a maximum rate of very little more. McCreary and Sisson put up a very feeble case against the well-prepared proposals of the promoters and the outcome of the inquiry was a unanimous decision in favour of the proposed township.[46]

Rathmines was now poised to become the first district in Ireland, according to the claims of Stokes, to withdraw from the grand jury system. The major objections to that system were outlined by him some years later. He stated that he and his fellow promoters of the township bill sought 'separation from the county' on the grounds that the grand jury system entailed government of the area by people who were unacquainted with it; the promoters however wished to 'secure constant supervision over a small area.'.[47] The district was one chiefly of house property and they wished to remove it from the jurisdiction of those operating in a rural environment. Stokes also had objections to the contract system of labour under which the grand jury operated. It was, he claimed, open to gross abuse and the ratepayers were heavily taxed while the work was hardly done.

While these deliberations were going on in Rathmines, the general act for consolidating in one act a number of provisions contained in various measures for paving, draining, cleansing, lighting, and improving towns was passed by parliament. This act, known as the Towns' improvement act, was to extend only to such towns and districts in England and Ireland as would adopt it by having a local act passed in parliament. According to Stokes, the efforts of the promoters met with general approval in the area and, despite opposition by the corporation in both commons and lords, the bill was passed at a cost of £900.

The area chosen to form the new township was quite compact. It was composed of that part of the barony of Uppercross which was in the parish of St Peter. The full title of the act, dated 22 July 1847, named the main districts which it would comprise: 'An act for better paving, cleansing, draining, regulating, lighting and improving the district of Rathmines, Mount Pleasant, Ranelagh, Cullenswood, Milltown, Rathgar, Harold's Cross and such other portions of the parish of St Peter within the barony of Uppercross in the county of Dublin and for otherwise promoting the health and convenience of the inhabitants' (10 & 11 Vict. c. 253). It went on to state that the area was made up of several villages and was a populous one, and that the work outlined above could not be carried out without the authority of parliament.

The promoters chose the area which was entirely in one parish because it was, they felt, a homogenous district as far as rating was concerned and did not include huge tracts of unbuilt land which would provide very little in rates, but enough for them to pursue their building programme. There is evidence, however, that the promoters deliberately avoided taking in poor areas which would also be a drain on the rates. As can be seen from Stokes' valuation figures, Harold's Cross was a comparatively poor area, especially the west side of Harold's Cross Green. Conveniently for the promoters, that side of the green was outside the parish of St Peter's, and was excluded. A Mr Connor of Harold's Cross objected, stating that both sides should be taken into the township. Stokes refused to budge, however, stating that the promoters were reluctant to encroach on the parish of St Catherine. Fearing that the interests of that part of Harold's Cross within the township would be swamped by the wealthier districts, Connor demanded that the area be assigned two commissioners – in effect that it form a separate ward; however it was pointed out to him that there was no precedent, at that time, for having electoral divisions in the appointment of commissioners.[48]

Another case was that of Milltown. Despite being mentioned in the act, and being in the parish of St Peter's and within the barony of Uppercross, it was not subsequently taken up by the commissioners, and was the only townland in that parish and barony which was excluded. A number of reasons were given for this. One was, according to Stokes, that the ratepayers of Milltown had objected. They attended the inquiry, and sturdily objected to being taken in, especially two local landowners, Harmon Hodges and Tighe Hamilton, and so they were left out. Stokes claimed that they later regretted this, and asserted that by 1879 the population of the area had fallen from 850 to 560. Stokes, however, later admitted that the village of Milltown was not included because it had a number of small houses and cottages which would be a burden on the ratepayers.[49] Consideration was given to including Terenure, and the major landlord, Sir Frederick Shaw, was favourable to it, but again a number of ratepayers opposed it and it was not included. [50]

The Rathmines act, besides incorporating the Towns' improvement act (1847), as already mentioned, availed of powers in a number of other acts which would facilitate the development of the township. These were the Commissioners' clauses act (1847), Lands clauses act (1845), which gave the new commissioners powers to purchase land by agreement, and certain clauses from the Waterworks clauses act (1847). An important element in the bill was the exclusion of the grand jury from the township area, although the commissioners would have to pay a levy as the areas contribution to 'county-at-large' presentments. Other Dublin suburban townships and a number of towns such as Belfast, Galway and Sligo subsequently followed the lead of Rathmines and removed themselves from the jurisdiction of the grand jury[51]

The fact that the Dublin townships obtained expensive local acts shows a degree of enterprising vigour and self-confidence, and a degree of support from their future ratepayers. It also resulted in the fact that each, while tending to uniformity owing to the incorporation and adoption of model general acts, ended up having its own constitutional history and indeed its own character. Of course, the fact that a local board adopted a piece of legislation from a wide menu at its disposal did not mean that it was enforced; indeed, many bodies worked at a snail's pace in undertaking the programme of work set out in their enabling acts.[52] The Pembroke township, for example, faced numerous complaints from the authorities in Dublin Castle in the late 1860s and 1870 over its tardiness in dealing with sanitary defects.[53]

Legislation such as that obtained by Rathmines could be very costly. To reduce the cost, the Towns improvement (Ireland) act of 1854[54] was passed. This legislation enabled towns in Ireland to obtain the powers of the English general act of 1847 without going to the expense of obtaining a private act. Many areas availed of this, including, eventually, all the Dublin townships: for instance, Kingstown in 1855, Dalkey and Kilmainham on their establishment in 1863 and 1867 respectively, and Killiney in 1870.

Under the new legislation, on the application of twenty-one or more householders who were rated to the value of £8 or more, the lord lieutenant could order a meeting to be convened to consider the adoption of the act within specified boundaries. The meeting was to be advertised in the press and notices posted on church and chapel doors. At the meeting householders valued at £8 or more were entitled to vote on whether to adopt the act in its totality, partially adopt it, or reject it. If partially adopted, further parts of the act could be adopted on a later occasion. A simple majority was sufficient to carry the proposals. A board set up under the act could have from nine to twenty-one commissioners and the new act nullified any previous local act. Voters had to have a rating qualification of £4 if they were resident within the boundaries, or £50 if resident within five miles of it. To be eligible to become a commissioner on the new local board, a qualification of £12 was necessary for residents and £50 for those within five miles of the area. The maximum rate that could be imposed was a modest 1s. 6d. in the pound.

This latter consideration was considered too restrictive in the rapidly expanding Dublin suburbs, and despite the cost many townships went on to obtain their own private act, having as a first step adopted the 1854 legislation. Such was the case of Kilmainham which adopted the 1854 act in 1867 and had its own act passed the following year. By 1912, 124 towns in Ireland were under some form of local government; eleven under the Municipal corporations (Ireland) act of 1840. Of these Dublin, Belfast, Cork, Limerick, Londonderry and Waterford were administrative counties, known as county boroughs. One hundred and four were administered under the 1854 act and only nine had special local acts.[55]

The foundation of the Kingstown township in 1834 has already been adverted to. Glasthule was added to it in 1855, and, by an act of 1861,[56] the management of the roads and bridges was transferred from the grand jury to the commissioners. Between 1860 and 1878 seven more townships were established in the Dublin area, making a total of nine bodies ringing the city (fig. 2).

The coastal area of Blackrock, close to, but separate from Kingstown, and on the railway line, was growing rapidly and wished to emulate its larger neighbour and become a township. The area was socially mixed and included the estate of Lord Cloncurry, the indigenous fishermen of Blackrock village and Williamstown, and a number of shopkeepers and publicans, largely based in Blackrock village. The Pembroke estate, of paramount importance in what would become the neighbouring Pembroke township, also held land in Blackrock (see fig. 2). The inspiration for a township came from the businessmen and shopkeepers of Blackrock village and was unsuccessfully opposed by the poorer residents of Williamstown. The township was established in 1860 and its area covered the village and surrounding land. The valuation threshold for franchise was low at £4, a concession to the poorer elements who had objected to the formation of the township. A substantial change came about in 1863 as a result of numerous petitions when the much more prosperous district of Monkstown became part of the township and the valuation for the franchise was raised to £8. The political consequences of this was that power which had been in the hands of the liberal, largely Roman catholic, interest transferred to a more conservative group with a much larger protestant presence.[57]

As areas adjoining Rathmines saw their neighbours taking their destiny into their own hands, it is not surprising that an aspiration to have the township extended to include them grew. As early as 1849, Terence Dolan was anxious for the extension of the township to the Pembroke district. This area flanked Rathmines and lay between it and the coast and was almost entirely part of the Pembroke estate. In November 1849 a bill for improving Upper Baggot Street, Pembroke Road and Waterloo Road was mooted in the *Dublin Gazette*. The Rathmines commissioners were open to the possibility of annexing the area, provided those promoting the scheme bore the expense of the legislation necessary. Dolan was deputized to confer with the agent of the Pembroke estate about the matter.[58] However, nothing came of the move and the area was never annexed.

In 1863, however, a private bill was obtained by residents of the Pembroke district and a township created. While water was the catalyst for the foundation of the Rathmines township, in the area that was to form the Pembroke township public lighting was the crucial issue. The Pembroke estate agent, John Vernon, described the casual process by which the township came into existence:

> The proprietor (the earl of Pembroke, then a minor), practically, had nothing to say to the original movement. There were several meetings of the ratepayers on the subject, and they objected to it ... After that the ratepayers appeared to have changed their minds, and to think they ought to have some form of government. The formation of the township arose in this way: discontent existed about lighting – portion of the township was lighted by subscription; a good many people put their names down and omitted to pay their subscriptions, and there was no means of compelling them. The ratepayers then met, and thought they would suggest some form of government.[59]

While the reaction of the Pembroke estate to the moves to create a township was passive, on its establishment the estate interest made sure that it had a good measure of control over the new board. Seven-ninths of the area of the township lay within the estate and the act stated that the first meeting of the commissioners should be held in the estate office, which, in fact, was outside the township boundary. John Vernon, the Pembroke agent, was *ex officio* commissioner until his death in 1887, fulfilling a similar, if less strident, role to that of Frederick Stokes in Rathmines.

The next area to seek local government was the coastal village of Dalkey. In 1860, the *Irish Builder* characterized Dalkey as comparatively neglected; it was 'still a wild barren place, a field whose apparent infertility seems, with few exceptions, to deter modern innovators and speculating capitalists from investment'.[60] Three years later it is apparent that all did not share these feelings; at a meeting held on 22 September 1863 in the Queen's Hotel, Dalkey, chaired by Milo Burke, proprietor of the Shelbourne Hotel, Dublin, the lighting provisions of the 1854 act were adopted.[61] In 1867, a move was made by the board to obtain a private act. This was motivated by alleged attempts by Kingstown to take over Dalkey; at the same time Dalkey hoped to take in the recently formed township of Killiney, claiming that it was defunct as a township, was not a town under the 1854 act and had not struck a rate for some time.

Killiney remained independent and the Dalkey act was passed, although it was opposed by a number of its inhabitants on the grounds that the area was not suitable for this status as it was too scattered. The act[62] gave the commissioners powers to build a town hall and a market house, as it now became a market town as legally defined. Powers were also obtained to erect two piers at Coliemore. A number of other Dublin townships, including Pembroke, also obtained powers to set up markets, but they were seldom used.

In 1871 the great scheme of Dublin corporation to obtain water by damming the Vartry river at Roundwood was completed and a special meeting was held in Dalkey to adopt the clauses in the 1854 act which would give the board powers to obtain water from the supply and to contract for gas. Dalkey was distinguished in having on its board two individuals who were to have a strong influence on the history of the Dublin townships in general – William Exham chaired the royal commission which sat in the late 1870s and early 1880s and conducted the largest inquiry ever undertaken into Dublin city and its surrounding townships, and Sir John Gray, who was responsible for the Vartry water supply to the city and the negotiations under which it was supplied to many of the townships, although his discussions with Rathmines, as we shall see, proved abortive.[63]

In 1864 the *Dublin Builder* lamented the fact that cheap and well-built houses could not be got for a reasonable rent in the suburbs especially those with a view of mountains and the sea: 'the lordly master of a thousand a year can hold the beauties of Bray or Killiney at command by renting small and inadequate houses at a fabulous price; why should the man of business, who works hard to eke out a subsistence upon two hundred, be excluded from a similar enjoyment?'[64] Killiney never reached the point where middle to low cost housing was built on a large scale. This was in part owing to the hilly nature of the terrain and its remoteness from Dublin. It is surprising that Killiney ever became a township as it had no recognisable nucleus and settlement remained scattered.

The Killiney township, which included both Killiney and Ballybrack in its title, initially had only limited powers when it was established in 1866.[65] The prime mover was Robert Warren, a director of the Dublin, Wicklow and Wexford Railway, a magistrate and deputy lieutenant of County Dublin. He became the first chairman of the board and remained in that position for almost a quarter of a century. In 1870, clauses in the 1854 act for the supply of gas and water were adopted. Before this, the water supply was very inadequate; Ballybrack, the poorer part of the township, had to rely solely on one well. Dalkey had already applied for the Varty water, and it had been piped to the boundary of that township so facilitating its extension to Killiney at a reasonable cost. As far as gas was concerned the Killiney commissioners' needs were modest, requiring only enough to light a few public lamps.[66]

Kilmainham was quite different in character from any other area that was to become a township. Settlement in the area was very old, perhaps even, as one recent author claims, older than Dublin itself.[67] By the 1860s it was dominated

Plate 3: Islandbridge, Kilmainham township, *c.*1905

by large institutions such as Kilmainham jail, Goldenbridge orphanage, the Oblate religious house at Inchicore and the large railway works of the Great Southern and Western Railway. Many of the residents were connected with these institutions, a large number making the area their home for a period of time, including workers from England employed by the railway. Housing in the area was of the modest variety; in 1868 only sixteen houses were valued at more than £20, and the district never became an affluent residential suburb. The initiative for the establishment of the township came from a number of industrialists such as Francis Moore Scott, the owner of Island Bridge Woollen Mills, David McBirney, a prominent city draper and textile producer and ex-member of Dublin corporation, and Samuel Shelly, an Islandbridge flour miller. The railway company originally opposed the establishment of the township and, when it failed in its opposition, had two of its staff elected to the board; a third's election was declared invalid.

The impetus for the establishment of the township was the deplorable sanitary condition of the area. The main problem was the presence of a huge open sewer into which the waste from Richmond Barracks was discharged. According to Dr E. Kennedy, who chaired the public meeting required under legislation before a township could be set up, three epidemics were directly traceable to that particular nuisance, cholera, fever and even, he claimed, some cases of what he termed 'black death'.[68]

The promoters realized that, owing to the small number of houses in the area and their low valuation, the revenue they would be able to raise would be small. The total annual income derived from a rate on the 3,776 houses and other buildings in the area valued at £6,255, would amount to only £520 a year. They hoped that government aid would be forthcoming to alleviate the severe sewage problem arising from the barracks. This had happened, they claimed, in other areas in which garrisons were situated, or which were affected by their presence. The second object of the promoters was the provision of a water supply, and after that the building of a better approach to the district. The only good access was through the Phoenix Park, and only a certain number of vehicles were allowed to pass that way, they claimed. The area was deficient in lighting, although the claim that it had none at all was disputed by the railway company.[69]

The Great Southern and Western Railway Company's works at Inchicore was very much a self-sufficient community. It covered 76 of the 534 acres within the boundaries of the proposed township. The company had invested over £228,000 in the works and on facilities for its workers, including housing. It had built 148 cottages housing 850 people. Its property was valued at £3,053, and, although land actually under the railway lines was rated at a quarter of the usual rate, it faced a large rate bill. The works' complex also had its own water supply and gas lighting; the gas it produced was more than sufficient for its own needs, and it supplied the village of Kilmainham, contrary to the claims of the promoters of the township.[70] The railway company had no desire to be rated to pay for such facilities for the general area. In its opposition to the proposed township it claimed that it would be liable for two-fifths of the rates but, out of an electorate of around 110, it would control only five votes.

The initiative of Scott, McBirney, Shelly and others resulted in the adoption of the Towns improvement act (1854) for the area in 1867 and in the following year the passing of their own private act.[71] The latter act limited the board's borrowing powers to £10,000, a very modest sum. Apart from the prominent businessmen who founded the township, and continued to play a prominent part in its administration, the railway company had a strong, if limited, presence on the board. Some of its representatives were prominent in the history of Irish railway engineering, such as Alexander McDonnell, the Great Southern and Western's chief engineer.

The township, in its short existence, never built a town hall, and its board met in Kilmainham courthouse. Its nine members set about their task of developing the area without delay. They immediately obtained a loan of £2,800 from the National Bank to cover the expenses of the enabling legislation and lay in mains in preparation for the Vartry water. The water mains cost £1,200 and the rest went on legal expenses, which were high owing to the original opposition to the act by the railway company. The institution that caused the greatest problem to the township, Richmond Barracks, with its 1,600 inhabitants, including married women, continued to prove contentious. The matter rankled all the more as the military authorities were not obliged to pay rates; an *ex gratia* payment of £100 made by them to the township, was regarded by the board as totally inadequate.[72] As the township was prevented from allowing its sewage to enter the Camac river, and a main drainage scheme was never undertaken, the area continued to harbour cesspools. Not surprisingly, the township was subject to only moderate population growth, and between 1861 and 1871, it grew by a total of only 224 persons. It remained an area different in character from the other townships and it never developed into an affluent residential quarter.

Of all the suburban districts, Clontarf seems to have come into existence as a township most reluctantly. Approached through tenements, docks and sloblands, the area was not favourably situated for suburban housing.[73] The optimism shown by the Great Northern Railway in opening a station there in 1844 proved untimely, and the station was closed in 1855 owing to under-use.[74] The derelict condition of the area regularly featured in the pages of the *Dublin Builder* in the following decade.[75]

The area consisted of a long stretch of unproductive land facing Dublin bay and was protected by a crumbling sea wall. The expense of erecting and maintaining the wall had fallen on the barony of Coolock, which was anxious to throw it on the parish or any local body foolhardy enough to take it on. Prospective township promoters knew this and it dampened their appetite for the adoption of local powers.[76] The district was dominated by the Vernon estate and the property of Arthur Edward and Benjamin Lee Guinness, with the Howth estate infringing on its northern limits.

In 1865, a grave threat to the area arose which galvanised these reluctant interests to action when proposals were drawn up by a private company to rid the corporation of the problem of sewage in the city by dumping it on the shore at Clontarf, and flooding part of the low-lying land there for this purpose. Local landowners, including John Vernon and Benjamin Lee Guinness, petitioned the corporation against such a move.[77] The vulnerability of the area became plain also to a number of middle-class inhabitants and these became motivated enough to promote a township bill in 1869.

The large property interests in the area regarded this as going too far, and at first opposed this move, knowing that they would bear the brunt of the improvement rate. George Tickell, later a long-serving member of the township board, originally opposed the formation of a township fearing that the future of the area would end up 'not in the hands of people who were interested properly in the township'.[78] Vernon, explaining how he had opposed the bill, gave the background to the foundation of the township. There were, he claimed two parties with regard to the making of this township – one was in favour of it and one against it. There was a public meeting held in the parish, and there it was decided to form a committee of gentlemen to inquire, and investigate, and look into the matter thoroughly, to find out what the cost would be of keeping up the township. They reported at a future meeting the result of their investigations – we got all the information we could, and came to the conclusion that it would not be a judicious thing to form it into a township. We considered it was a long sea board, an unproductive property, and that it would not be of advantage to the district to have the township. There was a stormy meeting after our report, and after discussion they carried a vote in favour of promoting it. I opposed it to a certain extent, because I considered we were not, after the enquiry had been made, justified in promoting the change. After some discussion they gave way on certain points I insisted on, and I withdrew my opposition, and the bill was passed.[79]

The net effect of the opposition to the bill was to add an extra £400 to the parliamentary expenses, a not inconsiderable sum for an area which would never have a high income from rates.[80] The extra cost was incurred as a result of the necessity of sending a legal team to London to fight the promoters' at every stage of the bill's passage through parliament. Eventually the Clontarf act[81] was passed; it named the area comprising the township as that of Clontarf, Dollymount and Ballybough. It was removed from the jurisdiction of the grand jury and a market town created. To complete the takeover of the new board by the landlord interest, John Vernon was appointed chairman for life.

Drumcondra was the last of the suburban townships to be established. Two builders, J.F. Lombard, a director of Arnotts, the retailers, and Edward McMahon, a Home Rule MP, were the founding fathers of this north Dublin township. From the mid-1860s they were building modest houses to the north of Sackville Street, eventually expanding beyond the city boundaries. By 1878, they had, between them, built about 600 houses and opened about 30 streets around the Blessington Street and Eccles Street area.

As the building activities of this entrepreneurial partnership expanded beyond the city, the nature of the rural area they were entering threatened to curtail their activities. Drumcondra is part of the Tolka valley, a river which at that time was no more than an open sewer, causing huge drainage problems. The option of annexation to its neighbour, Clontarf, was considered, but Clontarf was struggling with its own newly-acquired responsibilities and in no position to take on more. A drainage scheme, to connect the waste of Drumcondra to Dublin, was turned down by the local government board, and efforts to obtain water did not succeed. By 1878 the only option left was to establish a separate township. Increased credibility was given to the project by the extension of the tram service to the district at this time. Once again, large property owners did not approve; in this case, the inhabitants of villas in the Glasnevin district of the proposed area.

Even more so than Kilmainham, the area had a large Roman catholic institutional presence, with All Hallows and Clonliffe Colleges within the proposed boundary. The township promoters were greatly encouraged by the influential support of Cardinal Paul Cullen, archbishop of Dublin, for their bill.[82] With this support, the opposition of the property-owners, none of whom were in the same league as the large landed interests of Clontarf, was unavailing, and a private act of parliament was passed in 1878.[83]

Shortly after its formation, at the time of the Exham commission, it was reported that the Drumcondra township had a population of 3,200, and its 854 acres had a valuation of £12,000. It was divided into three wards, Drumcondra, Clonliffe and Glasnevin, represented by five, five and four commissioners respectively. The township had borrowing powers of up to £7,000, which it proceeded to utilize by obtaining a loan of £5,000 from the Patriotic Insurance Company.[84]

Dublin corporation's attitude to the setting up of Rathmines township has been already outlined. The future implications for the development of the city in the establishment of a plethora of townships surrounding it did not appear to dawn on the corporation. No coherent policy is evident in the city fathers' attitude to new townships. The main opposition to the establishment of the Clontarf and Kilmainham townships and increased powers for Kingstown came from the corporation waterworks committee. Similarly, the only objection to the Blackrock and Pembroke bills was that they interfered with what the corporation regarded as its exclusive right to supply those districts with water. The pattern which emerged was that, when it was clear that a township would be set up, the corporation moved to ensure that the corporation would supply it with water and not its rival, the Grand Canal Company. For instance, the city fathers moved swiftly to agree with Blackrock and Pembroke to supply them with twenty gallons per head of the population per annum at a cost of 3s. 2d. in the pound on all rateable valuation in the districts. It also undertook to bear the cost of distribution and maintenance, and the local authorities of the new administrative areas would undertake to collect the charges.[85]

No further townships were ever created in Ireland. The only other urban area that was comparable to Dublin in the extent of suburban development outside its municipal boundaries was Belfast. Questioned in relation to the proposal to extend Belfast's boundary, a witness at the Exham commission in 1878, Samuel Black, described the area of Sydenham, outside the town (Belfast did not obtain the status of a city until 1898) and other similar areas:

> it is really a suburban district of building ground rapidly being built upon. There are some buildings that are old, but the greater number are new residences. Immediately over the present borough boundary is

Connswater; there are rows of houses and streets which have been built within a very short period, and laid out as the owners themselves pleased, without supervision or control. Take Strandstown, there are rows of houses there and from that up to the proposed extended boundary the ground is substantially villa or building ground, and following the line then up towards Belmont the same observation applies. When you come down again to Knock there are a large number of houses built there within the last few years, a very large number indeed.[86]

The board of poor law guardians of the area in which Sydenham was situated was approached in regard to the sanitary condition of the area and with the possibility of having building bye-laws drawn up, but it refused to have anything to do with such matters. It was stated that an application was made to the local government board to form a township but it was not followed up.[87] This is the only recorded instance of a township being mooted in a suburb outside the Dublin area.

In conclusion, it can be seen that by establishing townships local élites of middle-class residents were responding to immediate needs incapable of being supplied by existing structures. Weak opposition by established local government bodies, local residents or landlords did not present a serious obstacle to township formation. While increased fragmentation in local affairs was common in Britain and Ireland at the time, the weakness of Dublin corporation and the low esteem in which it was held and an out-dated grand jury system left a vacuum filled by the establishment of townships. This was particularly the case in the 1840s when the crucially important Rathmines township was established. The internal politics of the corporation in the 1840s also meant that it was weak in opposing bodies which would siphon off much-needed revenue. At the time of the founding of the Rathmines township the corporation's energies were taken up in promoting a bill to increase its powers and in opposing a rival bill, so that it was, despite later claims by Frederick Stokes, desultory in its opposition to the township bill. No opposition was voiced by the municipal body at the royal commission inquiry held in Rathmines in 1847. The concerns of large property-owners were allayed by ensuring that they obtained a controlling interest in the new bodies as happened in the Pembroke and Clontarf townships, with the vested industrial interest in Kilmainham having only limited influence.

CHAPTER TWO

Township administration, finances and staffing

The personnel, *modus operandi*, financing and development of the Rathmines township and the other Dublin townships are examined in this chapter, and their relations with each other and other bodies explored. As regards financing, a key question examined is that raised by John McEvoy, an ex-chairman of Kingstown township, when he argued at the royal commission on municipal boundaries, the Exham commission, in 1879 that the townships were too small and consequently their ratebase too low to carry out the numerous functions with which they were charged. This lack of resources led, he claimed, to a duplication of staffs and the employment of personnel of less than professional standards. Did this dearth of resources seriously affect the workings of the townships? This question is examined in relation to services, administration and staffing.

The eighteen members who were to make up the first board of Rathmines commissioners were named in the private act of 1847 (fig. 4). At least half of them were speculative builders possessing large amounts of house property between them. The rest was made up of businessmen and professionals, especially in the legal and medical professions. The act stipulated that one-third of the commissioners were to go out of office, in rotation, every three years. To be eligible for election as a commissioner, candidates had to be rated in the district to the value of £30 and be resident there. Non-residents could stand if they enjoyed profits or rents from property in the township to the value of £200. The electorate consisted of all male persons of full age rated to the relief of the poor within the township for property to the value of £10; electors had to be resident in the district for at least six months and have their rates paid up to date.

The first Rathmines board did not delay in establishing its administrative structure. On 23 July 1847, the day after the enactment of the Rathmines township legislation, a notice appeared in the *Irish Times* advertising the posts of surveyor, secretary and two rate collectors for the new township. Replies were to be sent to 9 Harcourt Street, the offices of Frederick Jackson, solicitor, one of the proposed commissioners named in the act and a substantial property owner in the Leinster Road area.

The first meeting of the new board took place on 8 December 1847, with fifteen of those named in the bill present. Jackson had been proposed as chairman by the commissioners prior to the meeting, but on the day he was away on business in the country, and asked the others by letter to reconsider their choice, stating that over the coming winter he would be away much in London or the country, and would not be able to attend. He proposed Frederick Stokes as chairman, stating that 'the attention which Mr Stokes has given to local taxation, his full and intimate knowledge of the subject and his habits of business give him claims to the place.'[1] He was so adamant in this matter that he stated that he would vote for Stokes against himself in a division. In the event, Stokes was elected as chairman in a division with Dr Christopher Wall, by eight votes to seven.[2]

Figure 4: Property within township area owned by members of the first board of Rathmines commissioners, 1847

Name	Address	No. of houses owned	Valuation
John Butler	Rockville	28	£1,031.25
Terence T. Dolan	Mt. Pleasant Square	38	£893.45
William Todd	Foreesque Terrace	16	£639.40
John Sibthorpe	Epworth Terrace	8	£375.35
John Connor	Harold's Cross	22	£357.25
Frederick Jackson	Leinster Rd.	17	£339.25
Henry Reid	Elm Park	8	£239.40
Andrew Gill	Erin Terrace	6	£195.25
Frederick Stokes	Eton Terrace	4	£131.40
Patrick P. Bacon	Euston Terrace	0	0
John H. Evans	Mount Harold	0	0
Alexander Parker	Turner's Buildings	0	0
Christopher E. Wall	Fortesque Terrace	0	0
Edward E. Galavan	William's Park	0	0
John Purser	Rathmines Castle	0	0
John Scally	Rathmines Terrace	0	0
Thomas McEnery	Newington Terrace	0	0

Source: Rathmines township act 1847, 10 11 Vict., c.253 Griffith's Valuation (those listed as owning no houses in the township had property in the adjoining area)

As the board was largely composed of men of business, it became their custom from the start to meet early in the morning; indeed for many years they met for breakfast at their own expense at eight a.m., and held their meeting. This was later changed to nine o'clock, but no business of which notice had not been given at a previous meeting was discussed after ten o'clock so that members could leave and attend to their affairs in Dublin without fear of missing any unscheduled items.[3]

Mary E. Daly states that suburban politics to the end of the 1870s do not merit being described in party-political terms, and that until then Dublin local bodies were dominated by conservatives.[4] However, an examination of the existing evidence shows that religious and political differences played a part in civic life at township level. This evidence comes from sources other than township minutes, which are silent regarding religious and party-political matters. This silence is explained by the fact that it was common for such matters to be debarred from discussion; in Rathmines this bar was referred to as a standing rule.[5] There are some pointers towards the political make-up of the inaugural Rathmines board. At a meeting called in the Roman catholic parish of St Peter and St Mary, Rathmines, in November 1847 to collect money for a monument to Daniel O'Connell, recently deceased, four subsequent Rathmines commissioners were prominent. John Scally was appointed secretary to the committee formed, Edward Galavan became treasurer and Thomas McEnery and Terence T. Dolan were members, as also was S.A. McIvor, who was to be appointed a rate-collector for the township.[6] It can be taken for granted that these five had what was termed at the time 'liberal' leanings in politics and as admirers of O'Connell, were more than likely repealers, and probably Roman catholics. Frederick Stokes stated that six of the eighteen seats on the first Rathmines board were reserved for 'liberals'. It would appear that the above-mentioned group, already active in the religious/political sphere, swung in behind Stokes in the founding of the township. It is interesting that the idea of reserving a one-third block of seats for a religious minority was mooted in Dublin previously. When Daniel O'Connell was mayor of Dublin, he expressed the wish to be succeeded by a protestant and took up the proposal by Sergeant Jackson that one-third of the seats on the corporation be reserved for them. The offer was subsequently rejected but was put into effect in Rathmines for Roman catholics, although, as will be seen, it did not survive for long.[7] Terence T. Dolan together with Frederick Stokes can be considered the founding fathers of the Rathmines township. We will subsequently see that Stokes was conservative in politics. It would appear then that a deliberate attempt was being made to include both liberals and conservatives, catholics and protestants in the moves to found a township and on the first board. We shall also see that Stokes openly admitted that continuous efforts were made to reserve a certain number of seats on the township board for Roman catholics.

There is a degree of uncertainty over trends in the protestant population of Dublin over the course of the eighteenth and nineteenth centuries. While David Dickson claims that protestant numbers continued to rise over the late eighteenth and early nineteenth century,[8] Patrick Fagan, looking at the somewhat longer period of the whole of the eighteenth and the first half of the nineteenth centuries, has charted a steady decline of the protestant population of Dublin city. According to Fagan, between 1695 and 1798 the total population of the city grew from about 47,000 to 180,000. The decline in the protestant population is seen after 1733. In that year the number of protestants stood at about 75,000, levelling off to 58,000 in 1766 and had been reduced to 54,000 at the end of the century. In relative terms the protestant percentage fell from approximately 67% in 1715 to about 30% in 1798.[9] Fagan estimates that this had fallen further to 26.4% by 1831. Using returns quoted in the report on religious public instruction in Ireland of 1835 he calculates that of a population of 250,245 there were 183,931 Roman catholics (73.4%), 62,782 members of the established church (25%) and 3,429 dissenting protestants (1.4%).[10]

According to the more accurate figures provided by the census of Ireland of 1861, in that year Church of Ireland numbers in Dublin city had fallen to 49,251 with almost 6,800 presbyterians and methodists. This census also returned numbers for the Dublin suburbs (the townships): these amounted to 17,668 members of the Church of Ireland and 2,304 presbyterians and methodists.[11] Although the numbers were continually falling this was still the largest concentration of members of the established church in Ireland. By 1891 the Church of Ireland population of Dublin city had fallen to 35,125, while the township of Rathmines contained 10,758 members of the established church, 13,884 Roman catholics, 1,108 presbyterians, 801 methodists and 1,272 members of other denominations.[12]

Figure 5 shows that the protestant (Church of Ireland and presbyterian) presence in the seven largest townships was high compared to that of the city; taking the townships as a whole in 1871 the protestant percentage was 37% compared to 18% in Dublin. These figures had fallen to 31% and 14% respectively by 1911. At the beginning of this forty year period, Rathmines, with 46 per cent had the highest proportion of protestants. In all of the other townships existing in 1871 the protestant proportion ranged from 30% to 40%. Between 1871 and 1891, the proportion of protestants fell in all of the individual townships then in existence, except Clontarf, where it went up by almost three percentage points, reflecting the building of new middle-class housing there in those decades. The fall in the protestant component was most spectacular in Pembroke, nearly ten percentage points. Drumcondra township, which did not come into existence until 1878, had the lowest proportion of protestants (23%), reflecting its lower middle-class and artisan character. The drop in Kilmainham was small, as the protestant population there was largely working class, associated with the railway, and its vocational nature gave greater stability than that given by a purely residential status.

It should be pointed out that the proportions given above are for the total population, men women and children. A large proportion of the Roman catholic population was made up of domestic servants and the poorer sections of society who would not have attained the £10 property qualification for the right to vote existing in most of the townships. In 1911 in Dublin there were 12,322 indoor domestic servants. Nearly all of what were classified as the 'upper class' (98%) kept servants, 71% of the middle class and 23% of the lower middle class.[13] The vast majority of the first two categories lived in the townships. While no figures are available, a disproportionate number of the electorate in the townships was protestant.

Subsequent political allegiances of Rathmines commissioners can be difficult to determine. According to Stokes, only six of the original commissioners were liberals, probably Roman catholic. As will be seen, these liberal members found it difficult to retain their seats. Standing orders, adopted in the early years of the board, forbade the discussion of political matters, and this was stringently enforced for many decades. However, contentious matters purely relating to the business of administering the township arose from time to time. As will be seen when financial matters are discussed, a disagreement over the handling of payment of rates by Portobello military barracks caused a split on the board. Relations with ratepayers in general tended to be fraught, and some of those who had opposed the setting up of the township continued their opposition for some time after its establishment. At the first annual meeting of the commissioners, which took place in June 1848, with about forty ratepayers present, a contentious note was struck. A vote of thanks to the commissioners for their work over the year was proposed; however an amendment was tabled thanking them for the 'peculiar care and attention of Rathmines Road'. It was supported by a ratepayer from Ranelagh, who felt that area was being neglected, and by Thomas McCreary, who had opposed the setting up of the township. McCreary kept up opposition to the board over a number of years and refused to pay rates. In 1849 his arrears had accumulated to such an extent that the board succeeded in winning an order for the sale of his house to meet his rates' bill. This appeared to bring McCreary to his senses and he appealed to the board for a delay so that he could put his affairs in order.[14]

The whole Rathmines area formed one constituency for the election of commissioners to the board. The question of dividing the township into wards did not arise until Rathgar was annexed in 1862. The new area was made into a separate ward and was represented by three commissioners, with the original area still having eighteen. This was re-arranged later when the whole township was divided into two wards, east and west, both of almost equal valuation. The arrangement did not cause any contention until the arrival of nationalist opposition at the end of the century.

Rathmines and Rathgar had no great pre-existing population of poorer people who might hold differing political views to the newly arriving middle classes. However, the situation was different in an area like Blackrock where a large indigenous population resided in Blackrock village. When the township was extended in 1863, it was divided into three wards, and at the same time the township franchise was raised to £8. This brought about a change in the nature of the electorate: a catholic/liberal majority lost out to a conservative and protestant one. Daly quotes a disgruntled pamphleteer who claimed that Monkstown was made a separate ward to secure a majority for the 'ascendancy' on the board.[15] So, it appears, in Blackrock at least, nationalist/unionist tension was present from the start. Inter-ward rivalry, based more on social division, arose in Kingstown in 1869 when the township was divided into four wards and there was, according to a witness at the Exham enquiry, 'much trouble in doing so'.[16] The wards were Monkstown, Kingstown east, Kingstown west and Glasthule. Monkstown was given three seats on the board and the others six each. The trouble arose over the low-valuation ward of Glasthule being allocated six seats.

Pembroke, with its large population of poor people residing in Ringsend and Irishtown, was not divided into wards until the shake-up instigated by the 1898 local government act. Many of these poor did not have a vote as they did not reach the rateable valuation needed. Those few who did were squeezed out by affluent Ballsbridge. Unlike the poorer areas in other townships such as the Blackrock village area in Blackrock, and the town of Kingstown and Glasthule in Kingstown township, Irishtown and Ringsend did not have a large element of small traders and shopkeepers who were more likely to hold different views and have distinct interests from the middle and upper-class residents of the squares and avenues.

Access to township boards was often not by election but by co-option, a procedure allowed under the township acts. It became a common practice when a vacancy arose on the Rathmines board, owing to resignation or death, to co-opt a new member who would hold office for the duration of the term of the deceased or retiring member. Stokes made a virtue out of this practice by stating that it was the commissioners' custom from the inception of the township to co-opt a Roman catholic in such cases. This was done, he claimed, because, as the majority of the ratepayers were 'conservative', catholics found it difficult to get themselves elected. This would lead us to believe that in Stokes' time at least, catholics tended to be non-conservative. When such a co-optee's tenure was up, he was usually rejected by the electorate although endorsed for re-election by the board. Stokes claimed that it was the general policy of the board that those who held strong political opinions were avoided when co-option arose.[17] He also claimed that three or four seats were reserved for non-property owners in the township, that is those who were renting their houses. It was claimed that these, when they were supported by the board, were re-elected when they stood in an election. This is in sharp contrast to the experience of Roman catholics, who although supported by the board at election time, were, if what Stokes states is correct, not generally elected. This suggests that in Rathmines social divisions were not as important as political and religious differences.[18] Co-option was used quite cynically early in the life of the board. Stokes himself was never very popular with the ratepayers, and was, in fact, rejected at the first election; however a member of the board resigned to allow him to be co-opted.[19]

Figure 5: Dublin city townships: percentage of protestants, 1871–1911

Township	1871	1891	1911
Rathmines	46	43	39
Pembroke	40	36	30
Clontarf	35	38	–
Blackrock	34	31	28
Kingstown	33	30	28
Kilmainham	31	30	–
Drumcondra	–	23	–
Dublin	18	16	14
T'ship Total	37	33	31

Source: Mary E. Daly, *Dublin: the deposed capital* (Cork, 1984), p. 149

An insight into the purpose of co-option and how it was operated can be gained from the experience of Mark C. Bentley, a commissioner who subsequently became one of the greatest opponents of the Rathmines board. Bentley was a speculative builder in the Kenilworth area of the township. He received a letter from Stokes stating that a vacancy had come about on the board and that as a large property owner he was 'entitled' to a seat. He let Stokes know that he did not like co-option as he felt that it constrained members, and that once they took their seats, they lost their independence. However, friends prevailed on him to take the seat, asserting that the board was a 'self-elected body', and that if he did not take up the opportunity he would never get another chance of becoming a member. He took the advice and accepted the offer.[20]

Bentley claimed that once he became a member, he threw his weight behind reform, and supported the campaign of like-minded candidates for membership of the board. He characterized the board as a 'perpetual cabinet star chamber', and claimed that its members met in one another's private houses to draw up agreed addresses to the ratepayers. He himself and Commissioner Holmes were, he asserted, the only members not part of this group and opposed it on the question of the failure to introduce water from Dublin corporation's Vartry scheme, an issue dealt with in Chapter 3.[21]

From the experience of Bentley, it would appear that a number of ratepayers believed that the Rathmines board operated as a self-perpetuating clique, and while elections were duly held every year to replace one-third of the commissioners, those recommended by the board were usually elected. If a vacancy arose in mid-term the board selected a co-optee. The only time this arrangement broke down and the wishes of the board not fulfilled was when a Roman catholic co-optee was in due course put before the electorate.

While middle-class conservatives dominated the boards at this time, in the townships including large landed estates, landlords took steps to ensure that they were in positions of authority. The landlord interest prevailed in Clontarf where Vernon, the largest landlord in the area, was chairman for life, and in Pembroke, where the estate agent was an *ex officio* member of the board. Sectional interests of a different nature tried to gain some control in Kilmainham. The tussle between the promoters of the Kilmainham bill and the Great Southern and Western Railway Company continued for some time. When three members of the Kilmainham board offered themselves for re-election in 1869 they were opposed by three candidates put up by the railway company: its traffic manager, its paymaster, and one of its best-known engineers, Alexander McDonnell. The other commissioners tried to prevent their candidature on the grounds that their proposers did not pay rates but that they were paid by the railway company on their behalf. On advice, their nominations were accepted; however, they were not elected and the outgoing commissioners were returned.[22]

Many key founding members of townships remained on their boards for a lengthy period of time. Milo Burke was the guiding spirit in Dalkey for ten years and, in Killiney, Robert Warren remained at the helm for twenty-five years. John Vernon, the Pembroke agent, was *ex officio* commissioner until his death in 1887, and his namesake (no relation) in Clontarf, John E. Vernon, was, by statute, chairman for life; his colleague on the Clontarf board, George Tickell, was another long-serving member.

In 1877, as the result of a paralytic stroke, Frederick Stokes stepped down as chairman of the Rathmines board and resigned his seat. So ended an association which had lasted for thirty years, during which he had almost continuously been chairman. A special presentation was made to him in the town hall on 19 June 1878 where his public work in connection with the board of guardians, the Hospital for Incurables, Donnybrook, and especially, the Rathmines township, was recalled. A presentation of a library of books and a fine illuminated address was made to him before his retirement to England.[23] As will be seen when his examination before the Exham commission is discussed, Stokes appears to have been a very authoritarian figure. His extensive knowledge of local government and taxation was deferred to by other board members and he held strong opinions. This aspect of his character is also borne out by what we know of his time as a governor and chairman of the Royal Hospital, Donnybrook. He remained chairman even after moving to England, and while there, vehemently opposed changes to bye-laws drawn up by him many years before. He resigned shortly after these changes were made.[24] In 1883 he was forced to come out of retirement to face a committee set up to look into the management of the hospital while he was in charge.[25] This is remarkably similar to what happened in the case of his tenure on the Rathmines board. He had to come back to Ireland to face cross-examination at the Exham commission as a result of complaints by ratepayers over how the township had been run under the his chairmanship. However, some doubt must be cast on the efficacy of the Royal Hospital committee as a number of its members were close associates of Stokes, including Edward Fottrell, his chosen successor as chairman of the Rathmines board, Orlando Beater and T.S. Sibthorpe, two other Rathmines board-members. Stokes eventually returned to Ireland and died at Monkstown, County Dublin, in 1898.

Stokes was succeeded by his protégé and business associate, Edward Fottrell. The fact that Fottrell was a Roman catholic was a sign that things were changing in the township. Like Stokes, Fottrell was prominent in the business life of the city. He became chairman of the Alliance and Dublin Consumers' Gas Company in 1874 and remained in that position for many years. He had been elected to the Rathmines board in 1872 and, on attaining the chair, held it for twenty years.[26] So, for the first half century, except for a short period during the illness of Stokes, the township had only two chairmen, Stokes and Fottrell. Figure 6, based on Appendix 1, examines the duration of service of Rathmines commissioners for the first thirty years of the township's existence. It can be seen that many commissioners served for long periods of time on the board, up to ten years being very common, with nineteen serving for over twenty.

Figure 6: Duration of service of Rathmines commissioners, 1848–77

Years	Commissioners	Years	Commissioners
1–5	26	21–5	7
6–10	18	26–30	11
11–15	8	31+	1
16–20	2		

Source: Rathmines township minutes; *Thom's directory* 1847–77

The qualifications for the franchise and for membership of the township board in Rathmines were outlined on page 62. This was, of course, a time when there was no universal suffrage and men such as Frederick Stokes were firmly of the opinion that local government should be in the hands of those with a stake in the area, property-owners like himself; so the townships were not 'democratic' by modern standards. Taking the year 1885 as an example, a glance at the size of the electorate compared to population (fig. 7) shows, however, that some authorities were more democratic than others. This depended on the precise property qualification for the franchise and the social mix in the area concerned. Nowhere did the electorate reach 12% of the population, although Clontarf came close to this, with Drumcondra and Blackrock not far behind. In descending order, between 8% and 5% came Rathmines, Kilmainham and Killiney. The electorate of Dublin Corporation, with a large concentration of poor in its area was less than 3% of its total population.

Figure 7: Electorate as percentage of population, 1885

Town	Electorate %	Town	Electorate %
Clontarf	11.54	Kilmainham	6.3
Drumcondra	10.53	Kingstown	5.7
Blackrock	10.32	Killiney	4.83
Rathmines	7.53	Dublin	2.66
Pembroke	7.04		

Source: Return of taxation in Ireland, H.C. 1886 (4810) lvii, pp 2–7

A profile of commissioners before the widening of the franchise in 1898 shows the presence of professionals, businessmen, builders, and in the case of Kilmainham, industrialists and engineers. A notable member of the Pembroke board was Edward H. Carson, father of the unionist leader, Edward Carson. One of the founder-members of the township, he had been commissioned as architect to a number of domestic and ecclesiastical buildings in the Rathmines and Pembroke area in the late 1850s and early 1860s. He remodelled St Peter's parish church in Aungier Street and worked on a prestigious terrace of houses, Warwick Terrace, on the border of Rathmines and Pembroke, which greatly enhanced his reputation as an architect. He collaborated with John Butler, a builder and one of the founder-members of Rathmines township, in this scheme. The *Dublin Builder* saw Warwick Terrace as a perfect example of the type of housing 'suited to the highest gentry in our land', which were springing up in the new Pembroke estate.[27] Carson was the designer of Pembroke town hall and worked on many other projects in townships ranging from Clontarf to Blackrock.

The financial basis underpinning all the work of the townships was the rates levied on the townships' valuation. The township acts set limits to the amount of the rate which could be struck, often quite restrictive. The principal weakness in the financing of the townships was the limited revenue available to the various authorities owing to the low rate base and consequent restricted borrowing powers. The piecemeal manner in which the townships had developed, and the consequent fragmented structure of local government in the Dublin area, left each township with very limited resources. This retarded the ability to provide the necessary services. A strong case was made against fragmentation, especially in the coastal townships, by John McEvoy, who had been a Kingstown commissioner for eight years, and chairman for two. Outlining to the Exham commission in 1879 the weaknesses of the current local government structure in the coastal townships, he pointed out that there were four boards and sixty-two commissioners supported by a population of only 30,000, and that if the same representation was given to Dublin city there would be 600 instead of sixty councillors.

McEvoy cited the case of Killiney, which had not a large enough population to be deemed in law a sanitary authority, and where most of the work was done by the board of poor law guardians. The guardians, he claimed, accomplished this more economically than similar work done in neighbouring Dalkey and the other coastal townships. He went on to point out that each board had a secretary, surveyor, law agent, consulting sanitary officer, executive sanitary officer, medical officer of health, collectors, water inspector and minor officials. They had quite numerous and formidable acts of parliament to implement, including the Towns' improvement act and the Public health act, the latter with 293 clauses. The onus this legislative burden placed on the townships required skill and competence. If the other acts which needed to be adopted urgently were taken on, a heavy burden would be placed on areas of small taxation, and so the work remained undone; the whole situation amounted to 'local government on paper only'. As an example of this he cited the Artisans' dwellings act which was not adopted simply because townships were too small. Another area neglected because of lack of financial resources was drainage, and he saw, as a solution, making Blackrock, Kingstown and Dalkey one drainage area. Lack of funding led to the employment of a less than professional staff, characterized by McEvoy as amateurs, 'numerous gentlemen', who in some cases for only £10 a year, were 'willing to allow themselves to be called by high sounding titles'. In some instances, he claimed, these incompetents did not perform their duties at all, and in others, in only a perfunctory manner.[28]

Before examining the argument of McEvoy it would be useful to look at the mechanics of revenue-raising, taking Rathmines as an example. In Rathmines by law the rate was not to exceed two shillings in the pound per annum, but could be increased by a further 6d. if two-thirds of the ratepayers at a special meeting agreed to it. At the first meeting of commissioners, the township was divided up into two equal parts for the purposes of collection. The rate of 1s. was collected in two moieties, in March and September of each year. Figure 8 shows how the valuation in Rathmines grew at a steady pace reflecting the sustained development of house property up to the beginning of the twentieth century.

The Rathmines board promptly set about collecting its first rate. The funds available for improvements would prove meagre as, from the 1s. available, 6d. would go towards the costs incurred in preparing the township bill. The question of an accurate valuation of the district arose. The surveyor was directed by the board to see whether the poor law valuation was satisfactory, and, if not, to draw up a new valuation. The result of this investigation was that the poor law valuation was accepted with certain modifications. At the same time a new general valuation was being prepared by Richard Griffith and the board decided to accept this when it became available.[29] Property owners were eager to exploit any loophole to avoid paying rates. In the early years some householders on the margins of the township attempted to maintain that they did not reside within the township boundary. However, an appeal by the board to Griffith in the valuation office gave an assurance that the use of the ordnance map to settle such questions had the backing of the law.[30]

Figure 8: Rathmines township valuation, 1850–95

Year	Valuation	Year	Valuation
1850	£28,364	1875	£89,751
1855	£37,072	1880	£102,058
1860	£43,313	1885	£114,989
1865	£67,707	1890	£121,389
1870	£79,850	1895	£128,280

Source: Return of taxation in Ireland, H.C. 1886 (4810) lvii, pp 2–7

The 1847 Rathmines act stipulated that occupiers were to pay the rate, and in the case of unoccupied houses, the owner. In an area such as Rathmines, where at any one time a large number of houses were being built, a question arose as to when a new house became suitable for occupation, and so liable for rates. The commissioners sought legal advice on this and decided that 'a stringent rating of such property (untenanted) would operate as a discouragement to outlay in building in this township and that therefore the law of rating shall always be interpreted in the landlord's favour regarding unoccupied property'.[31] A clear conflict of interest for a number of commissioners engaged in building houses did not prevent all board members heartily agreeing with this motion. This is an example of the thinking in the Rathmines township which always tended to keep the rates' bill as low as possible for property owners and occupiers. While in this case the sums involved were small, the overall policy, as will be presently seen, starved the township of revenue and greatly affected the provision of services.

The low rates policy of the board prompted strong opposition to the government's proposal for a rate-in-aid for distressed areas in February 1849. It was intended to transfer half a million pounds to areas still suffering famine at this time by placing a rate of 6*d*. on a nationwide valuation of £9 million.[32] The house of commons was petitioned on behalf of the ratepayers; it was claimed that the proposed measure would take away protection for industry, and tax the Rathmines district for the support of remote and neglected areas. This very negative response was in fact the only time that the famine crisis in the country was adverted to in the minutes of the board.[33]

By March 1851, Griffith had completed his valuation of the township, but it did not meet with the commissioners' approval, as they thought it was too low. When Griffith refused a request for a revision of the new valuation before it was finally decided, the board considered a petition to parliament.[34] Fears of a sizeable reduction in the valuation of the township were realized when the new rating was published in February 1852. The valuation was reduced from £40,680 to £35,320, a figure, which, the board claimed, would allow it to maintain the improvement of the district, while adhering to a rate ceiling of 2*s*., only by the 'strictest economy'.[35]

A long-running dispute over rate payment also seriously affected the finances of the township. This arose when the barrack-master at Portobello military barracks, Colonel Farquarson, refused to pay rates on houses which he regarded as official Board of Ordnance property. The commissioners, on the other hand, regarded some of these as being private and therefore liable for rates. Unwisely, as it turned out, the case was pursued by the commissioners through the courts. A number of hearings, unsuccessful from the township's point of view, resulted in high legal expenses being incurred. By 1854, a total of £360 had been expended in an abortive attempt to recover the half yearly rate on the property concerned, a sum of £1. 16*s*. 8*d*.

The expenditure of such a large sum by a body of very limited resources prompted the commissioners to set up a special committee to report on the matter. It concluded that such a large sum should not have been spent on a case which had not even the benefit of being a test case, and so of no benefit to the township, as no other cases would be influenced by it. The committee recommended that heavy law expenses should be avoided in future, and, moreover, that various law suits pending be terminated. The blame was laid on the permanent law officer employed by the board; it was claimed that he had too much influence, and it was recommended that his post be abolished. The committee felt that such a post was unnecessary since there were several men on the board with legal experience. In contrast to the Portobello case, it was pointed out that a dispute with Lord Palmerston had been settled for an outlay of £5. In place of the law officer, a permanent legal committee was proposed to deal with such matters in the future.[36] This recommendation caused a split on the board which led to the resignation of three commissioners in 1855, John Connor, Edward Wright and John Butler; Butler and Connor had been named as commissioners in the 1847 Rathmines act.

While ratepayers' money was being expended in this imprudent way, the commissioners closely scrutinized the spending of others which may have affected the state of the township's hard-pressed coffers. By the enabling legislation, the first call on the township rates was the county at large presentments made by the County Dublin grand jury. The sum varied from year to year according to the presentments made. It became the practice of the commissioners to watch closely the proceedings of the grand jury and oppose any large presentments liable to place a heavy burden on its funds.

The auditing of accounts was a cause of much dissatisfaction among Rathmines ratepayers. The 1847 private Rathmines act specified that two auditors were to be elected at a public meeting of ratepayers. The auditors had to have the same property qualifications as commissioners – £30 for residents, £200 for non-residents. They were not required to be qualified professionally in any way, although, according to Stokes, they were usually 'persons of high standing, the accountant of the Bank of Ireland, or someone in that capacity'.[37] The auditors chosen were usually those picked by the board itself, and up to 1876, it had happened on only one occasion that there had been a competition and those recommended by the commissioners not chosen.[38] When it was decided to reorganize local government in Ireland and place the structure under a local government board, two of the provisions in the bill stated that the accounts of townships should be placed under the new state board. Rathmines immediately saw this as gross interference in the management of its affairs and lobbied to have the provisions made optional.[39]

The cogent argument of McEvoy is borne out by an examination of financial problems faced by the Rathmines, Pembroke and Clontarf townships. In Rathmines a predicament arose when it became clear that a policy of strict economy resulting in a water supply of dubious quality was no longer acceptable to ratepayers (examined in more detail in the next chapter). Because of problems in the construction of a new waterworks and the ensuing long drawn out dispute with millowners on the Dodder, the Rathmines commissioners found themselves in financial difficulties in the early 1890s. By that date they had exceeded their borrowing powers under the Public health act of 1878, the Waterworks act of 1880 and the Improvement act of 1885. The local government board refused to sanction further loans and Rathmines, like Pembroke, considered new legislation. In this case the legislation was approved and an act to enable Rathmines to amend and define its borrowing powers and to enable additional money to be borrowed was passed.[40]

Clontarf was almost bankrupt at the end of the 1870s, and the decade of the 1890s proved to be one of serious financial difficulty for both Pembroke and Rathmines. The Pembroke situation was more serious and it is worth looking at it in a little detail as it highlights the contrast between a board like Pembroke, which was prepared to spend on services and facilities, and a township firmly in the hands of an 'economy party' like Rathmines. The Pembroke board was lulled into a false sense of financial security by the patrician generosity of the Pembroke estate, which contributed a free site and funded two-thirds the cost of a town hall, financed up to 20% of the cost of main drainage, provided funds for Ringsend technical school and donated the land for Herbert Park.[41]

The Pembroke financial crisis had its origins in the provision of the relatively expensive Vartry water, which the township bought from Dublin corporation, while Rathmines relied on the cheap canal supply. Pembroke also was more conscientious in implementing public health legislation and embarked on an ambitious public housing programme. As a result of this, the Pembroke board applied to the Bank of Ireland in 1892 for an overdraft facility of up to £6,500 to meet current expenses and cover the excessive expenditure of the previous year. The problem was exacerbated by the fact that the township secretary had absconded with some of the funds. The board stated that two independent auditors were being appointed and a private loan was being sought. Measures were also being taken to reduce current expenditure by dispensing with staff and reducing the wages' bill.[42] However, when the bank sought assurances as to the board's credit balances, the board was forced to admit that they were not satisfactory, but that steps were being taken to increase the yield from rates during the coming year and to recoup certain capital expenditure.[43]

The bank agreed to the overdraft provided that the board prepared an estimate for the coming year and that the rate it struck was submitted to the bank's directors. The bank continued to warn the board over the state of its finances and had itself appointed the township's treasurer in 1894 at a fee of £150 a year. The financial situation had not been alleviated by 1902 and a letter was placed in the newspapers requesting all who had liabilities against the board to inform it of them.[44] As the financial crisis continued legal opinion was sought, and the obtaining of new legislation was recommended. When the commissioners sought advice from the local government board as to how they should proceed to 'extricate themselves from their embarrassment', the board replied that it regarded them as solvent but did not recommend new legislation, as it did not believe that it would succeed.[45]

In response to the ongoing financial problems a ratepayers' association ran a number of candidates in local elections. In 1901, the Pembroke estate, which had over the years injected funds for particular projects like the town hall and technical school, refused further assistance. The following year the rate stood at 11s., more than double that of Rathmines. A desperate, but dubious, measure was resorted to when it was discovered that £33,000 borrowed for the establishment of the electricity works was not sufficient, and over £4,000 more had to be borrowed. It was proposed to recoup this liability in the board's no. 1 account by transferring the amount from its no. 2 account, although it was pointed out that no. 2 account was set up for artisans' dwellings in Ringsend, and this procedure would be improper. The chairman of the council, George Perry, a resident of Elgin Road and a portmanteau manufacturer of Grafton Street, was completely opposed to this move. Although the funds were transferred on a majority vote of the council, Perry signed the cheque under protest and had the following statement recorded in the minutes:

> I, George Perry, chairman of this board, having been required by a majority of the board to sign cheques for £4,740/10/9 hereby state that I have done so in obedience to the said resolution, but absolutely under protest as to the legality of such transfer.[46]

At the time numerous requests for settlement of accounts were coming in, including a writ for over £4,000 from Dublin corporation. The board's exact liability was difficult to determine; the chairman stated that it was £37,187, while other board members maintained that it was not nearly half that.[47] The crisis, especially the very high rate of 11s., led to the resignation of board members and culminated in the stepping down of Perry from the chair. An appeal by the board for the earl of Pembroke to act as guarantor for its advances from the bank met with a negative response. However, the new chairman, Robert Gardner, agreed to loan the board between £4,000 and £5,000 'to remove all pressing liabilities'. As the new century dawned, any lingering hope that the council had that the Pembroke estate would help in a financial crisis had evaporated.

On the larger political front, in the 1890s, the prospect of home rule caused some anxiety to the townships in general over the continuation of exchequer funding. The Blackrock board agreed to petition parliament in March 1893 against the insertion of a clause in the home rule bill which would deprive them of exchequer funding and so increase local rates.[48]

The extension of townships, or attempts to extend them, was an important element in the development of a number of the local authorities. Despite being hampered by lack of resources leading to ongoing criticism by people like McEvoy in Kingstown and Bentley in Rathmines, those living in the areas adjoining the townships were envious of the improvements being made under township boards compared to the relative inactivity of the grand jury. It is therefore not surprising that adjoining areas wished to avail of the benefits of better local government and come under township control. The annexation of Monkstown by Blackrock has already been alluded to.

As early as 1849, Terence Dolan, the builder of Mount Pleasant Square and a founder member of the Rathmines township, was anxious for the extension of the township area to include the Pembroke district. In November 1849, a bill for improving Upper Baggot Street, Pembroke Road and Waterloo Road by the extension of the Rathmines township to include those areas was mooted in the

Dublin Gazette. The name and address of a firm of solicitors were appended to the notice (Woodroofe & Wilson, 30 Upper Mount Street, Dublin), but the promoters were not named.[49] The Rathmines board let it be known that those who were promoting the scheme would have to bear the expense of promoting the bill. Dolan was deputized by the Rathmines board to confer with the agent of the Pembroke estate in relation to the matter, but nothing came of the moves.[50]

In 1850, the possibility of an extensive enlargement of the Rathmines township took the commissioners by surprise. Without the knowledge or consent of the board, Frederick Jackson, the solicitor who had seen the Rathmines legislation through parliament, now no longer a Rathmines board member, placed a notice in the newspapers to the effect that an application would be made at the next session of parliament to extend the Rathmines act to the townlands of Baggotrath East and North in the parish of St Peter, and to the townlands of Donnybrook West and Sallymount in the parish of St Mary's, and to the townlands of Donnybrook and Rathgar in the parish of Rathfarnham. The two latter townlands were in a different barony, Rathdown, from that of the rest of the existing township and the other new areas proposed for extension.[51]

The commissioners disapproved of this extensive scheme, struggling as they were to look after the area already in their care. Their immediate worry was that it be made clear that they would not be in any way liable for the expense of promoting such a bill in parliament. They placed a disavowal in the press, pointing out that they had nothing to do with such a move and that the bill was the sole responsibility of Jackson.[52] By the end of the year, they had heard from Jackson that he did not wish to proceed with the bill as he was unwilling to incur the expense. Tribute was paid to his good work for the township and the commissioners pointed out that there was nothing personal in their opposition to the bill.[53] It is difficult to determine what the motives of Jackson were. It is evident from his involvement in the promotion of a bill to reform the administration of Dublin city that he had a keen personal interest in local government and improvement and perhaps his maverick move was inspired by the purest motives.

In 1852, a number of inhabitants of Rathgar met to consider having the township extended to the area. A deputation met the commissioners and a number of meetings took place. Nothing came of this move either, once again the cost of promoting such a bill probably dissuading the inhabitants.[54]

In 1853, moves were afoot again in Rathgar for annexation; this time the deputation that came to see the board included Sir Robert Shaw, a large landowner of Bushy Park, Terenure, who had wished to be part of the township from the start. The response of the commissioners was equivocal. They would facilitate a bill for the improvement of Rathgar provided it was for a separate township with power to amalgamate with Rathmines in the future, but a bill for immediate amalgamation would be resisted.[55] This reluctance on the part of the commissioners arose from the fact that they were at the time borrowing and spending huge sums on the canal waterworks scheme. After a motion against amalgamation had been passed, a number of commissioners changed their minds and called a special meeting of the board where their previous objections were rescinded, and it was decided to seek the inclusion of Rathgar in the township. It is not clear why they changed their minds, however it is likely that negotiations took place between the Rathgar party and the commissioners whereby the ratepayers of the new area would bear the bulk of the financial burden involved in annexation. This is what transpired when the area became part of the township some years later.

However, in 1853, formidable opposition to the proposed extension came from Frederick Stokes. With his usual energy and thoroughness, he drew up a list of grounds for objection. He reminded his colleagues that the main reasons why Rathmines had been separated from the county in the first place had been to remove it from the jurisdiction of people who were 'unacquainted with it' so that a small area could be 'secured by constant supervision' over it. The proposed new area was also mainly made up of land rather than houses and was too far away from the town hall. He pointed out that the original Rathmines commissioners had excluded part of Harold's Cross at the time of the inception of the township for the latter reason. He went on to claim that Rathgar had nothing in common with Rathmines; it was in a different electoral division for poor law rates, and indeed paid up to 50 per cent more than Rathmines; it was in a different parish for ecclesiastical rates, and in a different barony for county rates. It was, moreover, half the size of Rathmines but had more than half the length of roads to be maintained and it was less than quarter the valuation. He foresaw that there would be dissatisfaction in the new area, and that the ratepayers there might be hostile to the present commissioners, and, indeed, might try to oust them.[56]

Such was the influence of Stokes that, despite the resolution of the board in favour of an extension to Rathgar, the matter was let drop for seven years. When the matter arose again, the Rathgar promoters agreed to several conditions laid down by Stokes. The Rathmines board would not be the promoters of the bill or liable for costs, but assenting parties. The preparation of such a private bill incurred high legal costs and it was agreed that these would be levied on the new district only. The improvement rate for the new district would be 6d. in the pound for five years, which would be collected in Rathgar in addition to the existing Rathmines rate. To ensure that there would be perfect equality as to rating there was to be no exception in favour of land. The new district was to be a separate ward with three members representing it on the board. It was also decided that the small townland of Sallymount would be added to the township 'to square the boundary in that district', but that the townland of Terenure would not be taken in, in whole or in part, on any terms (fig. 9).[57] The Rathgar

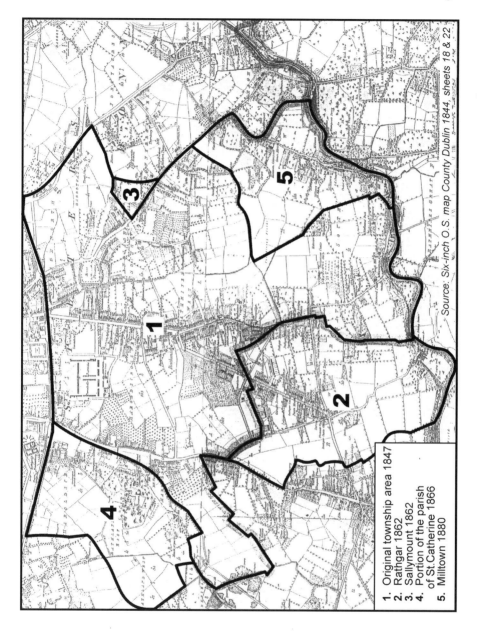

Figure 9: Rathmines townships showing annexed area

and Sallymount improvement act received the royal assent on 11 June 1862, and the new representatives of the Rathgar ward, Commissioners George Sykes, Maxwell McMaster and Henry W. Todd took their seats on the board.[58] All three were wealthy city businessmen residing in suburban Rathgar and were involved in the promotion of the bill.

The rateable valuation of the new district was £8,100 and its population in the 1861 census was 1,806. The new area, especially Rathgar, developed greatly in the years after amalgamation and by 1879 its valuation had doubled.[59] In 1866 a portion of the parish of St Catherine was added to the township,[60] and Milltown was added by the Milltown extension act of 1880 (fig. 9).

Figure 10: Dublin city and townships: valuation, population, no. of houses, voters and representatives, 1885

Town	£ Valuation	Population	Houses	Voters	Representatives
Dublin	675,673	249,602	24,211	6,644	60
Rathmines	113,969	24,370	3,946	1,836	21
Pembroke	96,980	23,222	3,537	1,636	15
Kingstown	78,053	18,586	3,074	1,060	21
Blackrock	49,450	8,902	1,464	919	24
Clontarf	18,522	4,210	727	486	12
Drumcondra	17,978	4,878	715	514	14
Dalkey	14,184	3,234	582	582	12
Killiney	10,690	2,607	343	343	12
Kilmainham	10,178	5,391	662	340	9

Source: Return of taxation in Ireland, H.C. 1886 (4810) lvii, pp 2–7

After all the townships had been established, a return of various statistics relating to the city and the suburban bodies compiled in 1885 provides an opportunity for comparison (fig. 10). As can be seen the city far outstripped any individual township in valuation and population, although the combined figures of the townships are a fair match for the corporation area: while the townships had a combined population of only 95,4000 compared to 249,602 in the city, their combined valuation amounted to £410,004, that is, 60.68 per cent of the city valuation of £675,673.

Each township found itself working within a nest of local bodies such as the county, parishes, poor law unions, very often with competing interests. There was very little co-ordination between them until the establishment of the local government board in 1872, although a certain amount of co-operation on matters of mutual interest was proposed and occasionally took place. In 1864 Stokes hosted a meeting of a newly formed committee of commissioners from Rath-mines, Pembroke, Kingstown and Blackrock to adopt a united approach to such matters as opposition to publicans' licenses and keeping a watchful eye on grand jury presentments. Four years later the boards of Kingstown and Rathmines were corresponding with County Dublin members of parliament with a view to investigating the possibility of creating a new parliamentary constituency in the area of south Dublin formed by the two townships. Strained relations between Dublin corporation and the townships, especially Rathmines, precluded much co-operation. As will be seen, the provision of water bound the corporation and all the townships, except Rathmines, together, although the relationship was strictly a business arrangement and, in fact, often led to contention.

A professional gulf, played up by people like Stokes who wished to keep the corporation at bay, was developing between the members of the corporation and the township boards. The larger businessmen were often willing to play their part in the suburban board rooms but kept themselves at arm's length from the municipal body. The corporation tended to be left to smaller businessmen, often grocers and publicans. There was also a noted absence of builders and proper-ty speculators on the corporation, a class that played a key role on many town-ship boards, the suburbs of course providing much greater scope for their activities.[61] The municipal body was increasingly used as a debating chamber for nationalist grievances. In 1850 Frederick Stokes was an enthusiastic supporter of a campaign by the Dublin Chamber of Commerce against the corporation being used as a nationalist platform and for a demand for a revision of the burgess-roll, the list of those entitled to vote for seats on the corporation.[62]

Antipathy towards the corporation was widespread in the townships, even in a less affluent one like Kilmainham. The Reverend Thomas Mills, rector of St Judes in Kilmainham, claimed he was summing up popular feeling towards the corporation in his evidence at the Exham commission. He stated that at corpo-ration meetings 'if there is a question of freedom of education, or political pris-oners, instead of freedom from dirt or dust, there is more interest shown in it by the members than anything else'.[63] The corporation attempted to contradict this impression by statistics. John Norwood, an influential member of the corporation and a lawyer, stated that in 1878 there had been eighty-six corporation meetings at which not a single political subject was mooted and 483 committee meeting at which only the business of administering the city was discussed. Mills weakly defended his accusation by stating that he was speaking in general, causing Norwood to retort that 'common reputation is, they say, a common liar'.[64]

Frederick Stokes, the Rathmines kingpin, had a strong personal dislike of Dublin corporation, as he revealed to a select committee on local government and taxation in 1876. When asked if he had thought of becoming a member of the corporation and changing it from the inside, he replied that nothing could induce him to go into it; he never took part in municipal affairs 'except to fight them' (the corporation); he had taken part in every fight with the municipal body over the past thirty years.[65] He believed that one man could not change the municipal body. He had often been asked by both parties to become a member, by which he meant, one supposes, conservatives and liberals. Both, he claimed, had promised him mayoralty, but he had refused. Revealing something of his personal ambition, he stated that he would rather be 'first in a village than second in Rome'. He claimed that the publican interest was much too strong on the corporation. Stokes had a personal dislike of the drinks trade and was a strong supporter of the temperance movement. On many occasions he proposed that publicans' licenses be opposed in Rathmines and at the township board he supported the movement for Sunday closing of licensed establishments. He attributed the success of the suburbs to ratepayers being driven out beyond the city boundaries by the high poor rate and the city rate.[66]

Apart from a growing difference in the make-up of the corporation and township boards, the main contention between them arose from the desire of the corporation to extend its boundaries and so extinguish some, or all, of the townships. As early as 1853 the city engineer, Parke Neville, in his first report, recommended extension of the boundaries. He cited the case of similar English cities to Dublin and the unfair taxation placed on the city. This suggestion caused the Rathmines board to form a committee to rebuff the corporation which resulted in an undertaking elicited from city hall stating that the corporation in fact had no 'present intention' of interfering with the township.[67] However, in the following years the corporation would return to the same arguments on many occasions.[68]

Specific contentious issues led to differences between Rathmines and the corporation. In 1861 an attempt was made by Dublin corporation to levy £8,877 over the whole metropolitan police district for a new bridge and wall at the Great Southern and Western Railway station at Kingsbridge. The police district included the city and all the townships and the new tax would entail a levy of around three pence in the pound in the township. The move was strenuously opposed by the Rathmines commissioners and they sought the support of the poor law unions and the grand jury for their stand. There was also opposition to the corporation's attempt to lay pipes for its new water supply through the township. The board saw it as affecting the independence of the township – an encroachment, allegedly, paving the way for absorption.[69] A public meeting was held on the issue at which a ballot was taken, the result of which was that 299 opposed a corporation bill giving it powers to lay the pipes, with only seventeen in favour. Of more weight with the board was the amount of property these figures represented. It was triumphantly announced that property-owners to the value of £9,227 opposed the corporation and those representing only £526 10s. were in favour.[70]

Despite differences, many of the townships' commissioners were prominent members of other local government bodies and occasionally of the corporation itself. In 1879 three Rathmines and four Pembroke commissioners were elected members of the corporation.[71] Alexander Parker, a prominent Rathmines commissioner, was a high sheriff of Dublin city in 1872[72] and board members were frequently poor law guardians. In 1869 no fewer than four of the Rathmines board members were on the dispensary committee of the south Dublin union.

Parish vestries retained certain local government powers, albeit much weakened, and they could still impose a parish cess. In 1861 the vestry of St Peter's voted £300 for four fire escapes (ladders made portable by wheels), the Rathmines board agreeing to pay one-quarter of the cost. The commissioners, however, resented the fact that they had no representation on the vestry, and hence no say in where the escapes would be placed. Payment was only made when a commissioner was appointed to the vestry and it was agreed that an escape would be located in Rathmines.[73]

To enhance its identity, Rathmines sought for many years to have the portion of the Church of Ireland parish of St Peter, in which the township was situated, made into a separate parish, but the Dublin archdiocesan authorities were opposed to this. The board then memorialised the lord lieutenant and privy council to rectify this, but was unsuccessful. In 1868 the setting up of a commission on disestablishment of the Church of Ireland was seen as an opportunity to press this matter and the commission was petitioned by the board. It was claimed that there were 7,000 members of St Peter's parish in the township, and that there was no Church of Ireland parish in the country as populous, not even the city portion of St Peter's. The township now encompassed a number of parishes and six places of worship of the established church. These were not sufficient to cater for all who wished to attend Sunday worship. The churches referred to were Holy Trinity, Belgrave Road, the Rathmines chapel of ease for St Peter's, which had opened in 1828, Zion church, Rathgar, Harold's Cross church at Mount Jerome cemetery, the Molyneux Institute, Sandford and St Philip's, Milltown; the last named was small and recently built. In all there was accommodation for 4,000 people, which was 'clearly inadequate'.[74] The request fell on deaf ears until 1883, when Holy Trinity became a separate parish.

Almost annually, Rathmines sought representation on the presentment sessions of the County Dublin grand jury, in order to be in a position to oppose any large expenditure which would entail cost to the Rathmines ratepayers, but be of no benefit to them. In 1854, four Rathmines commissioners were on the county grand jury but wished to be represented on the presenting grand jury, where the funding was allocated. The grand jury's invariable response was that only baronies were represented and it would not deviate from that precedent. At barony level a close watch was kept on any extraordinary presentments which would entail great county at large costs and these were usually opposed by Rathmines commissioners. They claimed that their opposition often resulted in the amount of a presentment being reduced. Due to continuous pressure, Stokes

Figure 11: Rathmines Urban Council, equalisation of the rates inquiry, 1911. 'Surveyors department – rate of wages per week'

Particulars	1906-7		1907-8		1908-9		1909-10		1910-11		Average number of men				
	s.	d.	s.	d.	s.	d.	s.	d.	s.	d.	1906-7	1907-8	1908-9	1909-10	1910-11
Overseer	77	0	77	0	77	0	77	0	80	0					
Carpenter (Head)	40	0	40	0	40	0	40	0	40	0					
do. (Assistant)	12	0	17	0	17	0	17	0	21	0					
Blacksmith	24	0	24	0	24	0	24	0	26	0					
Engine driver (steam rollers)	30	0	30	0	30	0	30	0	30	0	2	2	2	2	2
Yardman	18	0	18	0	20	0	20	0	20	0	1	1	1	1	1
Timekeeper	25	0	25	0	25	0	21	0	25	0	1	1	1	1	1
Stableman	25	0	25	0	25	0	25	0	25	0	1	1	1	1	1
Carters	19	6	19	6	20	7	20	7	20	7	26	26	26	26	26
Day Labourer	18	0	18	0	18	0	19	0	19	0	84	99	95	102	86
Plumber	33	0	33	0	33	0	33	0	36	0	1	1	1	1	1
Water Inspector	30	0	30	0	31	0	31	0	36	0	1	1	1	1	1
do. (Assistant)	17	0	17	0	19	0	19	0	20	0	1	1	1	1	1
Ganger (two)	30	0	30	0	37	6	27	6	27	6	2	2	2	2	2
Painter	25	0	25	0	22	6	25	0	25	0	1	1	1	1	1
Fire Brigade (Supt.)	25	4	25	4	25	4	25	4	25	4	1	1	1	1	1
do. (Assistant)	65	0	65	0	65	0	65	0	65	0	1	1	1	1	1
Water Works (Supt.)	34	6	34	6	34	6	34	6	34	6	1	1	1	1	1
Fire Brigade Men	40	0	40	0	40	0	40	0	40	0	2	2	2	2	2
	25	0	25	0	25	0	25	0	27	0	5	5	5	5	5
Parks' Gardener	30	0	30	0	30	0	30	0	30	0	1	1	1	1	1
	18	0	18	0	18	0	18	0	19	0					
	—		—		—		20	0	18	0					

Source: Dublin City Archives

was appointed a member of the board of superintendents of the grand jury in 1856, where he would have some control over county at large expenditure. There were continued complaints over the years that people in commerce were excluded from the grand jury and that it favoured large landowners. Rathmines also complained that the north county was over-represented, although it was far inferior to the south 'in valuation and educated persons'.[75] It was usual for the chairman and one or two of the commissioners of Rathmines to be on the bench of magistrates appointed by the government to administer justice in local areas. In 1859 the board was represented on the bench of county magistrates by three but it made representations to have the number increased.

In 1872, the poor law board was replaced by the local government board and given increased powers to co-ordinate and oversee local government in Ireland. The functions of the lord lieutenant, the privy council and the chief secretary relating to the government of towns, the administration of the poor law and sanitary laws devolved upon the new board. The new legislation made it easier for a local body to obtain extra powers. Provided the ratepayers consented, this could now be done without having to go to the expense of obtaining an act of parliament. If extra powers were now sought, an application could be made to the new board and a local inquiry held at little expense to the locality concerned, and if no objection was made and sustained, the powers were given. This was done by means of a provisional order, which passed through the legislature, usually without discussion, and without expense to the parties asking for it.[76]

Decisions made by township boards of commissioners, later known as councillors, were implemented by a number of salaried officials and a workforce of waged artisans and labourers. Township officials included a secretary, treasurer, a position sometimes entrusted to bank officials, and surveyors. Later, as services expanded, officers of health, sanitary officers, various clerks and inspectors were added, as well as engineers in charge of waterworks and electricity stations. An indication of the complexity of staffing reached by 1911 can be seen in the details of those employed in the Rathmines surveyor's department (fig. 11).

Some of these posts, even in the larger townships, were part-time. In 1891 when Henry Johnston, the Rathmines surveyor retired, it was decided that his successor would be obliged to give his whole time to the post.[77] Some of the key posts, such as secretary or surveyor, were held by the one person for long periods, and the holders had a strong influence on the development of their areas. Another major change in personnel had come about in Rathmines in 1888 when John Drury resigned as secretary and shortly afterwards resigned from the board.[78] Frederick Fawcett got his job as secretary and Sir Howard Grubb was co-opted in his place on the board – the motion that they wait until the next election being defeated.[79]

The contract system of labour, that is voting a certain sum of money for a project and hiring a contractor to carry it out, was associated in the minds of

many, Frederick Stokes of Rathmines in particular, with the evils of the grand
jury system. The system had led to much alleged corruption on grand juries and
the Rathmines board and the other township boards preferred to use direct
labour, employing their own workforces for the purpose. Stokes, however,
believed that the direct labour system could also be faulty and was critical of the
quality of Dublin corporation's labour force, on one occasion disparagingly referring to the corporation's labourers as 'St Vincent de Paul's men'.[80] With the
increased unionisation of labourers in Irish cities, friction developed between the
Rathmines board and its workforce. A dispute arose in 1888 when the township
scavengers refused to wear numbered badges dispensed to them. When they
declined to work rather than be badged they were replaced.[81] These rather
primitive industrial relations had given way six years later to a process of nego-
tiation. When the workmen requested that they get a half-day on Saturdays, finishing at two o'clock, a compromise was reached by which they would be free at
three.[82] While the board was prepared to negotiate, it was not yet ready to
recognise a union. In 1896 the workers sought to have a union recognized, but
were refused, the board insisting that there was no need for one as it had always
treated its workers fairly and reasonably.[83] Insurance for death and injury came
about slowly. In 1887, a request from a Mrs Searls for compensation for the
death of her husband while in the employment of the commissioners was not
entertained.[84] However, by the end of 1889 a scheme had been provided for the
insurance of the workers against injury.[85]

**Figure 12: Rathmines township: number of labourers and
artisans, and rates of pay, 1896**

44 labourers	at 2s. 6d. a day
21 "	at 2s. 8d. "
1 labourer	at 3s. 2d. "
2 "	at 3s. 4d. "
1 "	at 3s. 8d. "
1 "	at 4s. "
1 "	at 5s. "
1 carpenter	at 5s. 9d. "
1 mason	at 6s. "

Source: Rathmines News & Dublin Lantern, 4 Jan. 1896

By 1896, a workforce of seventy-three labourers and artisans was employed
in the township. Their designation and rates of pay are shown in fig. 12. The
forty-four labourers sought an increase of 3s. a week which would give them
rates of pay equal to those being paid in the city and by those working for pri-

vate firms.[86] They also requested that the cleansing of ashpits should be distributed amongst all the men and that all men should be allowed go to mass on
holy days.[87] Frederick Dixon, the township engineer, replying to the mens'
demand, stated that many of the labourers on 2s. 6d. could, with overtime, earn
from 15s. to 20s. a week. With regard to the demand by the men that they be
allowed go to mass on holy days, he stated that they had always had this privi-
lege, so long as they went to early mass.[88]

The Dublin Trades Council took up the grievance of the workers. It pointed out that a number of the Rathmines board members were large employers
and were paying their own employees rates of pay that they were not willing to
give the township workers. It congratulated Dublin corporation for paying its
labourers union rates and criticised Rathmines for giving its secretary an increase
of £50 a year, while at the same time, refusing a modest wage increase to its
labourers and artisans. In particular, it highlighted the plight of the township
scavengers; they existed on a 'miserably small pay', 3s. a week less than their
counterparts in the city, and their work was every bit as arduous. The trades'
council sent a deputation to meet the township board, with no result.[89]

Matters came to a head in May 1896 when a number of public meetings were
held under the aegis of the United Corporation Workmen of Ireland Trades'
Union. At one of these meetings over 400 members of the union were present
and, it was claimed, representatives of all sections of the ratepayers of
Rathmines. There was also political involvement; some of the leading organisers
of the meeting were prominent members of the Rathmines and Harold's Cross
branch of the Irish National Federation, including Dr Francis Adye-Curran and
Arthur Hanlon, treasurer of the federation. Many of the members of this organization were also active in the Rathmines Ratepayers' Association, which also
supported the workers. At the first of the meetings, Thomas O' Connell, ex-
president of the Trades' Union Council, castigated Rathmines for being under-
staffed. He claimed that it was the dirtiest township in Europe and, to great
amusement, suggested that it should be prosecuted by the corporation for all the
mud being brought from it into the city. It was pointed out that 15s. a week, the
wages of some of the labourers, was wholly inadequate for survival, particularly as 90% of the men were married, most of them with five or six children. The
cottages at Gulistan, which the commissioners had built, were not occupied by
their own men; most of them were still living in 'huts' and had to pay rent of
4s. 6d. a week for them. The differential in the wages paid by the Dublin corporation and Rathmines was in some cases close to 5s. a week. How inadequate
wages in Rathmines were could be seen when they were compared to other cities
in Britain and Ireland. The average wages in these was between 26s. and 28s. a
week, and even in a medium-sized town like Dundalk, it was 17s. a week. Adye-
Curran described the board as 'an unapproachable body in many ways – a
miniature co-opting house of lords', which used its surplus of funds to increase

the salaries of its top officials.[90] There was much substance in the point that the grudging concessions made to the workers contrasted starkly with the way in which the professional officials were treated. When Henry Johnston, the township surveyor, resigned in 1891 he had received an allowance of £266 per annum.[91] In May 1896 further pressure was put on the commissioners to grant the workers what was seen as a fair wage in a petition signed 'ratepayers', and the *Rathmines News* recommended that it would be gracious of the council to agree to the workers' demands.[92] Whatever the outcome of the 1896 dispute, the council was dealing with a workers' union two years later, so victory had been gained by the workers on the question of union recognition.[93]

By the early twentieth century the township councils were co-ordinating their approach to questions such as the length of the working day, uniforms, the payment of bonuses and other matters. In 1916 a conference was held between Rathmines, Blackrock and Pembroke councils to decide on a joint policy on these matters.[94] The workers saw the benefits of joint action also, and in 1920 employees of Kingstown, Blackrock, Rathmines and Pembroke, members of the Irish Municipal Employees' Trade Union, went on strike in the four townships.[95]

The workforce of Rathmines had steadily grown over the years as the area changed its status of a township to an urban district. Some idea as to the size of the Rathmines urban district council's workforce shortly before retrenchments necessitated by the first world war began to bite can be gleaned from a report on the increase in wages obtained by workers in 1912 and 1913. Thirty-eight labourers obtained an increase of from 18*s*. to 19*s*. a week and twenty-three drivers an increase of from 19 to 21*s*.[96] A fuller breakdown is available for the following year; as well as the labourers and carters, the following were also granted increases: stone-spreaders, watermen, sewermen, pipe-layers, foremen, a horse-keeper, painters, storemen, and park assistants. These increases brought the labourers' wages up to £1 a week, all the other categories were receiving more than this, with the horse-keeper and the painters being paid the optimum of 26*s*. a week. The labourers and carters were also granted one pair of trousers and one vest annually.[97] The differential in pay between the workmen and the senior officials of the council can be seen in the fact that when Frederick Dixon, the surveyor, resigned his post with the council some months later his salary stood at £600 per annum – almost twelve times the wages of a labourer. While this salary was in keeping with professionals of his standing at the time, it was a huge expense for a relatively small local government unit like Rathmines to bear. The situation was replicated in the case of other council officials and gave ammunition to the case of Dublin corporation and others for one body to govern greater Dublin and eliminate expensive duplication.

As we have seen, the council at this time agreed to recognise a union – as long as it was confined to employees of the council and that it (the council) had the right to employ anyone it thought fit.[98] Towards the end of 1917 there was much industrial unrest among the council workmen. They were seeking the same rates of pay that workers had in other urban councils in County Dublin. Matters dragged on without resolution and a strike took place in the electricity department among stationary engine drivers and stokers, the refuse destructor men and the workers in the surveyor's department. The council opened negotiations with the Corporation of Dublin Workmen Trades' Union and the Dublin United Trades Council Labour League, despite a plea from Councillor William Carruthers that the council look for other men to carry on the work.[99] The talks broke down and the strike dragged on until August when a deputation of residents requested the council to re-open negotiations but the request was refused. Arbitration finally settled the dispute but, unfortunately, the terms have not been recorded.

Major strikes of the workforce took place in the summer of 1920 and in 1921. Deputations of prominent ratepayers and others, including on one occasion the well-known Dublin politician Alfie Byrne, later lord mayor of Dublin, appealed for negotiations. A financial settlement was reached on both occasions and in 1921 the men's request for a forty-four hour week agreed to, although the council stated that forty-seven was not unreasonable in summer.[100]

To conclude, the charges of Mark Bentley at the Exham commission that the Rathmines was a 'star chamber' – a proverbially arbitrary and oppressive body, and a nationalist description of it as a 'mini-co-opting house of lords' can be perceived as not entirely groundlesss. As we have seen catholics found it difficult to hold seats there in the early days. Many key individuals were in power for long periods, the first two chairmen of the Rathmines board for half a century between them, and many members served on the board for long stretches. Businessmen held the key posts in Rathmines, while in Pembroke and Clontarf the landlord interest was paramount. The railworks in Kilmainham was less successful in gaining control there.

The low-rates policy of Rathmines condemned its residents to a suspect water supply, while townships like Clontarf and Pembroke, which contracted with Dublin corporation for a pure but expensive supply found themselves in financial difficulties. When Rathmines was eventually forced to build its own waterworks, it too ran into financial problems. One solution to the problems of scale was the enlargement of the townships. If the attempts to extend the Rathmines township to include what later became the Pembroke township had succeeded that large area would have had a better chance of success. These two townships were forced to pool their resources later to build a main drainage and a hospital. The Rathmines annexation of Rathgar, which should have been beneficial was ill-timed and caused problems related to the water supply.

Lack of resources meant that a number of key salaried positions on the Rathmines board were part-time. There was an interchangeability between staff positions and membership of the board, confirming suspicions of a star chamber. The parsimony of the board was felt by the township workers who fought a long battle to obtain pay comparable to levels being paid by Dublin corporation and other townships.

CHAPTER THREE

Health and wholesome water:
the fight for environmental control

Having overcome the legal obstacles surrounding their creation, the Dublin townships, with varying degrees of urgency, set about utilising the powers vested in them by their adopted acts of parliament to provide the services expected by their ratepayers. These services can be divided into two kinds and, roughly, into two phases. The first could be termed 'sanitation' and the other 'civilization'. The first dealt with environmental control – infrastructure, building regulations, water supply, sewerage, drainage and public health – and will be reviewed in this chapter; the other was concerned with the social and cultural sphere such as the provision of public libraries, parks, technical education and swimming baths.

The overseeing and maintenance of roads and the supervision of building gave to the townships the power to plan the physical development of their areas. The result of this regulation can be appreciated today in the wide roads and large houses to be seen in many of the suburbs. The provision of water and a drainage scheme was more vital to the health of the inhabitants of the areas under consideration. These sanitary measures fall into the category of prevention of disease; the remedial aspect, especially the provision of hospitals will be dealt with in a later chapter. A fundamental question relating to the establishment of townships is whether such small areas that only generated a modest revenue from their rates could successfully provide these services? The spectrum of services provided by the Dublin townships grew over time as more and more powers devolved upon local bodies. At present, the provision and regulation of the most basic services, roads, a water supply and drainage, is examined.

Infrastructural development, in particular the maintenance of roads and the regulation of building, was a major responsibility of township boards. In the first year or so of its existence the Rathmines board had the heavy costs of its bill to defray; because of this, and as a result of indulging in imprudent law cases, funds were in short supply. The board therefore, instead of dispersing the meagre resources ineffectively here and there throughout the district, opted to expend funds on Rathmines Road only. This, predictably, led to complaints from ratepayers not privileged to live on or adjacent to it. Within a short period of time, however, funds became available for outlay on other thoroughfares. The Rathmines township act included clauses relating to the layout of new roads and buildings and the board set about implementing these. Many of the commissioners, in their private capacity, were involved in the business of opening new roads and building houses, and now found themselves supervising their own operations, a far from ideal situation, and one complained of many times over the years. The provisions of the act laid down general regulations such as that no new road was to be built with opposite rows of houses less than thirty feet from its centre. The board set up a 'new roads' committee' which drew up further regulations in the form of bye-laws governing the creation of such, and, in particular, their state of completion before they were adopted by the board as public roads. Every road had to be opened at least one month before being adopted and had to be properly gravelled and drained with footpaths properly formed according to a sketch prepared by the township surveyor; sewers were to be placed in the middle of the road. Developers could enter negotiations with the board and, on payment of an agreed sum, grant the tender for finishing the road to the commissioners.[1] Once again, as many of the roles of developer and commissioner overlapped, the scope for mutually beneficial deals was great.

As well as new roads being adopted by the board, under the fifty-fourth clause of the Towns' improvement act of 1847, the commissioners could adopt any established private road, on the application of the ratepayers holding more than half of the valuation of the houses or land on such a road. Up to the enlargement of the township in 1862 about a dozen new roads were taken into the hands of the commissioners, a number of them being built by individual Rathmines commissioners (fig. 13).

While plans of new buildings were supposed to be submitted to the townships' surveyor, this did not always happen in Rathmines. Apart from condemning dangerous buildings, the powers of the commissioners to regulate building work were weak. Complaints were often made about the erection of inappropriate structures such as shops on Rathmines Road, but the board pointed out that there was little it could to do about such development, as long as the builders complied with public health regulations.[2]

The late 1850s and 1860s saw a boom in house building in the Rathmines township; the *Irish Builder* was enthusiastic about the nature of the development taking place:

> The approaching season promises to be a busy one, and now that the last vestiges of winter have faded away, architects, builders and building speculators are bestirring themselves. At Rathmines, Rathgar etc. even despite the unprecedented inclemency of the last few months, ranges of dwellings have been pushed forward, and will shortly be ready for occupation. Every inch of available ground is sought after by eager capitalists, more especially in the neighbourhood of Kenilworth Square, where it is taken at prices of 2s. to 5s. per foot; and as quickly do half-finished houses find ready ten-

Figure 13: Roads adopted under seal by Rathmines & Rathgar township and urban district council, 1862–1924

30 Apr. 1862	Belgrave Square South	3 Aug. 1892	Charleston Avenue
5 Nov. 1862	Chelmsford Road	4 Apr. 1894	Temple Gardens
3 June 1863	Cambridge Road	4 Apr. 1894	Palmerston Park
3 June 1863	Leeson Park Ave.	6 June 1894	Rostrevor Terrace
11 Apr. 1866	Temple Road	1 Dec. 1897	Annesly Park
29 Aug. 1866	Temple Road	2 Nov. 1898	Mount Pleasant Parade
9 Oct. 1867	Brighton Avenue	3 Apr. 1899	Artisans' Dwellings,
3 Feb. 1869	Garville Ave. Upper		Harold's Cross
3 Feb. 1869	Brighton Square	1 Nov. 1899	Ashworth & Drummond
3 May 1871	Belgrave Square West		Place
4 Dec. 1871	Effra Road	3 July 1901	Edenvale Road
4 Mar. 1874	Ormond Road	3 July 1901	Albany Terrace
4 Mar. 1874	Palmerston Road	2 Dec. 1903	Summerville Park
3 Apr. 1878	Beechwood Road	2 Dec. 1903	Kenilworth Place
3 Apr. 1878	Beechwood Avenue	1 Sept. 1909	Hollybank Avenue
3 Dec. 1879	Oxford Road	6 Nov. 1912	Cherryfield Avenue
17 May 1882	Grosvenor Square	6 Nov. 1912	Park Drive
2 Nov. 1882	Dartry Park Road	7 July 1915	Cowper Gardens' Bridge
4 Apr. 1883	Coulson Lane	3 Nov. 1915	Casimir Road
5 Sept. 1883	Newington Lane	3 Nov. 1915	Casimir Avenue
3 Oct. 1883	Palmerston Estate Rds.	3 Nov. 1915	Wilfrid Road
7 Apr. 1886	Grove Road	3 Nov. 1915	Sion Hill Ave.
2 Feb. 1887	Killeen Road (part of)	7 June 1916	Wesley Road
4 Jan. 1888	Uxbridge Road	6 Aug. 1919	Sandford Terrace:
1 Feb. 1888	Castlewood Park		laneways at rere of nos.
5 Nov. 1888	Grove Park Rd.		12–18
6 May 1891	William's Park	4 Oct. 1922	St Kevin's Gardens
2 Sept. 1891	Beechwood Pk. Lower	3 Dec. 1924	Kimmage housing roads

Source: Rathmines roads list, Dublin City Archives

ants in occupation. This state of things savours strongly of ever-growing – yet overgrown London, and it affords an unquestionable evidence of our increasing prosperity. Contrasting, however, *our* general mode of building, and the character of the materials employed, with those of the *run-'em-up* structures – pasted over with bad cement to conceal settlements, having feather edged joisting for floors, poor zinc guttering, and insufficiently lapped slates for roofs, and with a variety of economical stratagems –

adopted by the 'short' leaseholders in some of London's suburbs, we have much reason to congratulate *our* modern house builders.[3]

An example of a commissioner who invested heavily in the area as a property speculator was Michael Murphy. He obtained Wingfield, a large estate in the township in 1849, and land at Kenilworth in 1852, amounting to some seventy acres. When he bought this land there was hardly a structure on it, but by 1878, in his own words, 'every inch' was covered by buildings. He opened the roads himself and laid the whole out in building lots. He developed house property amounting to £20,000 himself, and lessees of his invested a further £120,000 on his land.[4] Murphy was adamant about the rectitude of the board in dealing with these matters. He claimed that there was a very stringent rule among the commissioners to keep a close watch on any commissioner who speculated, to make sure that he did not get a penny of ratepayers' money to further his building interests.[5] This was not strictly true. Leinster Road was an important cross road linking Harold's Cross to Rathmines. Frederick Stokes was involved in its development and in the 1850s a number of Rathmines board members had property there, including John Evans, who became township secretary in 1862. In 1853 the Rathmines board entered into an agreement with the residents of the road to keep it in repair for a yearly sum of £10. This was highly irregular, if not illegal, and was condemned by the Exham commission.[6]

The maintenance of the roads in the care of the commissioners was a costly affair. The unsatisfactory state of a number of the main roads through the township had been one of the principal reasons for its establishment and the township struggled to keep roads in proper order as macadamising and paving were expensive. The advent of tramways in the early 1870s was a boon to the commissioners. Apart from the extra revenue gained from wayleaves, a rental paid by the tramway company to the township for the use of the roads, the company, under its agreement with the board, was obliged to pave the middle of the road over which the tram tracks ran. This relieved the commissioners of some of the upkeep of roads. As a result, the centre of the road was favoured by the drivers of heavy goods vehicles, but it had frequently to be vacated owing to the arrival of a tram.[7]

Much heavy traffic used the roads, as is clear from a traffic census taken at the point of entry to the township through its three main arteries, the canal bridges at Portobello, Charlemont Street and Harold's Cross. Over a period of three days, 13–15 May 1879, 1,285 goods wagons crossed over them from the city and 1,558 went to the city. They contained a variety of merchandise, including stone, bricks, hay, straw and coal.[8] Adding to the wear and tear on the roads were the herds of cattle being driven from the rural areas to the city market early every Thursday morning.[9]

In the late 1870s, the only part of the township that was paved with stone was the centre of roads on which trams ran, and crossings; about eight miles of footpath were asphalted. Even in the city very few roads were paved with stone flags or setts at this time. In 1880, 80 out of 110 miles of road were surfaced with macadam.[10] Although the initial outlay was high, stone paving greatly reduced the cost of cleansing streets. The use of macadam, crushed stone, while it served well villages and country roads, was unsuited to city streets with their constant wheeled traffic. Macadamized roads were also almost impossible to clean. An example of this was William Street in the city, a macadamised street. In 1877 it cost the corporation £68 to clean; however when it was paved the following year, the annual cleansing bill was reduced to £7.[11]

The mud in winter and the dust in summer made it difficult to cross roads without clothes becoming besmirched, particularly in the case of ladies in the long skirts of the period. This necessitated the placing of raised crossings of stone setts at strategic places. These included major junctions and at churches and other frequently-visited buildings. Much time was spent at board meetings dealing with requests for crossings from various interests and complaints at the upkeep of existing ones.

The upkeep of roads required the maintenance of a large staff and equipment. In the early 1880s the yard of the Rathmines commissioners housed eight horses, eight scavenging carts, eight watering carts, three ordinary drays, a one-horse brush, eight drivers and twenty labourers to keep about twenty roads in order. The horses were reported as being well-fed and the harness and carts well-kept, as was the yard itself.[12] Material used on roads was usually dry macadam. Footpaths were often asphalted, although it was claimed that Rathmines was applying its own cheap form of surface made of a mixture of tar, pitch and gravel, as a cheap substitute for real asphalt which was used in Pembroke, a claim difficult to substantiate from existing records.

Practical matters such as naming of new roads and numbering of houses had to be undertaken. Roads were named with an eye to increase their market value. Mostly English names were chosen, especially those based on desirable residential areas in London, the city in which many of Dublin's architectural and cultural influences lay. Belgrave Square and Grosvenor Square are examples of this. Also favoured were names culled from literature such as Kenilworth and Waverley from the works of Walter Scott. The downright quirky was also found; Patrick Plunkett, a prominent house-builder in the Belgrave Road and Palmerston Road area, named a new road of his Killeen Road after the pen-name used by his son, Count George Plunkett, who wrote poetry in his youth.[13]

Turning to health, the death rate in the city of Dublin was very high compared to other cities in the United Kingdom and was one of the reasons for the flight of the more affluent to the suburbs. The reputed, and much-flaunted, healthiness of the suburbs blinded those in authority in the townships to the need, as they became more densely populated, for sanitary services.

The question of sanitation was taken more seriously in Ireland from the 1850s on. The Public health act (1848) and the Dublin improvement act (1849) had the net effect of providing powers to town councils, and in the latter case, Dublin corporation, to take action when sanitary nuisances were reported to them. The corporation became more involved in the drainage, cleansing, paving and lighting of the city, work which had been in the hands of boards of commissioners, such as the paving board, up to then. As a result of these acts the city appointed inspectors of nuisances assisted by a small number of policemen. A permanent public health committee was established in the city in 1866.

In Rathmines, on the inception of the township, the board appointed Dr George Brassington as officer of health as the existing St Peter's parish officer of health was regarded as ineffectual in the area. Brassington was asked to include Rathmines in his dispensary district and to have a smaller dispensary at Harold's Cross; the dispensaries themselves were supported by the grand jury.[14] Brassington promptly made a report on the state of the district, as a result of which the board appointed a committee to look into scavenging, draining and promoting the general cleanliness of houses. Notices in relation to whitewashing and cleaning of houses were printed and delivered 'where needed' and implements were provided for this. Lanes were to be scavenged and notices warning parties against further accumulations of refuse erected. To facilitate the work, the township was divided into sanitary districts, each under the superintendence of a commissioner.[15]

A sanitary court, authorized by the public health acts, sat in Rathmines in the 1850s and had strong backing from the board, which made its own offices available for its hearings. At a sitting in February 1850 the presiding magistrates were Sir Robert Shaw and John Purser; Rathmines commissioners Wall and Evans were also present to observe matters. Eighteen cases came before the court and an order for abatement of nuisances was made in each case and fines imposed. It was reported that orders made by the court were usually complied with.[16]

In 1851 the post of officer of health was abolished 'as not necessary', with no dissent on the board.[17] This was probably a response to the Medical charities act which set up a system of dispensaries throughout the country under the poor law, with a medical officer in charge of each district. Sir George Grey, the secretary of state, wrote to the board signifying his approval of its decision to discontinue the post.[18] The sanitary powers of the board were greatly enhanced under the Public health act of 1874. Together with forty other towns in Ireland, the township became an urban sanitary district and could now set an unlimited rate for sanitary purposes.

Rathmines, however, was sluggish in availing of the powers of this act, as a scathing attack on the sanitary administration of the township in the Exham commission report shows. The report, published in 1881, compared Rathmines very unfavourably with Pembroke. A sanitary officer had not been appointed until 1879 and a sub-sanitary officer, who was also the porter at the town hall, had done all the work until then. No bye-laws had ever been made covering the five slaughter houses in the township. As far as the medical health of the inhabitants was concerned, there was no hospital in the township and the board did not contribute to any hospital in the city; no provision was made for disinfection and there was no vehicle for removing infectious patients to hospital[19] .

Further powers relating to public health were given to local bodies under the provisions of the Irish public health act of 1878.[20] Townships which had their own private acts became the statutory urban sanitary authorities in their districts; those that were under the 1854 act and had a population of more than 6,000 also became sanitary authorities. Under this act all the Dublin townships became statutory sanitary authorities, except Killiney, which was excluded owing to its low population.

The act contained a number of provisions which had a particular bearing on the sanitary development of the townships. With the permission of the local government board, authorities could unite under joint boards to carry out water supply, sewerage and other services. Regulations relating to sanitation were tightened; all houses were to have privy accommodation, either a water or an earth closet, and all houses were to be built with drains; sewage was to be purified before being discharged into streams. Authorities were given further powers to make bye-laws relating to building. New powers were made available relating to water supply and power to contract for gas was increased; if a gas supply was not available authorities could make their own. Regulations concerning common lodging houses, markets and slaughterhouses could be also drawn up.

Much of the sanitary work of the townships concerned the 'abatement of nuisances', and the 1878 act provided a list of the type of offensive situations met with under this heading; any premises in such a state as to be a nuisance or injurious to health; any pool, ditch, gutter, watercourse, privy, urinal, cesspool, drain, or ashpit, so foul or in such a state as to be a nuisance or injurious to health; any animal so kept and any accumulation or deposit which was a nuisance or injurious to public health. Also covered was any house or part of a house so overcrowded as to be dangerous or injurious to the health of the inmates, whether or not members of the same family; any factory, workshop or workplace not kept in a cleanly state, or not ventilated in such a manner as to render harmless as far as practical any gases, vapours, dust or other impurities generated in the course of the work carried on therein.[21]

The sections dealing with industry were relevant to parts of the semi-industrialized districts of Pembroke and Kilmainham. Deemed a nuisance was 'any fireplace or furnace which does not as far as practical consume the smoke arising from the combustible used therein, and which is used for working engines by steam, or in any mill, factory, dyehouse, brewery, bakehouse, or gaswork, or in any manufacturing or trade process whatsoever'.[22] Included was any chimney, other than of a private dwelling house, sending forth large quantities of black smoke. More stringent restrictions were placed on the establishment of offensive trades such as blood, bone and soap boiler, fellmonger, tallow melter and gut manufacturer. The penalty imposed on the detection of such trades being carried on was £50 with a fine not exceeding 40s. per day imposed for every day on which the offence was continued. In the case of infectious diseases, the authorities were given the right to cleanse and disinfect premises and, as sanitary authorities, powers to build hospitals and to act as a burial board.

As a result of this legislation the Rathmines board drew up new bye-laws relating to the cleansing of footpaths and pavements adjoining premises, the abating of nuisances, the keeping of animals, and the regulation of slaughterhouses. Rules were made regarding the erection of new buildings and their drainage, and measures for the control of water-closets, privies and ashpits were drawn up. Cess pools, still a common feature of many homes, were henceforth to be at least twenty feet from dwellings or public buildings.[23]

As a result of the criticism levelled at it in the Exham report, Rathmines, in subsequent years, made modest annual contributions to a number of Dublin hospitals. The sanitary officer became much more active in detecting and rectifying defects in sanitation in the township. In June 1886, he reported that fifty notices had been served, seven prosecutions and convictions brought, two fines imposed and 672 houses and yards inspected. In addition twenty-four houses had been limewashed, one dwelling disinfected, the township disinfecting chamber used by one person, and forty-one articles of clothing disinfected. Moves were made to have insanitary dwellings in an insanitary area, Spireview Lane, closed.[24]

The Dublin Sanitary Association, a watchdog body set up in 1872 by prominent citizens after a smallpox epidemic in the city, regularly pointed out sanitary problems to the board. On the other hand, opposition to the board's regulations came from the township's dairy association.[25] As a result of such opposition, it took some time before some important health legislation was adopted. While a registration clerk of dairies was appointed under the Contagious diseases (animals) act of 1878, it was not until 1887 that bye-laws were drawn up regulating milk sheds and dairies.[26] By 1893 the commissioners were taking a more direct approach to the question of public health. During a cholera outbreak that year they decided to erect sheds for cholera patients at the back of the town hall on land that they had purchased at Gulistan.[27] It appeared finally that the township was beginning to address the problem of the alleviation of sickness within its boundaries. However, this small gesture to treat those in ill-health instead of dumping them on the city, that is having them apply to the city hospitals for care, met with considerable opposition. Sir Howard Grubb, proprietor of an astronomical instruments' firm in the area, presented a memorial with 712 signatures objecting to the move; he later stated that Canon Fricker, the parish priest of Rathmines, wanted his name added to the list.[28] Lord Meath made one of his infrequent communications with the board, when he too complained of the erection of the sheds.[29] A motion was passed at a board meeting that the project should not proceed at Gulistan, but it is not clear whether cholera sheds were built elsewhere or not.[30]

While this controversy raged, the board appointed a superintendent medical officer of health. Dr Montgomery A. Ward, who had been a commissioner, resigned his seat and was appointed.[31] This would not be the last time that this kind of move, from commissioner to official, took place in Rathmines. It should be stated that much of the action taken on public health was at the prompting of the local government board, and with its financial assistance. By 1895 the salaries of sanitary officials in the township were jointly funded on a 50/50 basis by the Rathmines board and the local government board.[32]

By the early 1890s, all the townships had a some form of sanitary staff in place. The printed reports of the Kingstown township provide us with a summary of the duties of the three officers of health, the medical superintendent officer of health, the medical officer of health and the sanitary sub-officer of health. The duties of the medical superintendent officer of health were to attend meetings of the sanitary authority (the township board) whenever required to do so, and advise on all matters and proceedings requiring medical knowledge. He was also to give his advice on the administration of the sanitary laws and to report monthly on the general sanitary condition of the district and on the discharge of their duties by the medical officer of health and the sanitary sub-officers.

The following example of a monthly report of the medical superintendent officer of health, for Kingstown in 1887, is fairly typical:

> I have the honour to report as follows: the health of the township has been satisfactory, comparatively speaking. The number of births registered was 40, being 17 above the number for a corresponding period last year, and represents an annual rate of 28.0 per 1,000 persons living. The number of deaths registered was 39, being seven below the number for corresponding period last year, and represents an annual rate of 27.3 per 1,000 persons living. The death rate during the same period was 27.1 in London, 33.9 in Dublin, 22.3 in Rathmines, 20 in Blackrock. Of the 39 deaths registered in Kingstown, five were of infants under one year of age, and twelve were of persons of 60 years of age and upwards. There was no death registered from any zymotic disease during the period. There were seven deaths from diseases of the respiratory organs, including two from consumption, being 12 below the number of such deaths for a corresponding period last year. The duties of the medical officers of health and the sub-sanitary officer continue to be satisfactorily performed.
>
> J. Byrne Power.[33]

The duties of the medical officer of health were described as follows:

> When he is officially apprised or otherwise becomes cognisant of any
> matter demanding his attention, to visit the place as soon as practical, and
> if after due inspection, he finds such matter to involve danger to public
> health, to report thereon to the sanitary authority ... (with a) description
> of the nature and the remedy he recommends[34]

The duties of the sanitary sub-officer of health consisted of inspecting nuisances
and visiting such when they were reported and informing the medical officer of
health of the address of any premises needing attention by him. The sanitary
sub-officers were often policemen and sometimes remained in the post after
leaving the police.[35]

Dublin, Rathmines and Pembroke adopted early the Infectious disease (notification) act of 1889. This stipulated that every medical practitioner attending
a patient was obliged, on becoming aware that the patient was suffering from a
zymotic or infectious disease, to send to the local medical officer of health a cer-
tificate stating the disease from which the patient was suffering. This would be
an important tool in the fight against such disease, as a first step in such a campaign would be having a reliable estimate of the extent of its spread. However,
matters were different in the smaller coastal townships, which dragged their
heels on the matter on the grounds of cost. Kingstown pointed out that some
doctors were opposed to the act and that the cost of providing certificates would
be considerable. At the time the act was passed, Kingstown claimed that the
death rate from zymotic diseases in the township was small, only 0.8 per cent,
so it considered that no action was necessary. It is interesting that the medical
officer of health considered the 'almost unprecedented' low rate was a result of
the recent introduction of refuse collection in the township.[36]

It has been seen that the question of the provision of water was of crucial
importance in the foundation of the Rathmines township, and under their
enabling act the commissioners obtained powers to erect waterworks for the purpose of affording 'a sufficient and wholesome supply of water' for the district and
to enter contracts for such a supply. The act specifically mentioned the city watercourse, a distributary of the Dodder, and one of the sources of water for the city,
for the supply of the township, but this was quickly ruled out by the board. Prior
to the introduction of water from the great Vartry reservoir in 1871, Dublin city
relied on a supply from the watercourse and from the canals. Houses in the suburban areas relied on the collection of rain water, wells and pumps. The commissioners of Kingstown sank wells to improve the supply in their area, a remedy
to the water problem that would prove totally inadequate as the township grew.

From the start, the Rathmines board contracted with the Grand Canal
Company for a supply of water. Initially, this was not for drinking purposes but

for watering roads in summer, a very necessary service considering the clouds of dust which followed any animal or vehicle travelling the unpaved thoroughfares. In 1854 the township reported that no money to supply water to houses would be available for at least five years and that by then it was hoped that the city's new water supply would be available. Within two years the commissioners had decided not to negotiate with the corporation for drinking water, but to apply to the canal company for a supply of their own. The township surveyor recommended the building of a reservoir at the seventh lock of the Grand Canal and drew up plans for lines of pipes. The commissioners applied to the board of works for a loan for the scheme.[37]

As the city's plans for a major water supply from the Vartry river progressed, the township re-considered the matter. Frederick Stokes, an inveterate negotiator, was given the task of conferring with the city fathers on the question. The township feared giving the corporation power to collect water rates in the district, as they believed that it would give the municipal body a toehold there. The result of Stokes' deliberations was that the city agreed to supply water in bulk to the township on terms to be agreed and that the Rathmines board would distribute it and charge for it.[38] The board in its turn agreed to support the corporation's waterworks' bill.[39]

By January of the following year all this had changed; claiming that the city fathers had gone back on their agreement, the commissioners now opposed the corporation's bill and its right to lay pipes through the township, and negotiations were re-opened with the canal company. The stumbling block would seem to have been the refusal of the corporation in the end to supply the township in bulk, insisting that it deal with each individual house; this involvement in the township was, of course, repugnant to the board.

A last ditch effort was made by no less a person than Lord Redesdale, the chairman of the committees of the house of lords, to arbitrate between the corporation and Rathmines, but at a special meeting of the Rathmines board on 1 July 1861, it was decided to reject his intervention and issue tenders for a separate supply of water.[40] The offer of the Grand Canal Company was accepted; a half per cent on the 6d. water rate was to be paid to the company for every house supplied. A supply for the watering of roads and for public pumps would not be charged extra. The commissioners would build the filters and lay the pipes.[41] F.J. Bateman, the eminent engineer, who had built the Manchester waterworks, was given charge of the work.[42] Sir Charles Domville, a property owner in the township, gave one acre of land free alongside the Grand Canal for filter beds and a reservoir (fig. 14).[43]

The reservoir was situated at Gallanstown at the eighth lock on the canal. Having agreed with the county grand jury for permission, the work of building the reservoir and laying the pipes the four and a half miles to the township got under way in the spring and continued over the summer of 1862 under the

Figure 14: Rathmines township Grand Canal waterworks at Gallanstown near 8th lock, four and a half miles from Rathmines: built 1863, later sold to Dublin corporation

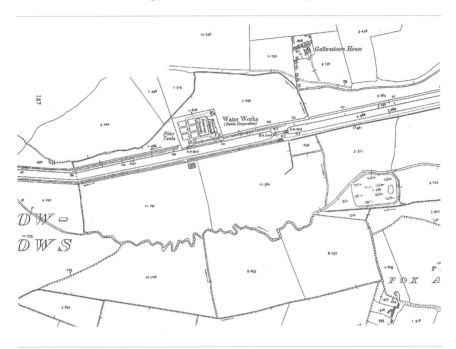

Source: O.S. map, sheets 16 and 17, 1908

supervision of Bateman. The sum of £12,000 was borrowed under the provisions of a new Rathmines and Rathgar act (25–6 Vict. c. 25) and debentures of £100 each were issued at 4.5 and 5% interest. Two members of the board, Brown and Parker, immediately subscribed for £2,000 and £1,000 respectively.[44] Orders for a supply were received from Portobello and Richmond barracks and the commissioners felt they could also supply the new Pembroke township, then being set up.

The summer of 1863 saw the completion of the new waterworks and their opening by the lord lieutenant on 23 July, the water flowing to houses connected in the township that evening. In an address the commissioners expressed the desire that their scheme would supply the great necessity of life to all parts of the township at high pressure and in the purest form, and all without increasing the 2s. rate. They touched on a matter which would cause controversy in the future when they alluded to the prejudice attaching to canal water, stating that they were confident that their purifying system would overcome objections. The

Plate 4: Watertower erected by Rathmines & Rathgar township to increase pressure to the Rathgar area

number of houses connected was very limited at first; by the end of 1864 only 171, but this had increased to 1,010 by the end of the following year.[45] The total cost of the works had been £17,800[46] and further loans were obtained from wealthy businessmen such as Brown and Sir Arthur Guinness.

The hope of the commissioners that the prejudice against canal water could be overcome proved unfounded. Indeed, events were to prove that the objections were based on more than blind prejudice. Almost immediately complaints were received about the purity and deficiency of the supply. A major problem was that the waterworks were planned without taking into account the new district of Rathgar, which is considerably higher than Rathmines.[47] The Rathgar district was too high for the pressure available and the supply tended to be intermittent, especially at night time. The commissioners countered criticism by stating that the problem only arose as the reservoir was refilling. Eventually a new pumping station had to be built at Harold's Cross on land rented from Mr Evans, a long-serving commissioner, and a water tower was erected in Rathgar.[48] The tank was sixty feet above the highest house in Rathgar and was filled at night. To facilitate this and avoid the huge waste the surveyor claimed took place at night, up to 50,000 gallons, the supply was cut off from houses from midnight to six in the morning. The tank held 102,000 gallons and was filled by a nine-inch main from Harold's Cross bridge. Two engines pumped all night at a cost, including coal, of £300 a year. The fact that the water was switched off from the district above the Roman catholic chapel on Rathgar Road caused concern to the residents as it would take half an hour to switch it on again in case of fire.[49] The new work cost a total of £11,000, bringing the overall cost of the waterworks so far to £29,000, £20,000 of which in debts was still outstanding by the time of the municipal boundary commission's inquiry of 1879.

Apart from the water rates there was no further charge to householders including those who had water-closets and baths, unless the number was excessive. A supply to stables was charged for however; those with up to five horses were charged at 3s. per horse per annum and those with more than five 4s. per horse per annum. The minimum charged for commercial premises was £1 per annum, with a rising scale depending on circumstances.[50]

In 1871 the Dublin corporation scheme for the supply of water from the Vartry river, by means of a reservoir at Roundwood, was completed. Many areas of the suburbs, including the Pembroke and Blackrock townships, contracted with the corporation for a supply (see fig. 15). However, the townships of Kingstown, Blackrock and Dalkey had clubbed together to provide their own supply. They engaged the services of a well-known engineer, Richard Hassard, and a bill was presented to parliament to obtain powers to carry this into effect. The scheme turned out to be to ambitious and was not proceeded with and the townships entered into contracts with the corporation.[51]

Figure 15: Dublin corporation water contracts with townships

Township	Act	Rate in £ charged
Pembroke	26 & 27 Vict. cap. 72	three and a half pence
Blackrock	26 & 27 Vict. cap. 121	"
Kilmainham	31 & 32 Vict. cap. 110	four pence
Clontarf	32 & 33 Vict. cap. 85	"
Kingstown	32 & 33 Vict. cap. 85	five pence
Dalkey	30 & 31 Vict. cap. 134	four pence
Killiney	Special deed of contract dated 19 Oct. 1871 usually for 20 gallons per head per day.	

Source: Various township minutes 1863–71

Relations between the corporation and those that had contracted for a supply of water did not always run smoothly. The corporation was anxious that the outlying areas did not take more than their agreed supply and was eventually forced to meter the townships' water, causing much friction in the process. A major row developed between Blackrock and the corporation over the charging of Blackrock three and a half pence a gallon for excess water. Blackrock brought the matter to court and it was found that, although the contract between the two parties was not binding and required re-negotiating, Blackrock, should, for the time being, pay the levy.[52] However, Blackrock for the second time entered into negotiations with Kingstown to build a separate reservoir, something that Kingstown was considering. The cost was to be borne by the two townships in proportion to their populations and the engineer Richard Hassard was employed to draw up plans.[53] The scheme faced many difficulties, not least being the fact that J.J. Robinson, the chairman of the Blackrock board, did not favour it; also Dublin corporation attempted to restrain the boards from promoting the bill. The scheme finally collapsed when Kingstown pulled out.

If Rathmines experienced difficulties of low water pressure owing to the elevation of certain parts of the township, the problem was even greater in a very hilly area like Dalkey, despite its source being the much stronger Vartry supply. The main problem arose in supplying a number of affluent residents who lived in villas on Mount Salus and Torca Hill, areas which were well beyond the gravitational supply. The corporation had laid a fifteen-inch main to Kingstown from its reservoirs at Stillorgan, the top water level of which was 271 feet; from Kingstown an eight-inch main was laid to the Dalkey township boundary. In order to service all its ratepayers a pressure produced by a fall of 350 feet would be needed. Various schemes to get round this were looked into by the Dalkey commissioners, and the least costly one was that proposed by the township engineer, Richard W. Walsh, that of using wind power to pump the water.[54]

Walsh claimed to have experience of wind power from his family's farm in his youth and was confident that it could work successfully in Dalkey. An American device, Halliday's Standard Windmill, was purchased, and installed by a local contractor, John Cunningham. The wheel of the windmill was twenty-two feet in diameter and consisted of ten arms made from ash. Instead of sails, two circles of light beech slats stretched over the arms, 140 on the outside and 100 on the inside. Walsh was afraid of straining in high winds, but the winter of 1886, the first year of operation, caused no problems. The fact that the speed of the wheel could be controlled by adjusting the slats helped to minimise the danger of damage. However, the windmills caused numerous problems over a period of years and were no longer in use by 1900.

Relations with the corporation over the water supply continued to be less than cordial. The townships often complained that the municipal authorities were not providing the supply contracted for, and the corporation for its part complaining that there was much wastage taking place in the townships. The suburbs greatly resented the action of the corporation in sending inspectors inside their boundaries to check on their water mains. Matters came to a head during a drought in 1893 when the supply to the townships was greatly curtailed. The townships complained that the corporation had failed to fulfil its statutory obligations to supply them with a continuous supply of water and appealed to the local government board. The board sided with the city however, agreeing that the drought was 'an unforeseen accident' and so relieved the corporation of responsibility. Kingstown regarded the situation as very serious and its medical superintendent officer of health reported:

> The partial, and threatened total failure of the Vartry water supply during the autumn was a very serious matter, and from a sanitary point of view, as, had a total failure ensued, no one can say what may not have been the disastrous results upon the health of the community [sic]; and it may be noted that this low condition of our water supply synchronised with the outbreaks of the infantile diarrhoea and whooping-cough epidemics and no doubt the water in the Vartry reservoir became impure as it decreased in quantity. I also remark, with regard to this matter, that the zymotic death-rate in the city, as well as in the suburbs of Dublin, for the year 1893, was the absolute highest, and considerably above the average for the last four years. An unlimited supply of pure water to the community ought to be the desideratum of all sanitary authorities, as a deficient supply is always felt most when it is most needed amongst the poor, who, unlike the well-to-do, have not the means of storing water convenient to their dwellings.[55]

This serious disruption, coming on top of the numerous disputes with the corporation waterworks committee, caused Kingstown to re-consider building its own waterworks. However, it faltered at the first step when the local government board refused it a provisional order to buy land compulsorily.[56]

While the problem in the other townships was mainly quantity, in Rathmines it was one of both quality and quantity. Despite further outlay by the board, it was clear to all that the canal water was still defective, and an increasing call was heard from ratepayers for the township to obtain a supply from the Vartry reservoir. Attempts were made by the commissioners to remedy the problems of low pressure by placing meters on larger pipes and so cutting down on wastage. The inadequacy of the Rathmines supply was tacitly admitted to by the commissioners when Stokes and Commissioner Fottrell began negotiations in 1872 with Sir John Gray of the corporation for Vartry water, however these discussions failed.[57]

Complaints continued to be voiced. A letter-writer to the *Freeman's Journal* claimed to express, in a very colourful manner, the views of many of the ratepayers. The correspondent had taken a sample of water from the tap in his house in the township. The water contained an 'active animal' of the kind he had seen many thousands in the water in the past; a tumbler-full would often contain over fifty. He expressed a dislike of swallowing 'live bait', which was also getting into his children's ears at bath-time. In order to use such water it had to be boiled and strained. The correspondent finished by wishing that the corporation would give up its opposition and provide the Vartry water to Rathmines, as it had done in every other neighbourhood of Dublin.[58]

A note from the editor of the paper pointed out that the corporation had offered Rathmines 'the blessings of pure water' on advantageous terms but had been refused. This pointed out that the city's water pipes were now at Leinster Road crossroads and would soon be at Rathgar crossroads, and if a number of residents of the township applied to the corporation for a supply, the paper would support their claim.[59] Stokes and Fottrell rushed to the defence of their stance in negotiations with the corporation, stating that the terms offered did not match those obtained by Pembroke and Blackrock.[60]

The water question would not go away. As a result of numerous complaints in the press about the quality of the supply the board finally decided to carry out tests. A deputation went to Naas, which was suspected by some to be a source of pollution of the canal water. Dr Charles Cameron, Dublin city analyst, and Dr Sandeman Bell, a prominent city practitioner, inspected the water, as a result of which it was decided to write to the Naas civic authorities to ask them to make sure that sewage from the town was not contaminating the canal. In an attempt to pacify ratepayers' anger over the breakdown in negotiations over the Vartry supply, the commissioners issued a statement rehearsing the history of the water question as they saw it from 1844 and had it circulated in the township.[61]

As a result of constant criticism, another special meeting of the township board to try to resolve the water question, including possibly taking the Vartry supply, was held in the Commercial Buildings, Dublin, on 24 October 1876. It was first of all resolved that whatever water would be taken would be the same for the whole township. The meeting listened to the surveyor's report and the position was summed up by Commissioners Fottrell and Parker in a very one-sided way. Parker had been a heavy investor in the Rathmines waterworks. They stated that it would cost the ratepayers £3,000 to avail of the Vartry water whereas, for an outlay of only £300, they could double their own supply and increase the pressure. When a vote was taken, it went 11 to 8 in favour of improving the existing scheme.[62]

In desperation, a number of very dissatisfied ratepayers formed a ratepayers' association to oppose the commissioners on the question of water. Twenty prominent ratepayers held a series of meetings at the houses of an ex-commissioner, Mark Bentley, Mr Archer of St Brendan's, Upper Rathmines and a Mr Bagnall. They organized two public meetings where much aversion to the canal water was expressed. The three strongly objected to the fact that the commissioners had spent up to £20,000 on an unreliable and polluted supply. Bentley pointed out that the £20,000 would need to be doubled by the time the work was finished; even the Vartry scheme itself had cost over £60,000 instead of the projected £30,000.

The dissidents appointed a prominent barrister and resident of Rathgar, Dr Launcelot Studdert, as their chairman as he had made a study of canal water and was not a property owner in the district, and so might be regarded as impartial. Studdert had queried the findings of Dr Emerson Reynolds, who had tested both the canal water and the Vartry supply on behalf of the commissioners. Reynolds had taken a sample of canal water from the tap in his own house in Upper Leeson Street which was within the township. He analysed this both before and after boiling. The specimen of Vartry water was taken from a house in Rathgar, also within the township. When the first sample of the Varty water revealed a higher content of 'organic contamination' than expected, a second analysis was made with nearly the same results. Reynolds' conclusion was that 'the Vartry water, while, undoubtedly, to be preferred on account of its great softness, is not superior in any other material respect to the well filtered supply of the canal'. These findings and the method by which they were obtained were attacked by Studdert. He claimed that Reynolds had compared boiled canal water only to an unboiled Vartry sample. Reynolds strenuously denied this and claimed that his results had been ascertained with the greatest care.[63]

The dissident ratepayers went above the commissioners and entered into negotiations with the corporation themselves. They succeeded in agreeing terms which they regarded as favourable; a daily supply of twenty-two gallons for every man, woman and child in the township at a poundage rate of 5d. on the valuation, which amounted to 2s. 4d. per 1,000 gallons.[64] Armed with this proposal they wrote to the board in December 1876 asking it to receive a deputation from them. The board grudgingly agreed to do so, stating that although it was contrary to the rule of the board to receive deputations, it would meet them before its next meeting.[65]

On the appointed day the deputation, which included prominent local residents and ratepayers, Roland Phillipson, Dr Studdert, Rev. Loftus T. Shire, Prof. Robert Galloway of Trinity College, a barrister, Stephen Elrington, and Mark Bentley, waited on the board. They read a resolution, which had been passed at a meeting of the group, demanding the Vartry water and protesting at any more expenditure on the canal supply. Professor Galloway spoke of the deficiencies of the canal water from the medical point of view and Bentley put it to the board that a house-to-house canvass should be carried out to inquire into the opinions of the ratepayers as to the merits of the two sources.

Stokes, without even consulting his colleagues, according to members of the deputation, refused to answer the deputation but referred to the written reply to their demands which he had handed to them when they entered the town hall.[66] This peremptory treatment of the objectors was continued when, some months later, the ratepayers' association was refused use of the town hall for its meetings.[67] The association considered taking action against members of the board who, they believed, held canal stock, particularly the secretary, Evans. Bentley claimed that canal stock to the value of over £600,000 was held by commissioners, and the ratepayers' association looked into the matter of obtaining an injunction excluding such members when the question of extra spending on canal water came before the board.[68]

While the objectors did not succeed in their battle on the water issue they did strike a blow for more accountability by the board. Up to then the commissioners appointed their own auditors to carry out the annual audits of their accounts. This was quite legal. However, the ratepayers' association called a meeting of ratepayers, which was attended by more than the thirty required by law, and a motion was passed requesting the board to adopt the 11th and 18th clauses of the Local government of Ireland act, which provided for annual independent audits of receipts and expenditure, and penalties for non-compliance. Shortly after, these clauses were adopted by the board.[69]

Prominent ratepayers did not desist in their efforts to obtain Varty water from the corporation. In 1882 Mark Bentley, Mrs Hanson of Rutland Square, Mr Holmes of St Stephen's Green and Mr Bailey of Thomas Street, (using their city addresses for their communication with the corporation, but all large property owners in Rathmines), wrote to the municipal council asking it to supply the township, and presenting it with a petition signed by fifty ratepayers; the corporation promised that it would negotiate with Rathmines on the issue.[70]

By the late 1870s, it was clear to the Rathmines board that reliance on canal water could not be sustained and it would have to be replaced. In 1844, long before the Vartry scheme was planned, a proposal for a reservoir on the Dodder at Glenasmole, near Bohernabreena, to supply the city had been made by Robert Mallet, one of the most distinguished engineers of the day. Mallet again considered the idea in 1860 but by then it was reckoned that the valley would not be able to supply the whole city.[71] The board of Rathmines in 1877 asked Richard Hassard to look into the feasibility of supplying the township either from the higher levels of the canal or from the corporation's reservoir at Stillorgan. He rejected these options in favour of a revived Glenasmole scheme. After a series of meetings the Rathmines board decided that it should embark on the scheme proposed by Hassard and in 1881 work began on an ambitious undertaking which would be the township's greatest achievement, but one which was to be fraught with many difficulties. As a result of the problems encountered, the scheme would not be completed until 1887.

In Glenasmole Hassard faced a number of difficult environmental and engineering problems. The main drawback of the area as the site of a reservoir was that the water from the upper reaches of the Dodder flows through peaty soil, and after heavy rain, takes on a brown coloration. With long and bitter experi-

ence of complaints from ratepayers over water quality the board wished to avoid
any such problem with the new supply. Knowing how its consumers would
react to discoloured water, the board was prepared to go to considerable extra
cost to avoid it. Hassard proposed diverting the river into an artificial watercourse which would by-pass an artificial upper lake. This upper lake would be
fed by draining the slopes of Glenasmole itself which lie on volcanic rock and
slate, and so produce water more suitable for domestic purposes. The river
would then flow into a lower lake of less pure water which would be allowed
flow downstream when needed by the millers and factory-owners who used the
waters of the Dodder and the city watercourse.

Legislation was prepared to allow the new work to proceed. The bill stated
that the board intended to impound the River Dodder and its tributaries. This
would provide both water for the township and, in the eyes of the commissioners, regulate and improve the supply to the mills and factories on or near the
Dodder and the city watercourse. It was proposed to charge the millowners for
this service. Not surprisingly they resented this attempt by the commissioners to
usurp their supply, which they had enjoyed free until then, and petitioned against
the bill. After negotiations, the commissioners agreed to allow not less than
14,700,000 gallons every week downstream. The commissioners also agreed not
to extract peaty water for the reservoir at all until the flow down a conduit
exceeded 1,500 cubic feet per minute, but would be at liberty to take any excess
above this. Having come to this agreement, the bill passed through parliament.

The year 1887 saw the completion of this huge undertaking by the commissioners. In November Hassard reported that the waterworks had been completed and that the water was ready to flow. In the same month a loan of £35,000 for
the work was received from the board of works.[72] The Bohernabreena water
flowed for the first time in the township on 12 March 1888.[73] When completed, the river-fed lower lake, which was know as the millowners' reservoir or compensation reservoir, drained 4,800 acres of peaty soil and was usually about fifty
feet deep. The service reservoir, supplying the township, drained 3,760 of gran-
ite soil; it was a mile long, thirty feet deep and at any one time, held an eight-day
supply of water.

If the commissioners thought that the vexed question of water had now been
laid to rest they were badly mistaken. A number of mill-owners on the Dodder
took legal action against the commissioners claiming that the work had not been
carried out in accordance with the law, and their business had been damaged
because of loss of supply. Hassard had many problems owing to the nature of the
ground at Glenasmole. This forced him to abandon the idea of placing an open
conduit for peaty water alongside the upper lake and put it instead below ground
under the reservoir. The mill-owners were very unhappy with the nature of the
work carried out and an injunction was brought by three of them, Sir Robert
Herron, who owned a flour mill at Harold's Cross, James Chaigneau Colville, and

Frederic W. Pim, owner of the large Greenmount Spinning Company also at Harold's Cross, restraining the commissioners continuing with certain work, interfering with the flow of the Dodder, and taking water from it except as authorized by the act.

In the ensuing high court action it was found that certain work had not been carried out in accordance with the terms and provisions of the act. On appeal in May 1892 this ruling was overturned on the commissioners giving an undertaking that minor additions to the works would be carried out. The mill-owners then appealed to the house of lords and the previous ruling was overturned with certain modifications. The injunction was lifted however until 1 August 1893. By May 1893 an agreement was reached and a new act of parliament passed. This act (56 & 57 Vict. c. 224) to 'confirm and legalise' the work carried out by the commissioners also gave them power to construct further necessary work to address the concerns of the mill-owners. It should be pointed out that a domestic water supply was slow to reach all parts of the township; it was not extended to the Milltown area until the 1920s. Water was also sold to the Dublin South Urban District Council, which was set up in the contiguous area of county Dublin under the local government act of 1898.[74]

One advantage, at least, which the Rathmines ratepayers had in having their own supply was that there was not the same pressure on users to conserve water as was evident in the other townships which received their supply from the corporation. These townships contracted for a fixed amount per annum and there were penalties if they were exceeded. In years of drought the corporation was forced to restrict the supply.

The battle for pure and adequate water in Rathmines had been a long one. The cry of 'economy' had held out against the health lobby there more so than in any other area of Dublin. In 1896, the medical officer of health of Kingstown pointed out the tangible benefits of an untainted supply. He stated that the Kingstown district had been visited by cholera in 1866 and in four months it had carried off 127 people, a rate of 70.3 per 10,000 persons living, while in Dublin, which had Vartry water during the same epidemic, the rate was 33.7. In 1871 the pure water had been turned on in Kingstown and the township had been free from serious epidemics from then on.[75]

Even more than the provision of a clean water supply, the lack of proper drainage was a serious danger to the health of those taking up residence in the new suburbs. While builders provided a primitive drainage system in individual houses built by them, the waste usually ended up in cess pools, and eventually found its way into local streams and rivers such as the Swan river in Rathmines or the Tolka in Drumcondra.

The whole system, if it could be designated as such, was a serious health hazard. Builders were sadly lacking in knowledge of the basic principles of good drainage or, more likely, were unwilling to bear the cost of undertaking the work in a professional manner. The *Irish Builder* summed up the situation in 1864:

> But of all the evils that arise from the economical and unprofessional style of building, the most incurable, the most fatal, and, unfortunately, the most frequent, are those which arise from ignorance of the principles of under-drainage. There is nothing more usual than to see a sewer placed immediately under a pump, immediately over the well, and the whole in close proximity to the walls of the house, with very often a cesspool only a few yards distant. Nothing more common than to see a channel not wide enough to admit a man's arm as the only passage for carrying off the drainage of the house. We have ourselves in several instances known the foundations of the house sewer to be laid *below* the level of the main sewer of the road, and when the connection was made the consequence was, of course, that the flow took place in the wrong direction, and the house sewer was constantly stagnant and overflowing. The practice of constructing cesspools in the immediate vicinity of wells, is in some places very extensively followed, and is gradually being attended with results that may prove little short of disastrous. By the constant soakage of liquid sewage the water becomes gradually permeated with solid matter, to such an extent as seriously to affect the sanitary condition of the district. We do not exaggerate in stating that we have known whole districts rendered objectionable to live in from this cause alone. It arises as a natural consequence that the occupants suffer ever afterwards from such a pernicious system of house-building, and fail to obtain the health and enjoyment which they chiefly seek in selecting a suburban residence.[76]

A decade and a half later the picture was, if anything, worse. While higher domestic sanitary standards were expected by householders in newly developing suburbs, the infrastructure to deal with the improved situation had not been put in place. When the medical officer of health of the newly-formed township of Drumcondra was asked to inspect the sewerage of the township, he found that there was none. Offensive matter ran into open ditches, which might, he explained, be adequate for a rural area, but not but for a district where between two and three hundred houses, each with a water closet, had recently been built. If remedial action were not taken the situation would worsen as a further 500 more houses were planned. He reported the alarming fact that sewage was being mixed with mortar for the new houses.[77]

The fragmented nature of the service-providing bodies in the Dublin area and the consequent piecemeal approach to the problem prevented the development of a badly-needed overall strategy on main drainage. While one body with limited resources struggled to put in place an efficient drainage system, its neighbours, especially if they were unlucky enough to be situated between the offending party and the sea, suffered as the effluent drained into their area. The corporation constantly complained of Rathmines waste being washed up on the shores of Dublin Bay, and Clontarf complained that sewage from the Liffey contaminated the shore of the township; indeed its medical officer, Dr W. Faussett, claimed that it had been the source of many epidemics in the area.[78]

The history of the provision of an effective drainage system in Rathmines was bound up with rivalry between the township and the city. Petty jealousies prevented co-operation between the two bodies and held back the provision of a main drainage system to the detriment of the health of residents in both city and suburbs.

Under the Towns' improvement act of 1847 all sewerage and drainage in Rathmines came under the management of the commissioners and they were obliged to divide the township into drainage districts, which they promptly did. Drainage and sewerage were primarily a health prevention issue, but also benefited those commissioners who were building houses in the area. The township was studded with cesspools and open sewers, and the most urgent work involved the closing in of these and the building of new covered drains. The overall plan adopted by the commissioners was to rectify the inadequate drainage in the lower parts of the township where the problem was most acute and work up to the higher ground. Much waste matter of all kinds, euphemistically called 'nuisances', built up in laneways and in front of houses, and steps were taken to have this removed.

Most of the township was drained by the Swan river, which was subject to frequent flooding in the parts of the township on low ground. The township surveyor reported that the river was the only outlet for the sewage of the township, and also for much of Harold's Cross, Roundtown (Terenure) and Rathgar. At its lower end, he reported, near Appian Way and Leeson Street, the river was an open sewer and was very offensive from stagnant and dangerous effluvia. To this point the river flowed through an arched tunnel large enough to take winter flooding and the problem arose in the open section beyond this. He reported that it was necessary to extend this tunnel to the rest of the river's course.[79]

In the long run, these arrangements were inadequate to cope with the increased sewage of the area, especially as water closets became increasingly common. The need for a main drainage scheme to carry the sewage effectively from the township to the sea was obvious. Main drainage posed a problem for the city as well. When the corporation investigated undertaking a main drainage scheme in the late 1860s, the estimated cost was considered too large for the city to raise itself. The corporation applied to the treasury for aid in 1871 and advanced a main drainage bill, but the £470,000 applied for was refused, the government considering the security the corporation was in a position to offer to be insufficient. Rathmines, Pembroke and the Dublin port and docks board had opposed the main drainage bill as it contained provisions for the drainage of much of the city and suburbs, which the independent-minded Rathmines board exaggeratedly regarded as amounting to a takeover by the corporation. The board vigorously opposed this, announcing that it would 'drain alone'.[80]

Negotiations were entered into between the corporation and the townships and agreement was reached when extensive concessions were granted to Rathmines and Pembroke. In effect this amounted to an agreement that the drainage rate in the suburbs would be capped at four pence in the pound but with no limit placed on it in the city. In a memorial by a number of citizens of Dublin protesting at such an arrangement it was pointed out that this was contrary to the precedent set in London.[81]

The experience of London, which had to grapple with problems similar to Dublin, but on a much bigger scale, should have been an example to Dublin city and suburbs. *The Times* of London had commented in 1855 that

> There is no such place as London at all ... (it is) rent into an infinity of divisions, districts and areas ... Within the Metropolitan limits the local administration is carried on by no fewer than three hundred different bodies, deriving powers from about two hundred and fifty local Acts.[82]

London managed to overcome its problems, in relation to drainage at least, by the creation of the Metropolitan Board of Works in 1855. The board had overall jurisdiction in sanitary matters in the City of London and in the seven parliamentary boroughs surrounding it. Each parish vestry, which alone held responsibility for sanitary regulation until then, appointed representatives to the new board. The board undertook the main drainage of the whole metropolitan area of London, a scheme which was completed in 1868.[83] The metropolitan board also had responsibility for roads, bridges, the building of artisans' dwellings and the creation of open spaces. Much work in the greater London area was undertaken in these areas of activity, the most spectacular being the creation of the Thames Embankment.[84]

In Dublin the agreement with the townships still did not meet the approval of the treasury and a further application for funding the main drainage was refused. Attempts were made by the corporation to obtain an improved financial deal with the townships but by 1875 it was clear that they would not be successful. In a letter from the chief secretary to the corporation it was pointed out that the security required would impose unacceptably high rates within the limits allowed to the corporation by legislation. In reply to this the Dublin town clerk, accepting defeat for the corporation on the issue, communicated a motion that had been passed at meeting of the corporation on 6 Nov. 1875, stating that:

> the only means which the corporation could devise to add to the security referred to in the letter, now read, would involve a costly and pro-

tracted contest with the townships, and of doubtful issue ...; the corporation decline the responsibility of entering upon such a contest.[85]

As a result, Dublin corporation dropped the issue of a main drainage for the city
for many years.

Faced with the reality of undertaking a costly main drainage scheme alone,
with the consequent burden it would place on ratepayers, the Rathmines board
reconsidered its lone stance and made approaches to the neighbouring Pembroke
township. The natural drainage of Rathmines was through Pembroke, which lay
between it and the sea. A joint approach to the solving of the costly drainage
problem made sense and negotiations were successfully completed. The two
townships went to parliament and had a joint drainage act passed in 1877
(Rathmines & Pembroke main drainage act, 40 & 41 Vict., c. 82), despite opposition by the corporation and the Dublin port and docks' board.

The act enabled the two boards to undertake an ambitious scheme to drain
the two districts. The matter of effective drainage depended very much on the
topography of the area of Rathmines and Pembroke. Apart from a small part of
the Rathmines township at Harold's Cross the whole of the area is in the basin
of the river Dodder. However, only a narrow strip to the south-east of the area
drains directly into the main river; two-thirds of the area forms the basin of the
Swan, a tributary of the Dodder. The watershed between the Dodder and the
Swan is followed almost exactly by the line of the Grand Canal.

The relief of the area varies considerably; parts of Rathgar reach a height of
150 feet above sea level, while a large part of Pembroke lies below the twenty-
five feet contour, and some even below the level of high water spring tides. The
underlying limestone is covered by glacial clays, thin in the higher Rathgar area
and quite thick in the low-lying district. From the twenty-five feet contour to
the coast, an area of about 900 acres, the clay is covered with a deposit of sand
and gravel. Indeed it appears that the low-lying part of Pembroke was once a
lagoon which formed behind the sand bar on which Sandymount is built. The
area was subject to much flooding in the past and had been nothing more than
a marsh. When the Swan was culverted in 1867 and the Dodder was embanked,
the drainage of the area was greatly improved.

A Rathmines and Pembroke joint drainage board with equal representation
from each township was established under the Rathmines and Pembroke
main drainage act of 1877. The work was carried out by Richard Hassard,
the engineer who would later design the Glenasmole waterworks. The
scheme involved carrying sewage from the townships to the estuary of the
River Liffey at the east side of the White Bank near the South Bull Wall.
For the effective drainage of the townships a two-part interconnecting system was devised, one for the higher district and one for the area below the
twenty five feet contour. The high area, consisting of about 2,400 acres, was

drained by gravitation. The sewage from this area found its way into the Swan sewer and was intercepted by a new sewer built at Clyde Road and brought to a new outfall, by way of an embankment across Sandymount strand. The new outfall was built near the Pigeon House Fort and involved widening part of the South Bull Wall.

The drainage of the 900 acres of the low-lying district involved building two sewers to bring the sewage to a pumping station which raised it into the high-level sewer. The low-level sewer commenced near Sydney Parade railway station and ran for over a mile to the pumping station, draining the Merrion and Sandymount districts. The second low-level sewer commenced at Elgin Road and passed by Pembroke Road, Northumberland Avenue and Lansdowne Road to the pumping station. The pumping station, built alongside the Dodder near Londonbridge, raised the discharge from the low-level sewers 15 feet into the main discharge sewer.

To satisfy the war department expensive work had to be carried out at the Pigeon House Fort, an army facility. The total capacity of the outfall sewer was about 360,000 cubic feet and the sewage of the area, as originaly estimated, was 150,000,000 gallons per day or 240,000 cubic feet. The total cost of the project, including purchase of land, construction, compensation and the costs of the act, added up to about £105,000. The scheme was completed in 1879. The corporation was still unhappy with the project and claimed that it was not satisfactory, as crude sewage was washed up on the foreshore at Merrion.[86]

The Public health act of 1878 facilitated co-operation between local authorities as regards drainage by making it easier to set up joint drainage districts, similar to the Rathmines and Pembroke joint drainage board. Two of the coastal townships, Blackrock and Kingstown, availed of the provisions of the act. The coastal townships suffered from the same drainage problems as elsewhere, but with the added problem that the foreshore along both townships was constantly being polluted by sewage. In the Kingstown township alone seven sewers discharged raw sewage on the foreshore between St Albans, the outlet of the Glasthule river, and Sandycove baths.[87] The problem was particularly embarrassing for Kingstown, which was promoting itself as a tourist attraction, and competing in this regard with other towns in England and Wales. Despite the option of a joint approach to the problem, owing to the high cost of the work involved it was not until 1893 that a Blackrock and Kingstown main drainage act was obtained (56 & 57 Vict. c. 224). The cost of the act was increased by clauses added to it by the Dublin and South Eastern Railway Company and the Kingstown Harbour Commissioners. The act resulted in a joint board being set up consisting of five councillors from each township.

The engineering problem was similar to that of Rathmines and Pembroke; Blackrock drained in a north-easterly direction through Kingstown to the sea. The scheme involved building a series of intercepting sewers along the Blackrock and Kingstown coast which conveyed all sewage to a huge tank, 240 feet long, 160 feet wide and twelve feet deep. This tank was hermetically sealed to prevent any escape of odours or noxious gases. At every ebb tide the tank was completely emptied and its contents discharged through a cast-iron pipe three feet in diameter at a point as far out to sea as the west pier at Kingstown and at a considerable distance north-west of it. The mouth of the pipe lay thirty feet below the surface of the water at low tide. The discharge took place strictly at ebb tide only, taking about one and a half hours and was designed to allow no return of sewage.

It was agreed that Blackrock and Kingstown would pay for the outfall works in proportion to their valuation, but as Blackrock was not as developed as Kingstown as regards the provision of sewers, it would have to pay more for its internal drainage.[88] This caused many misgivings on the part of Blackrock over the years, and finding that re-negotiation was out of the question the Blackrock board declared itself in favour of the abolition of the joint board. When the 1898 local government bill was in preparation, Blackrock sought to have a clause included dissolving the main drainage board, but Kingstown was not agreeable to that.[89]

Public lighting was also a major responsibility of township boards. Gas lighting was introduced in Dublin city in 1824 and, on being set up ten years later, the Kingstown township board immediately began to make arrangements to light its area.[90] The 1847 act gave the Rathmines commissioners the power to produce their own gas supply, but they never availed of this, as they believed that it would never pay. Public lighting of any kind was almost non-existent in the district when the township was set up. The commissioners immediately entered into a contract with the Alliance and Dublin Consumers' Gas Company, which supplied the gas to the city, for a supply to the township for public lighting. The first agreement required the company to provide 1,000 perches of mains in the district and 200 lamps, as well as lighters to light them. In November 1848 it was reported that mains were being laid in Cullenswood and Dunville Avenues. By 1852 there were 152 lamps in the township.[91]

Gas lighting was not provided on an equal basis to all areas. Areas described as 'poor', listed as Bannavilla, Tivoli, Shamrock Villas (Harold's Cross) and Westmoreland Park, had only two feet of gas, half the normal supply, allocated to them, and so their public lamps were never as bright as those in the more affluent districts. On the other hand, places of a completely different character were also given priority in lighting. Church Lane, a lane which ran behind Upper Rathmines Road, was lighted for the sake of 'health and morals'.[92]

The gas lighting available at this time was much inferior to the bright glow available from the 1890s on with the introduction of the incandescent mantle. It was dim smelly and smoky and often caused dissatisfaction among ratepayers and commissioners alike, although when the supply went to tender, as it did every few years, the Alliance company invariably won it. In 1854 the commissioners were so unhappy with the supply that they appointed an inspector to look into it. The main complaints were that the lamps did not throw enough light and that they were going out too early. The gas supply in the suburbs also tended to be dearer than in the city as the lamps were further apart and there was a larger area to be covered by the pipes, which led to an increased percentage of gas leaking.

Public lighting in Rathmines was raised at the Exham commission. John Beveridge, the Dublin town clerk who, it must be noted, was a hostile witness, claimed that going home recently from the city to Rathgar between 1.30 and 2.00 a.m., there had not been a single lit lamp on Rathmines Road, until he came upon one outside the pharmacy of Hamilton, Long and Company in the centre of Rathmines village. It appeared to him that nearly all the lamps were extinguished between midnight and 1 a.m., a situation he regarded as unsuited to an area with a large population.[93]

The Alliance and Dublin Consumers' Gas Company had a monopoly of gas supply in Dublin city and suburbs and the townships feared that Dublin corporation would make an attempt to take the company over and so extend its influence. When such an attempt seemed likely in 1873, Kingstown petitioned against it.[94] In 1864 an attempt was made to break the monopoly and a new gas company was set up to supply Kingstown, Dalkey and Killiney. Its directors claimed that the district was being lighted by an 'English' company (the Alliance and Consumers), whose directors met in London and had a monopoly in the area. The new company called itself the Commercial Gas Company of Ireland and informed prospective customers that it had secured a site for its works in the area.[95] The company apparently did not succeed and the Alliance and Consumers' Company retained its monopoly.

Following a tragic fire in the Kildare Street Club in 1860, Dublin corporation obtained an act of parliament, the Dublin fire brigade act, by which, two years later, a fire brigade was set up in the city. Up to this time firefighting was in the hands of the parish vestries which provided a patchy service on a local basis. The Dublin Metropolitan Police also kept an engine which inadequately served a vast area covering Kingstown, Blackrock, Pembroke and Rathmines, but not Clontarf or Drumcondra. Householders prepared to pay for insurance cover were also served by the insurance companies' engines.

In the early years of the Rathmines township the water carts, which were used for watering the roads during the day, were filled every evening in readiness for use in case of a fire overnight. A man was employed to sleep in accommodation in the commissioners' yard, where the carts were kept, and to be prepared to fight fires. Negotiations were entered into with various insurance companies to entice them to part-fund a fire engine. Fire plugs were fixed to the mains water supply and fire escapes, telescopic-type ladders on wheels, obtained. The early escapes, similar to those in use in the city, were found to be unsuited to the suburbs as the wheels were too far apart to pass through front garden gates to get near enough to houses.

Rathmines was reluctant to form its own fire brigade because of the increase in rates which would follow. The fact that many of the houses in the township were covered by insurance companies provided the commissioners with an excuse not to obtain their own fire engine.[96] The township supported the Dublin fire brigade bill, hoping to benefit from the provision of a city brigade, under its own terms of course. The commissioners reached an agreement with Sir John Gray of the corporation that the Dublin brigade would be paid £15 for every fire it attended to in the township, but the Rathmines township secretary, John Evans, stated at the Exham commission, without giving a reason, that this was not carried into effect.[97]

Rathmines was heavily criticized at the Exham commission for its lack of adequate provisions for firefighting. The township claimed that the twenty workmen under their inspector of waterworks were regarded as firemen, but not called that. It was subsequently admitted that they were not obliged to go to a fire in the day or night. However, according to the township secretary they did respond when summoned by a bell at night as most of them lived in the neighbourhood. He went on to admit that they were not trained, but twelve of them were 'conversant' with the work.[98]

J.R. Ingram, chief of the Dublin fire brigade, stated, in his evidence, that the Dublin brigade was called to fires in the suburbs, but had to have permission from the lord mayor to go to them. The Dublin appliances could not be used in Rathmines owing to the problem of low pressure. The occasion of a fire at a whiskey distillery in Harold's Cross in 1877 highlighted the problem. The antiquated Rathmines hand engine, which Ingram believed belonged to the Patriotic Insurance Company, was inadequate to deal with the fire and Rathmines had no trained men anyway. The city's apparatus, when it turned up, was ineffective.[99]

Powers were included in the 1880 Milltown extension act to establish a permanent fire brigade in Rathmines.[100] Three years later Charles G. Smith, together with his family, was brought over from England as lieutenant of the new Rathmines fire brigade at 35s. per week.[101] The strength of the fire brigade was brought up to six men in 1886 and one of them was instructed in the use of a steam fire engine.[102] A provision in the act stated that Pembroke township could have use of the Rathmines brigade. However, Pembroke remained aloof in this regard and established its own fire brigade the following year.

A survey of firefighting services in the townships in 1882 showed that only Kingstown had a fire escape, but had no man to take charge of it; Pembroke had ordered one, but Rathmines and the other townships had none. The vestry fire escape located in Rathmines twenty years previously would seem to have been no longer available. It was noted that not all of the townships that had high pressure water had a reel to avail of it from their street hydrants. Those townships whose

Plate 5: Rathmines Fire Brigade, 1920

Plate 6: Pembroke fire engine and ambulances at their fire station

water pressure was low used fire engines. Rathmines had an excellent steam engine 'of the latest approved pattern' besides one old hand engine which was regarded as useful to have if the pressure was low or use needed to be made of Dodder or canal water. Kingstown also had a hand pump as a standby. Both Rathmines and Pembroke had brigades; in Pembroke there were eight men 'under a very intelligent and efficient chief'.[103] Kingstown had no designated brigade at this time but the general workmen were trained to fight fires, and whenever there was a guard ship, a naval vessel appointed to carry out coastguard duties equipped with pumps, in the harbour, this was also relied on.[104]

By 1900 the Rathmines brigade consisted of only four men while Pembroke had seven. Rathmines also had auxiliary units consisting mainly of young gentlemen – medical students and the like, according to the captain of the Dublin city fire brigade. He depicted them as wearing 'immense brass helmets and axes' and stated that they 'go out on occasions'.[105] He was of the opinion that they were more a source of danger than the fire itself. He claimed that the Dublin brigade often had to go to the rescue of the townships and that on those occasions the township fire brigades were unco-operative as this was regarded as a poor reflection on themselves. On one occasion the Rathmines men turned their hoses on the Dublin firemen and the fire blazed on while the two brigades concentrated on each other.[106]

Rathmines, Pembroke, Kingstown and Blackrock all built fire brigade stations adjacent to their town halls. In Kingstown a handsome building with Corinthian columns was built at George's Place at a cost of £8,000 from plans prepared by Joseph Berry, the township surveyor. It housed a fire brigade station, stores and stables, and several men resided there to be ready in case of an outbreak of fire.[107] If the firemen did not stay overnight at the fire station they usually resided close by, often in township-built artisans' dwellings. Some of these houses were connected by electric bells to the station, as was the case in the firemen's houses in the township artisans' dwelling at Gulistan cottages in Rathmines.

A number of the townships erected fire alarm posts at strategic points where members of the public could communicate with the fire station by means of private telegraph lines. Rathmines had a number installed and in Blackrock they were erected at Booterstown, Sion Hill Convent, Belgrave Square and the Knox Memorial Hall. In Blackrock also a system of fourteen bell alarms connected the police barracks, the stables and the firemen's houses.[108]

Despite all these improvements the Dublin brigade was still being called to the smaller townships in the early 1900s. It was reported in 1904 that residents in coastal townships were grateful for the arrival of the Dublin fire brigade and its steam engine at a fire in Dalkey. Township brigades arrived but they had no steam engine.[109]

By 1912 the Rathmines fire brigade was still a very modest outfit. It had a captain, an assistant and five men. It had now no fire engine and only one horse was available to pull its hose carts. The council excused this state of affairs by stating that the pressure from its waterworks was so good that it did not need a fire engine. After the Roman catholic church in Rathmines was destroyed by fire in 1920, the firefighting services in the township came in for severe criticism, and in the following year a Leyland motor tender was acquired. By 1923 the motorised fleets stood at three in Rathmines and four in Pembroke, including ambulances.[110]

Looking at the provision of basic services outlined, a pertinent question to ask is whether the townships were suitable local government units for the provision of the services expected by their ratepayers. It is quite clear that on the crucial question of the provision of their own water supplies the townships were not successful. All of the townships, except Rathmines, recognised this very early and opted to contract with the corporation. This did not appear to result in any loss of independence as was feared. The independent stance of Rathmines on this issue was in keeping with the anti-corporation attitude of some of its dominant personalities, especially Frederick Stokes. This attitude condemned the Rathmines householders to suspect water for some years after a pure supply had been conferred on the city and other townships. When Rathmines finally decided to grasp the nettle the cost to its ratepayers of the expensive Glenasmole scheme was high.

In firefighting it can also be seen that a united approach over the whole greater Dublin area, as later recommended by the Exham commission, would have been a more sensible option. While it is impossible to say at this remove whether any lives were lost as a direct result of what its critics liked to call 'dirty water' and a poor firefighting service, it is evident that the residents paid for their independence with substandard services. This fragmentation of services also had an impact on the city. The loss of the substantial rates of the suburbs condemned the inhabitants of this area in the care of the corporation to poor services and led to the deferral of the installation of a main drainage system for the city. Both city and suburbs combined would have been able to provide a better service as had happened in London with the establishment of the London Metropolitan Board of Works. The fact that Rathmines was forced to pool its resources with Pembroke to undertake a main drainage scheme proved that its jealously-guarded self-sufficiency was not sustainable.

J.A. Hassan has pointed out that 'a poorly balanced programme of sanitary reform might exacerbate public health problems in the short term' and that the spread of piped water among the well-off could cause a deterioration in the environment of the poor.[111] Such an imbalance was found in the Dublin area due to fragmentation. The provision of a water-borne sewerage system in Rathmines and Pembroke left the city vulnerable to the end product of this being washed into Dublin bay and pollution of the Liffey and the shoreline.

CHAPTER FOUR

The royal commission on boundaries: the Exham commission 1878

While a process of fragmentation and proliferation of local authorities was still evident in Dublin with the establishment of townships up to 1878, in Britain the period 1855–80 saw the beginning of a movement towards consolidation. Indeed, about the time of the establishment of the Drumcondra township, it was becoming clear to Dublin corporation that such fragmentation was undesirable and would have to be reversed by extending the municipal boundaries. The corporation's arousal from its lethargy while it was inexorably deprived of *Lebensraum* was rather belated. However, it now saw a reversal of the process as part of a great 'social movement' by which municipal boundaries were being extended in from seventy to over one hundred cities in Britain at the time.[1] The experience of the sanitary commissioners for England and Wales on the question of boundary extension was quoted by agents of the corporation. A report by the sanitary commissioners in 1871 had stated that there was a general indisposition on the part of residents in the immediate neighbourhood of boroughs to their premises being included within the parliamentary boundaries, but in almost every case this indisposition was attributable to the fear that an extension of parliamentary boundaries would be followed by a corresponding extension of municipal area, and that consequently they would become liable for the payment of city rates. Indeed as early as 1837 the English royal commission on boundaries took as its guiding principle the extending of the boundaries to the 'continuous built-up area' and even when the area to be added was not continuous with the core would recommend inclusion if it believed that there was a 'community of interest involved'.[2]

The corporation argued that the English and Welsh commissioners found that in many instances the case for boundary extension was so manifest that their decision had been rather what the limit of the enlargement should be rather than whether an extension of the boundary was required. In the many cases where they had recommended an extension, they endeavoured to include none but urban populations or adjoining districts, possessing, or likely soon to acquire, the aforementioned 'community of interest' with the borough. This was the principle the corporation wished to follow in Dublin.

In the United Kingdom generally, the trend was for municipal boundaries to be extended. This was exemplified in the setting up of the London Metropolitan

Board of Works in 1855. In Dublin the extension requested by the corporation was denied to it as it had not the power to introduce such a bill, and the government was reluctant to move for a number of reasons.

In 1876 Dublin corporation drew up an improvement bill and considered including in it the extension of its boundaries, but was advised that it would be acting *ultra vires* in trying to do so by a private act. It then appealed to the government to bring in the necessary legislation.[3] At the same time, the matter arose during the proceedings of a select committee which sat to look into the taxation of towns in Ireland. When it appeared to the Rathmines commissioners that the committee's inquiry would be used by Dublin corporation to further its case for annexation of the townships, Frederick Stokes decided to make the case for the independence of the suburbs, after, at first, refusing a request to give evidence.[4]

The select committee on taxation reported in July 1876 that local investigations to look into the matter of municipal boundaries would be necessary before the question of local taxation could be satisfactorily resolved. When the committee was re-appointed in 1877 it reported that a detailed report by a local government board inspector was required.[5] The select committee finally made its report to the house of commons in July 1878 and recommended *inter alia* that the municipal boundaries of Dublin, Belfast, Waterford, Limerick and Drogheda required extension and those of Galway and Carrickfergus needed some readjustment. The report recommended that a commission be appointed to look into this matter. Ironically, as the committee was recommending an extension of the city boundary another township was being formed. A number of parties interested in obtaining local government for Drumcondra, Clonliffe and Glasnevin came together to promote the project. Despite objections from the corporation, the township was formed and came into effect on 2 September 1878.

The recommended commission was set up in October 1878. It consisted of William Allen Exham, senior counsel and resident of the Killiney township, William P. O'Brien, an inspector under the Irish local government board and resident of the Pembroke township and Charles P. Cotton, a civil engineer who lived in Dublin city. The inquiry was usually known as the Exham commission. In all, the commission investigated the boundaries of 113 cities, towns and townships throughout the country. In their Dublin investigations, which, the commissioners admitted, were the most important and pressing part of their inquiry, they examined eighty-one witnesses between April and July 1879.

Owing to the 'vast importance and magnitude of the interests involved, pecuniary and personal' the commissioners decided to hear counsel for the authorities in question, the Dublin townships and the corporation, something they had declined to do in relation to towns in the other parts of Ireland to which their inquiries took them. As well as looking at the townships ringing the city, the commissioners decided to include in their inquiry the townships of Kingstown, Blackrock and Dalkey as they quickly saw that a rational scheme for services for the Dublin area, especially in relation to a matter such as fire-fighting, would have to involve these townships.

A very important matter affecting the final outcome of the inquiry was remarked on by the commissioners in their report. They pointed out that in addition to hearing evidence on the main question, the extension of the municipal boundaries, a conflict arose in two cases, Rathmines and Clontarf, between their boards and a number of ratepayers in the townships regarding their management. The commissioners felt obliged to consider this question as the select committee on taxation had not held any enquiry into the Dublin townships, and so there was no report of their management before the house. As annexation to the city was the objective of the dissident ratepayers, alleging mismanagement in their respective townships, the commissioners took their views into consideration.[6]

Proceedings opened with the presentation of Dublin corporation's case in April 1879. The crucial issue, according to the corporation, was that the townships were an integral part of the city. While it was always the case that the men of business who lived in the suburbs went to their 'counting houses' in the city on a daily basis, the corporation contended that the coming of the trams and railways had bound the city and its outskirts closer together; the so-called suburban area was no longer a place of isolated villas but an area that was now largely built on. The suburbs had not arisen as the result of any indigenous trade or industry but were an extension of such activity from the city.

In the Dublin case, the corporation argued, the municipal boundary, set in 1840 after an investigation by Sir Thomas Larcom, was inadequate now nearly forty years later. The wealthiest people were escaping paying their fair contribution to the city. The city had crippling financial responsibilities and these needed to be lightened by those who were financially capable of doing so. The corporation listed the main areas to which township dwellers were evading contributing: firstly the maintenance of the public thoroughfares, which were being used as much by suburban dwellers as by those living within the boundaries; next the poor rate, which was not being contributed to fairly by suburban dwellers; similarly, taxation for hospitals, lunatic asylums, industrial schools and reformatories was being evaded. On the latter head the corporation pointed out that hospitals received £4,000 a year from the corporation, industrial schools and reformatories £7,900, and lunatic asylums £7,000, whereas the townships contributed almost nothing.

The corporation further contended that the principle of the entire metropolitan area contributing to common facilities had already been conceded. The metropolitan police district, an area which extended well beyond the city limits and including the townships, was rated for the maintenance of the Dublin Metropolitan Police. A rate of eight pence in the pound was exacted and taxes were also imposed on pawnbrokers, publicans and hackney car drivers, within the whole area. These were supplemented by fees and fines received from police courts in the extended district. In 1876, revenue for the police amounted to £57,120 of which £30,599 was collected as rates.[7]

The police district was a long-standing entity. As far back as 1837 legislation had set the boundary as far south as the Dodder river to the south and the Tolka to the north. Moreover, power was given to the lord lieutenant and council to direct that any parishes within certain limits could be added to the district (1 Vict. c. 25). The district was gradually extended until it reached the limits as already shown in fig. 1. In 1876 when that same extended area was used as the basis for taxation to pay the cost of the rebuilding of Carlisle Bridge and the erection of a swivel bridge near the Custom House (on the site of the present Butt Bridge)[8] the townships, despite further objections, had to accept it and a further two pence was added to the common police tax to pay for the work. The corporation asked logically if the greater metropolitan area was taxed for bridges why not for the roads leading up to them? It was also pointed out that other facilities were shared by the whole area, in particular the gas supply and, except for Rathmines, a water supply. The failure of the townships to provide a professional fire brigade in their areas also meant that in effect the Dublin brigade was shared, but with no contribution from the townships.

John Beveridge, town clerk of Dublin, identified another resource that the city provided for the townships, a labouring class. He claimed, a little disingenuously, that there were no poor in the townships; no artisan or labouring class, yet, he explained, the townships gained from the services of this class, who were forced to reside in the city tenements. The townships should, he stated, 'bear a proportion of the burdens which such classes entail'.[9] Another witness, pointing out that almost all of the building carried out in Rathmines was by workers dwelling in the city, went as far as to suggest that Rathmines should contribute to the building of artisans' dwellings within the city limits.[10]

On the question of the city streets, the corporation made much of the fact that the residents of the townships benefited greatly by their use but did not contribute a penny towards their upkeep. For example, distilleries in the townships got all their grain from the quays, as did householders their coal, all of which was hauled over the city streets without the suburbs sharing the expense of wear and tear. The provisions of the townships came from the markets in the city, which were exclusively funded by the corporation. The case of Samuel Bolton, a substantial Rathmines ratepayer and board member, was cited. He was a large building contractor and drew all his timber and building material through the city. At one time his yard was situated just inside the city boundary but he moved it across the canal to Rathmines to avoid paying the heavy city rates, including that for the upkeep of the streets.[11] The city engineer, Parke Neville, pointed out that because of lack of funding, the surface of the city streets was in a poor condition and their cleaning was inadequate. A further problem arose regarding refuse as there was no place to dispose of it, as all the vacant land in the city had been built on and it had to be dumped in the sea.[12]

The economic importance to the corporation of the acquisition of the townships was stressed. The increase in the city's valuation as a result of extension of the boundary would increase its borrowing powers. These powers had recently been greatly enhanced under the corporation's 1878 improvement act. Up to then its borrowing was limited to £100,000 but this had been increased to £1,200,000. Despite this increase, there were still huge problems in relation to security for borrowing, which the increased rate base would alleviate.[13]

The public health consequences arising from the current local government structure in the greater Dublin area were explained by Parke Neville. He alluded to the fact that he had recommended a public abattoir to cover the whole urban area some ten or twelve years previously as the fragmented rate base meant that funding was not adequate in any one of the local areas for such an enterprise. As a result, only private slaughter-houses existed in Dublin and they should be closed on health grounds. Already in Edinburgh and Glasgow no cattle were allowed to be slaughtered outside the public abattoirs.[14]

The public health argument was taken up by Dr Charles Cameron, the city's medical officer of health. He cited Liverpool and Manchester as his models, where there was one sanitary authority over the whole metropolitan area. As an example of the absurdity of fragmentation, he informed the inquiry that the corporation had installed at great expense a disinfection chamber, a device for dealing with infected clothes. This chamber was well capable of handling the needs of the whole metropolitan area, but was under-used and the corporation had to bear the whole cost.[15] The English experience was again cited when a city councillor, J.P. Byrne quoted evidence from Sir Henry Thring (parliamentary counsel to the government), before the English sanitary commissioners, that 'no system of sanitary legislation can be efficiently carried into effect, without a readjustment of the boundaries of towns, so as to include populous districts, which had grown up without the actual limits, and although constituting part of the town, neither share in its burdens nor submit to its control.'[16]

While the low density housing of the townships with their affluent residents was a world away from the abysmal death traps of the city, the fact that the townships lagged behind the city in installing such a facility as a disinfection chamber gave the corporation ammunition with which to attack them. The corporation claimed the absence of disinfecting chambers meant that the townships, highly-populated areas from which large numbers travelled to the city every day, were a potential source of infection to the city. Charles Dawson, a member of the corporation's sanitary staff, pointed out that his colleagues were required to go to townships to carry out disinfection in order to prevent diseases spreading to the city.[17] Their lack of facilities meant that the townships were failing to implement the Public health act of 1866. The poor water pressure in Rathmines was attacked also on health grounds. For a sewerage system based on removal by water to be effective pressure must be adequate, levels correct and connecting pipes and mains laid properly; such was not the case in Rathmines, where, it was claimed, the pressure was abysmal, especially compared to the area served by the Vartry supply.

Other grievances of the corporation concerning the townships came to light. The anomaly of the corporation having to pay for the upkeep of the Rock Road, one of the main arteries through the Pembroke township, was highlighted. It had been 'thrown on' the city and the grand jury when the valuation of that district was low; but now that the situation had changed, the corporation believed that Pemroke should take over responsibility for it.[18] Byrne asserted that the city was financially sound, but that in justice it should not have to pay for the benefit of others.

A number of independent witnesses, unconnected with either the corporation or the townships, spoke in favour of amalgamation. Joseph Todhunter Pim, a leading city businessman with a keen interest in local government, pointed out the waste of manpower which the current local government structure in Dublin entailed. The largest English town had only sixty-four representatives, while the corporation of Dublin had sixty and the townships combined fifty-seven. The fragmented Dublin situation also exacerbated the problem Pim perceived of getting enough suitable men to stand for elections to the corporation.[19] The duplication of administrative personnel was another undesirable side-effect and the dividing of the valuation between city and townships meant that no authority could afford to employ a staff of the highest quality.[20]

The problem of the townships siphoning off suitable personnel for membership of the municipal corporation was echoed by other witnesses. Mr Stephen Elrington, a barrister and ratepayer in Rathmines, speaking also in favour of amalgamation, was of the opinion that should it take place there should be proper representation for Rathmines on the corporation. He suggested a body of forty representatives with Rathmines and the other townships electing twenty, so having 'equilibrium' between the parties in the new body, and so inducing men of business to come forward.[21]

Pim fully supported the corporation's view that the move towards amalgamation was part of a 'social movement' then taking place in towns and cities all over Britain. A table showing the area of cities and towns indicates that Dublin was ranked with towns of much smaller population (fig. 16). The contrast with London could not have been greater. The metropolitan board of works in London was responsible for an area of 78,000 acres and three and a half million people.[22] It was revalued every five years and in twenty years its valuation had doubled.

Several witnesses expressed the dissatisfaction of ratepayers with the management of Rathmines. Mark Bentley, an ex-member of the Rathmines board, was particularly trenchant in his criticism. He claimed that he had originally come to the inquiry against annexation but the evidence he had heard so far had convinced him that the township must contribute to the metropolis or be annexed. He had been under the impression that the city was insolvent but the evidence he had heard had convinced him that this was not so. His main criticism concerned the water situation and the lack of accountability of the commissioners. He claimed that a majority of the ratepayers were dissatisfied with the water supply, but, as a majority of the board were landlords and as it was the custom of landlords to pay the rates in the township, they practised a strict economy and were not prepared to provide a suitable supply of water. Bentley alleged that there was a very powerful canal lobby on the board, headed by Evans, the secretary, and that this group had an investment of up to £600,000 in the Grand Canal Company and so had a vested interest in buying water from that source.

Figure 16: Area of some Irish and English towns and cities, 1879

Leeds	21,572	Liverpool	5,210
Sheffield	19,651	Dublin	3,805
Bradford	7,221	Hull	3,635
Belfast	6,805		

Source: *R.C. municipal boundaries*, H.C. 1880, (2725), xxx,: evidence of Joseph Todhunter Pim, para. 1025.

On the question of accountability, Bentley claimed that it was impossible to get information from the board, which met in secret and issued only a six-line or so statement about the deliberations at their monthly meetings, and this they had only being doing in the past three or four years. Prior to that they published nothing about their meetings, only an annual report. When asked to explain why, if the majority of the ratepayers were opposed to the board over the Vartry water, it was not turned out by them, he alleged that this was made difficult by the existence of a 'house list' or panel of like-minded candidates presented at election time. He explained how this worked:

> The board consists of twenty-one members, eighteen for Rathmines and three for Rathgar – and seven of these gentlemen go out each year. The board is supposed to be renewed every three years, under the local acts. When these seven gentlemen go out, the whole board combine to return the six for Rathmines, and one for Rathgar; they use every influence in their power – and it is a very influential board and they not only do combine, but they send out, as they did at the last election, circulars. All except Mr Parker and Mr Fottrell, who did not take any part in the mat-

ter, sent out private circulars, which, I believe, the board had prepared;
Dr Ward and other gentlemen sent out private circulars, saying they
would feel much obliged if you would vote for so and so. Thus in point
of fact, you have the combined forces of the board against any new blood,
or new member, entering.[23]

More seriously, he alleged that a form of vote-rigging went on. The
Rathmines act of 1847 obliged the occupier to pay the rates, but Bentley claimed
that the owners paid it in many cases and, one supposes, included it in the rent
charged to occupiers. The led to electoral abuses. The rates in Rathmines were
paid in two six-monthly instalments; Bentley claimed that if the two moieties of
rate were not paid by 31 August each year the tenants were deprived of their
votes, and that they were deliberately not paid on many occasions as they were
in the hands of landlords. He claimed that bitter complains were made about
this practice at every election.[24] Bentley's contention was disputed by John
Saunders, one of the rate-collectors for Rathmines. In the part of the township
in which he collected, only £317 out of £5,500 remained uncollected by 31
August of the previous year. He explained also that landlords in any case paid
only a small proportion of the rates; in the current year, out of about a thousand
receipts for rates not more than forty were for landlords.[25] These figures of
Saunders were not questioned leaving the claim of Bentley hard to prove.

Regarding the manner in which business was introduced at board meetings,
Bentley's depiction of proceedings painted a picture of strict control by a cabal,
led by Stokes:

> A gentleman I endeavoured to get into the board, Dr Harvey, after he
> became a member, handed in a motion to Mr Stokes in connection with
> some reform about water or something of that sort and Mr Stokes hand-
> ed it back, saying 'we don't do business in that way'. There was hardly
> any question put to the vote, with the exception of two occasions, during
> eight or nine years, and one of these was as to the election of a collector,
> and the other was on a resolution which Mr Hodgson moved for a road
> committee up to that time. Mr Hodgson was as dissatisfied as I was.[26]

Bentley alleged that Stokes had threatened to resign over the question of a
roads committee as he regarded it as a vote of censure on himself and Mr
Johnston, the surveyor. He went on to claim that he 'never knew anything to be
carried at the board against Mr Stokes wishes, except on that occasion'. The
accusation of secrecy was followed up by Bentley. He stated that the press were
barred from meetings of the board. Nine-tenths of the board, he claimed, were
of the opinion that if the press was admitted it would lead to speechifying on
political issues in the manner of the dreaded Dublin corporation. We have seen

earlier that one of the chief criticism's of Dublin corporation by many suburban township commissioners was that the corporation wasted its time by engaging in political speechmaking and passing resolutions unconnected with the administration of the city. Bentley accused the Rathmines board of using the excuse of this happening at its meetings to bar the press from them. Bentley believed that the idea of any political or religious matter coming up was 'perfect nonsense'. He referred to the standing rule that no political or religious questions were to be discussed at the board. Certainly a reading of the minutes of the board shows that every time a resolution of a political nature was broached it was ruled out of order by the chairman, and, as Bentley put it 'no man could be eloquent on sewage or paving stones and such unsavoury subjects'. In Bentley's view the board hid behind the false fear of 'speechifying' in order to exclude information from ratepayers. Summing up his views on the situation in Rathmines he stated that 'the governing power is in the hands of the landlords, and they are in the main, with some exceptions, against the Vartry water and every other expense, and the householders are in favour of it. That is the plain English of the case.'[28] He went on to allege that deputations were not met nor complaints dealt with. Indeed the board had refused him access to documents to help put up the ratepayers' case at the present inquiry.

The personal record and integrity of Rathmines township personnel, especially the secretaries, were called into question. Bentley alleged that it was widely believed in Rathmines that the secretary in office before Evans (Henry Richards) had absconded with £2,000 of the ratepayers' money.[29] Evans, on the other hand, claimed that the sum in question was only £50 and that the affair was only a small matter. Evans went on to put up a poor defence of the record of Rathmines on matters of public health. The health acts required houses within in a hundred yards of a main sewer to drain into it and if they did not do so the commissioners were to undertake the work and charge the owners of the houses for it. Evans stated that this was never done in Rathmines as 'they did not like to use such powers'.[30] Worse than that, he had not any idea as to how many houses in Rathmines did not drain into the public sewers at all.[31]

The Rathmines surveyor came in for heavy criticism also from Bentley. He was not a full-time official and it was claimed three-quarters of the work undertaken by him was not for the township at all. Some of this work was carried out privately for individual commissioners and in fact Evans himself was building houses in the township.[32]

In defence of the township, Samuel S. Bolton, who had been accused of moving his builders' yard across the canal into the Rathmines township for pecuniary gain, summed up the feelings of the Rathmines board and many of its ratepayers by describing the corporation's attempt at amalgamation as a 'monstrous scheme of "beggar my neighbour"'.[33] Representatives of the township went on to point out that the corporation did not wish to annex Rathmines in

1847 when the area was poor – the same reason it did not wish to annex Clontarf now. Now, however as the township was growing in affluence, things had changed. Evans defended the officers of the township by pointing out that their salaries amounted to £807, which was considerably less than the 10 per cent of the rates allowed for salaries by the act.[34]

The townships countered the corporation's argument about wear and tear of its roads by claiming that as much traffic entered the city from the townships as the other way around. Indeed the Rathmines surveyor proved his point by conducting the traffic census already referred to in Chapter 3.

The corporation side had made much of the claim that the residents of Rathmines used the roads of the city without contributing to their upkeep. The Rathmines commissioners countered this by pointing out that many members of the Rathmines board were senior members of large Dublin companies which were heavy contributors to the city rate. Among others cited were William Todd of Todd, Burns and Co., Alexander Parker of Ferrier, Pollock and Co., Hugh Brown of Brown, Thomas and Co., William Aitken of McBirney and Co. and Thomas Sibthorpe of Sibthorpe and Company. Ferrier, Pollock & Co. alone was valued at £410 and Brown, Thomas at £470.[35] For their part the townships attempted to discredit the corporation by targeting its inefficiency and the parlous state of its finances. Rathmines attacked the corporation over the failed joint main drainage scheme, by claiming that when an agreement between the corporation, Rathmines and Pembroke was reached and an act of parliament obtained in 1871, the onus was on the corporation to carry out the work. However by 1875, the end of the time stipulated, nothing had been done, and the townships withdrew.[36]

The importance of Frederick Stokes in the development of Rathmines was demonstrated by the fact that he was called out of retirement in England to appear at the inquiry. Stokes had appeared at the local taxation hearing and made his strong feelings about the corporation known there. When asked if any proposal had ever been made by or on behalf of the corporation to annex Rathmines to the city, he replied: 'often; like the sword of Damocles it is constantly hanging over our heads. It has been threatened but they never made any real attempt'.[37] When probed, Stokes revealed his conviction that the corporation was a failed entity; he believed that the annexation proposal was like 'annexing a municipality distinguished for success to a municipality which is distinguished for want of success'.[38]

He answered the questions put to him in his usual forthright manner and was very frank about the way in which the township was administered and in particular about his role in it. He was asked if it was true that the Rathmines commissioners were mainly landlords and that they kept the taxes in the township low because they had a paramount interest in reducing taxation to the lowest possible limit and in effect 'starving the district' by their operations. His reply was particularly candid:

> There is no doubt, to some extent, that is so. The board always contained a considerable proportion of owners of property, and I am of opinion ought to do so; but there was also a considerable proportion of persons who had no interest in house property save the houses they lived in. As to keeping down taxation, I am the principal person to blame for that.[39]

From a list of current commissioners called out to him he stated that eleven of them were landlords and ten were not.

Responding to charges that Rathmines was a self-perpetuating oligarchy, Stokes admitted that it was true that at the first election he himself had lost his seat and that another member of the board resigned so that he could be co-opted. He claimed that that was the only occasion on which this was done.[40] Over the next fifteen years there had been only one contested election. This he saw as not being a bad thing, as otherwise Roman catholic commissioners such as Dolan, Plunkett and Murphy, all very active over the years, would have been rejected by the conservative electorate.

The other township which came in for close scrutiny by the commission, owing to the dissatisfaction expressed by its ratepayers, was Clontarf. From the evidence presented by its chairman, John E. Vernon, the impression is unavoidable that the township was in dire straits. Vernon claimed that the corporation did not want to annex it because 'Clontarf is practically a bankrupt concern'.[41] The problems besetting the district seem to have curbed his enthusiasm for the job in hand: 'we are struggling,' he stated bluntly; 'if any gentleman thinks it to be a pleasure to be a town commissioner, I advise him to try it. I can assure you it is a very troublesome and irksome occupation, and a very thankless office, without any remuneration'.[42]

It is thus not suprising that a number of the witnesses from Clontarf wished the township to be taken over by the corporation. Their argument was based on the infrastructural deficiencies of the area; there was no police as it was not in the metropolitan police area, and no lighting, making it a dangerous area at night. Not surprisingly, it had no fire brigade, and indeed had no fire appliance of any kind. A ratepayer, Bartholomew Hynes, was in favour of amalgamation, as he believed that a township like Clontarf was too small, and consequently the taxation too limited, and that the township lacked sufficient power to borrow money to carry out necessary improvements. He went on to claim that 'such a township is too local, and the management frequently too personal, whereas the corporation of a large city acts more on general principles'.[43]

Despite the admitted problems, Vernon wished to protect the township's independence and claimed that a memorial in favour of amalgamation, signed by 38 residents (out of a township total of 4,000) was got up by publicans. He claimed that the petition emanated in particular from the house of a certain Mr Carey, who wished the more liberal licensing laws of the city extended to Clontarf.[44]

Drumcondra was in such a position that if the inquiry recommended the extension of boundaries in its direction, it would be almost still-born as it had only just been set up. The secretary of the township, Michael Pettit, reported to the commission that it had carried out a plebiscite on the question of amalgamation with the city. The area had 500 ratepayers but only 400 circulars were distributed, the uncanvassed hundred being 'occupiers of small houses, cottages, and the like';[45] 225 circulars were returned, and of these only 25 were in favour of annexation.

The coastal townships of Blackrock, Kingstown, Dalkey and Killiney had only been included in the commission's investigations as an afterthought, as it became clear that they would have to be included in a greater Dublin fire brigade area. These townships did not consider it likely that the commission would recommend that they should be abolished and that they become an integral part of Dublin city. They did believe that there was a probability that Exham would recommend that they amalgamate with each other, a prospect which the coastal townships were prepared at least to consider. A special meeting was held by the Blackrock board to consider the matter while the Exham inquiry was meeting. The general opinion was against the establishment of an enlarged authority, since such a development would be too big and members would not be able to attend its meetings. The fact that the government now allowed townships to form joint drainage boards lessened the need for amalgamation, it was claimed. Indeed talks were already going on between Blackrock and Kingstown in this regard.[46]

There is evidence that at least one key individual in township administration was suspicious of the impartiality of Exham and his fellow commissioners. John Vernon, the Pembroke township chairman, appeared before the commissioners for two days. He later stated his reservations about the proceedings, claiming that the outcome was 'with Mr Commissioner Exham from the beginning a foregone conclusion, so much so that having been two days before him I called upon the learned counsel, one of whom is now a distinguished servant of the government, to withdraw from the enquiry because I said that it was absolutely useless for us to argue a foregone conclusion'.[47] Vernon admitted that that was a strong statement to make; however, he did not give any evidence to back up the allegation.

The Exham commmission reported that in the case of most Irish towns and cities examined, property within certain distances varying between a mile and two miles of their boundaries benefited from such proximity. This proximity generated higher rents for house owners, and residents benefited from such amenities as schools, shops, markets, places of worship and railway stations. Landowners were seen to benefit also from the greater value of land near towns. It also worked to the advantage of all if towns were kept clean and well-lighted. The commissioners felt that the cost of providing services and amenities should not be placed exclusively on the shoulders of the town ratepayers.[48]

Many of the objectors to the extension of the boundaries of rural towns had been open and honest to the commission about their motives. They claimed that they had built their houses outside the boundary to avoid paying rates and regarded it as unjust that they should now be brought into the net. In most cases the roads of the town were under the juristicion of the grand jury rather than a municipal body, so those outside claimed that that they were already paying for their upkeep.

However, the main objection of both rural and suburban dwellers close to municipal areas was that they were to be taken into the new extended areas without their consent. The commission completely dismissed this objection on the grounds that it was not in the brief given to them to consider consent or non-consent in determining their conclusions.

In line with this thinking, the commission recommended the extension in the case of vitually all the boundaries of the towns investigated to include quite extensive areas of agricultural land within the new taxation districts.[49]

The case of Dublin and its suburbs was unique. The only urban area coming close to it was Belfast. Belfast was beginning to spill out beyond its boundaries and was experiencing all the problems that that entailed. The areas of Strandstown, Belmont, and Knock were covered in building sites and newly-built villas. The suburban areas of Sydenham and Connswater were being rapidly developed and most of the buildings there were new. It was claimed that rows of houses and streets had been built within a very short period 'as the owners themselves pleased, without supervision or control'.[50]

The report of the Exham commission recommended that the boundaries of Dublin be extended up to four miles from the city centre on the south side and up to three miles on the north side, so amalgamating the townships of Rathmines and Rathgar, Pembroke, Kilmainham, Drumcondra and Clontarf with the city, together with parts of the adjacent county. The report even more strongly recommended the amalgamation of Kingstown, Dalkey and Blackrock. It pointed to the new town hall at Kingstown as being a suitable centre for a new enlarged area, and rejected claims that the future commissioners of the enlarged district would have difficulty attending meetings owing to the distance to be travelled by pointing out that the railway connected the three townships. Killiney was left out of the proposed enlarged township, but a proposal that Dalkey and Killiney be joined as a separate township was rejected, stating that it could not be said that one was the suburb of another as they were separated from each other by a range of high hills.[51]

Apart from these main recommendations, the report, most pointedly, made a scathing attack on Rathmines, which it compared very unfavourably with Pembroke. No sanitary officer had been appointed until 1879 and a sub-sanitary officer, who was also the porter at the town hall, had done all the work up to then. No bye-laws had ever been made covering the five slaughter houses in the township. As far as the medical health of the inhabitants was concerned there was no hospital in the township and the board did not contribute to any hospital in the city. No provision was made for disinfection of clothes or houses and there was no vehicle for removing infectious patients to hospital.[52] In effect the report found that in Rathmines there had been 'not the slightest real compliance with the public health acts of 1866 or 1874'.[53]

Inevitably the report had something to say on the question of canal water. The water pressure in the township was only eighty feet, completely inadequate for the high Rathgar end of the district and in some areas the water was turned off at night. The report expressed surprise at a provision in the Rathmines and Rathgar (Milltown) extension act, 1880, which was going through parliament while the commissioners deliberated. By this provision the improvement rate to be levied thenceforth would seem to be unlimited in amount, a power which did not exist in any town in Ireland. It was also noted that there were about 300 houses in the township, found chiefly in lanes, which were occupied by labourers, although they were unsuitable for habitation. Also commented on disapprovingly was the fact that the township surveyor, who had been employed for several years but did not give all his time to township work, had no map drawn up as required by the Towns improvement act and Public health act of 1878. In fact, apart from 700 to 800 houses, which drained into the public drains, the surveyor stated that he was ignorant of the drainage arrangement of the township.[54]

The report also criticised Rathmines in that although the commissioners were prepared to light and repair by contract some of the private roads in the district, they did not feel obliged to clean them or prevent nuisances building up. The royal commissioners commented that, in their view of the law, the reverse of the Rathmines board's actions was the legal one. Leinster Road was particularly referred to, and it was pointed out that the ratepayers of Rathmines were losing money each year on a private arrangement made with its owners. In general, financial arrangements in Rathmines were seen as lax. The board was not complying with the act of 1862 regarding £20,000 which had been borrowed; a sinking fund had not been set aside; had it been done, the mortgage would already have been paid off.[55]

The recommendations of the report were never acted on by government. This was as a result of strong opposition in the townships, especially Rathmines. There was a precedent for such inaction in England. The royal commission set up in 1837 to look into the question of municipal boundaries in England and Wales recommended that boundaries should be extended to include contiguous built-up areas and 'communities of interest', but its recommendations were often not implemented owing to strong local opposition.[56] Dublin Corporation lacked the powers to promote an annexation bill itself. This was in contrast to a township like Rathmines which was permitted to promote successfully three bills for its own extension.

An attempt was made in Blackrock to have the proposals of the boundary commissioners carried out by which the township would be amalgamated with Kingstown. Those in favour of this on the Blackrock board gave two reasons for the move: firstly on the grounds of economy, the annual cost of employing a surveyor (£430), would be saved; and secondly it would (harking back to the argument on the franchise when the township was extended) give the vote to inhabitants who were rated at £4 and above, as was the case in Kingstown. However, a motion at a meeting of the Blackrock board for the amalgamation of the two townships received little support and a motion objecting to the Exham proposals passed.[57]

Dublin corporation undertook a long campaign to have the recommendation of the Exham commission acted on. A deputation from the city and a combined Rathmines and Pembroke deputation waited on the lord lieutenant, Earl Spencer, respectively promoting and opposing such legislation. The corporation also sought reforms of the rating system.

John Vernon, the Pembroke chairman and estate agent, was chosen to state the townships' case. He did not mince his words on the differences between the corporation and townships and the consequences of amalgamation. He stated that the deputation

> differs from most deputations before him (the lord lieutenant) in that they do not come to ask the government for money and don't come to ask the government for help – on the contrary we deprecate the latter. We come as men of business and ask the government to allow us to manage our own affairs as we have managed them for many years, harmoniously and prosperously. We ask that the government will leave us to deal with our own duties, and will not asssent to the prayer of the corporation to bring in a bill to compel us to be united to them. Your excellency is no doubt perfectly acquainted with the character and constitution of the corporation of the city of Dublin. It may possibly have reached you that some of the very able men ... from that body have not infrequently subordinated their more menial duties pertaining to the municipality to the higher instincts of their patriotism. With that we have nothing to do, but I would merely say this, that between the gentlemen who manage the corporation of the city of Dublin, and the gentlemen who manage the townships, there is not one link of affinity, there is not one touch of sympathy, and if the government should unfortunately compel us to be united in one body, I am satisfied the result will be internecine warfare which will be fruitful of disaster to our townships, as well as to the city.[58]

Vernon's comments on the corporation very much echoed views he had already expressed at the Exham commission, where he stated that 'it would be the millennium' before Dublin corporation abjured politics and religion. He characterized the corporation as a 'first-class political organisation, but equally they are a very bad local administration'.[59]

Vernon went on to inform the lord lieutenant that he failed to find in the history of the annexations that had been made in England any case in which a larger body had annexed a smaller body without bringing to that smaller body some substantial advantage, whether it was gas, water or sewerage, or else it had been able to show that the administration of the larger body was far superior to that of the smaller body. In the present case as regards Pembroke (he did not mention Rathmines) that had not been attempted to be shown. He claimed that the report of the Exham commission had made manifest that in its administration Pembroke was a model township.

Vernon went on to claim that the corporation was now seeking to annex the area of the Pembroke township after the Pembroke estate had invested heavily in it. He pointed out that when Lord Pembroke came of age in 1841 he commenced to spend money on the area – especially to protect it from the sea. He had spent about £50,000 to entice builders into the area and since then about one million pounds had been invested by developers. From 1841 to 1863 the district improved steadily. In 1863 the valuation had been £60,000 – a vast increase from the £1,600 valuation of 1835. The inhabitants had then gone to parliament and obtained a township bill, which was largely unopposed by the corporation, and the improvement continued.

In his reply to the deputations, the lord lieutenant avoided dealing with the municipal boundaries issue by stating that a bill would be brought before parliament in the next session dealing with defects in the rates and that until that was done 'the question of extension of boundaries of Dublin is not ripe for settlement'.[60]

Despite further memorials from the municipal body to the lord lieutenant in 1883 and 1884, Dublin Castle was unwilling to interfere. A growing disenchantment between the government and the corporation owing to the municipal body's growing nationalist militancy no doubt contributed to the administration's attitude of indifference. The Castle deferred passing judgment on the matter by claiming that nothing should be done until the whole question of the rating system of the city was improved.

The township argument all along was that there was no precedent for annexing to another body townships constituted by private act of parliament against the wishes of its ratepayers. This stance was supported by the principal private bill clerk in the house of lords when the report of the royal commission on the housing of the working class also recommended extending the Dublin city boundaries in 1885.[62]

The continuous threat of annexation goaded the Rathmines board into an address to the lord lieutenant which openly fell back on a comparison between itself and an unloyal Dublin corporation. The government was urged not to lend assistance to any act of parliament which would be 'an act of spoilation and subjection of a township ... which has always been loyal and law-abiding, and thus assist in furthering the designs of a body such as the corporation of Dublin, the majority of whose members have so recently done all they could or dare venture to parade their disloyalty to crown and constitution'.

As it turned out the first real attempt at annexation since the township's inception took place in 1886 in the form of a private bill promoted by the Dublin city members of parliament on behalf of the corporation. The bill sought an extension of the boundaries as recommended by the Exham commission and in accordance with resolutions of the corporation on many occasions. The bill was introduced by the nationalist MPs, T.D. Sullivan, lord mayor of Dublin, E. Dwyer Gray, T. Harrington and William Martin Murphy. The extended area would include the five inner townships and parts of the county. The bill failed and in the following year the corporation passed a motion asking that 'the attention of the government be directed to the pressing necessity of carrying into effect the recommendations of the municipal boundaries commission with regard to the city of Dublin'. It went on to appeal to the city's representatives to once again introduce and press forward such a bill. This met with no success either.[65]

In the meantime, a large number of English cities had availed of the provisions of the local government (England) act, 1888 to extend their boundaries; these included, Canterbury, Coventry, Huddersfield, Manchester (1890), Birmingham (1891), York (1893), Liverpool, Plymouth (1895), Hartlepool, and Hastings (1897).[66] When the boundaries of Belfast were extended in 1896 to double its area, it surpassed Dublin as Ireland's most populous city. This goaded Dublin corporation to attempt once more to have the city boundaries extended, and in so doing take over the townships. An opportunity arose when it became clear that a restructuring of local government in Ireland was about to take place. A number of the city wards, through their ratepayers' associations, petitioned the corporation to have the extension of the city boundaries included in the comprehensive 1898 bill.[67] This bill proposed a complete reform of local government in Ireland, including the abolition of grand juries and the introduction of county councils, and urban district and rural district councils. The Kingstown board sent a deputation to Blackrock and Dalkey to consult on the question of amalgamating the three townships and petitioned the government to grant county borough status to this new amalgamated area. It argued that the area deserved this status owing to its population and position as a royal mail station.[68]

A rather belated attempt was made to have the boundaries of Dublin extended when the local government bill came before parliament. At the behest of the corporation, John Redmond, nationalist MP, agreed to bring in an amendment to the bill to this effect.[69] The corporation had received a certain amount of support for its objectives at a meeting of the association of municipal corporations held at the Guildhall in London. The lord mayor of London, Sir Albert Rollit, moved a motion supporting Dublin which was seconded by the lord mayor of Manchester. When the amendment was moved in July, Redmond pointed out that the Exham commission had recommended extension twenty years before. The objections to this recommendation, namely that the rates in the former township areas would increase now no longer held as the township rates had gone up considerably since then. Referring to the financial problems of Dublin city, Redmond claimed that the corporation had spent two million pounds on the city in that twenty-year period, but its valuation had gone up by only £2,000. If it were allowed to extend its boundaries to those recommended by Exham its valuation would increase by £130,000 or £140,000.[70]

The unionist, Colonel Saunderson, speaking against the amendment, pointed out the corporation's neglect; he claimed that the Liffey was a sewer whereas the townships of Rathmines and Pembroke had installed an excellent main drainage system at enormous expense. The first lord of the treasury wrapped up the argument by stating that the many interests involved needed to be thrashed out before a private bill committee as the matter was too important to be introduced as an appendix to a public bill. Redmond weakly agreed that the timing was not right for the matter to be gone into (the house was discussing the issue at ten to five in the morning) and he withdrew the amendment.[71]

In conclusion, it is evident that as early as 1837 a sensible theoretical framework had been laid down by the royal commission on boundaries in England for the extension of municipal areas. At the same time a working model of such an extended area had been set up in Dublin – the police district. The Exham commission followed the guidelines of the English body and recommended the extension of the Dublin city boundaries to limits very close to those of the police district.

The Exham commission investigated the whole local government of Dublin with admirable fairness and thoroughness. The failure of the government to act on its recommendations can be attributed to the strong political opposition mounted by the influential suburbs. It is likely that such a move would have failed in the house of lords. The royal commission's stinging criticism of Rathmines was well justified; in particular in relation to the township's almost total non-compliance with the health acts. From now on Dublin corporation possessed a stick with which to beat the townships. However, having moral right on its side was far from enough to win the argument and obtain redress. The English experience suggested that if there was stiff opposition to extension of boundaries the government was slow to act. Certainly in Dublin the well-argued case for greater economy and efficiency was lost in the need to satisfy local vested interests.

CHAPTER FIVE

From township to urban district council

When legislation was introduced creating elected county councils in England, Wales and Scotland in 1888 it was only a matter of time before similar legislation was brought in for Ireland. Land agitation, however, meant that the measure for Ireland came later rather than sooner. Arthur Balfour, the chief secretary, introduced a bill in 1892 to establish county councils on the English model. A joint meeting took place between the Rathmines and Pembroke boards calling for modifications to the bill – for instance, that the townships have more control over the expenditure of funds raised by county at large charges, if such a levy were to be continued; the townships also sought representation on the new Dublin county council.[1] Nothing came of this particular measure, but in 1898 a bill completely re-organizing local government in Ireland was introduced. The main thrust of the measure was to transfer the powers of the grand jury to new county councils, Balfour stating that 'you cannot put old wine into new bottles'. Existing townships and sanitary authorities became urban or rural district councils, and powers for making and collecting the poor law rate were transferred to them from the poor law guardians. As far as the Dublin townships were concerned, the main change was the extension of the local government franchise, giving women the vote for the first time.[2]

The anxieties of the townships in relation to the bill were expressed at a conference of representatives of six suburban townships (Pembroke, Clontarf, Drumcondra, Blackrock, Dalkey and Killiney) and the commissioners of Bray, which was held in Pembroke town hall. Amendments on a number of points were sought, mainly relating to financial provisions. It was felt by the townships that the proposal in the bill for the amalgamation of local improvement rates and the poor rates would lead to an increased financial burden on suburban ratepayers and relief was sought from the funds established by the act to allieviate such a burden. Also, the relief granted to rural districts on a rate levied for railway or harbour purposes was sought for urban districts. The bill provided for payment by urban districts to the county councils for county at large charges, and the townships requested that these financial arrangements be more clearly defined.

One of the principal effects of the 1898 act on the townships was the enlargement of the electorate to the wider parliamentary franchise. From now on men, and most significantly in a township like Rathmines with a large number of female owners and occupiers, women, in accommodation rated £10 or more

127

could vote for the new councils.[3] Attempts had been made by nationalists before this to achieve a wider franchise. Five years previously, when the Blackrock and Kingstown main drainage bill was going through the house of commons, T.M. Healy and the Irish parliamentary party inserted franchise clauses into it without discussing it with the townships. This liberty was resented by Blackrock in particular, which had a history of affluent ratepayers in Monkstown resenting extending the franchise to poorer areas of the township. The township then had the option of opposing the franchise clauses in the house of lords, but Healy stated that if this course of action was taken, he would wreck the bill. It was also quite late in the session and any opposition would probably result in the loss of the legislation, so Blackrock decided to let the bill proceed without hindrance. Horace Plunkett claimed that there was an agreement between the unionists and the nationalists on the bill and that Healy had reneged on it by introducing the offending clauses. Apart from the franchise clause, the other clauses seem quite innocuous, such as that relating to tenants not losing the vote as a result of moving house, a practice which, it was claimed by Healy, had been in existence in all Irish municipalities since 1842.[4]

After the 1898 bill became law the first meeting of the Rathmines and Rathgar Urban District Council was held in the town hall on 23 January 1899 with Edward Hodgson in the chair. From 1899 on, the local government franchise in the townships was exercised by rated occupiers, leaseholders, freeholders and lodgers, whether male or female, of full age occupying rooms to the value of 4s. weekly (£10 per annum) and satisfying a one year residency; so for the first time women obtained a say in civic affairs, both as voters and as prospective councillors. In general however, women were slow to participate in local government, and even by 1913 there were only five women among 1,361 urban district councillors in Ireland.

The year 1898 saw in Ireland the establishment of the United National League by William O'Brien and in 1900 the healing of the Parnellite split in the Irish parliamentary party. In the townships greater nationalist organization among the new increased electorate was met by an energetic unionist response. With this growing polarisation of political feeling, elections became more hotly contested. The Rathmines council remained under unionist control until 1920, although they did not attach a political party label to themselves until 1908. In 1899 the nationalists organized themselves to fight the Rathmines elections of early that year. The Rathmines branch of the South County Dublin National Registration Association, an organisation set up to maximize the nationalist vote in the area, selected twenty-one candidates, including the lord mayor of Dublin, Daniel Tallon, to contest the election. This was seen as the first election fought 'on straight political lines', and resulted in a complete defeat for the nationalists with not one being elected.[5] Fourteen members of the old board were re-elected and the seven others were approved of by members of the old board.

The existence of an agreed 'ticket' was clearly reported in 1902. This election was the first held under another electoral innovation for Rathmines. From the inception of the township one-third of the board members had retired every year necessitating an election if the seats were contested, as they increasingly were. To avoid the disruption caused by this and to minimize expense, the Rathmines council received sanction from the local government board to hold elections for the whole council every three years instead of for one-third every year. As a consequence of this, the first election for the whole council took place in January 1902 and subsequently every three years.[6]

The extension of the franchise did not make a huge difference to the composition or indeed the age-old electoral practices of the Rathmines board. In 1902 all the members of the old board were returned, except a small number who wished to retire. These were replaced by candidates who 'threw in their lot with the old board'.[7] Two candidates who refused to sign a common address by the old board and their allies were not returned.[8] Some disquiet was expressed at times that the 'ticket' did not include enough local traders as opposed to big businessmen who resided in the township; but the old system (the election of 'non-political' but in reality unionist councillors subscribing to an agreed agenda) remained intact during these years.

Of particular concern in suburban areas was the question of registration, especially now that the large shifting population of lodgers had the vote. A nationalist registration association was set up in Rathmines in 1902 and strove over many years to marshall the nationalist turn-out. It was equally as strenuously opposed by a similar unionist machine. The nationalist association invited residents who shared its views, especially lodgers, to visit its offices in Rathmines where its inspectors and agents were in attendance 'ready to afford all information regarding the franchise'.[9]

The rivalry engendered by this partisanship led to over-zealousness. In 1904 two members of unionist associations in the townships were suspected of tampering with the register and charged with forgery. A revisions court sat in the town hall in Rathmines each autumn and the register, with objections, was placed before a solicitor or barrister. This was a tedious procedure. In 1904 there were 2,700 objections to names on the register, 1,400 by the unionists and 1,300 by the nationalists. Many objections were made to attempts by householders to register their sons and other family members as lodgers, or to lodgers who were not paying enough rent. John Baker, of Ranelagh Place, for instance, claimed to be a lodger in a house occupied by his wife; however, the unionist agent pointed out that Mrs Baker had stated to him that her husband never occupied a separate room from her, and never paid her anything, and the claim was disallowed.[10]

The two unionist agents charged with forgery were an election agent named Macartney (no first name given) of Rathmines and Thomas Ladd of Kingstown. Macartney would call on houses, known to him to be nationalist, in which the rate collector of Rathmines had left a registration form to be filled in a few days previously, and collect the forms. Telling the busy householders that he would fill them in for them, he would then do so deliberately incorrectly. When the authorities in Rathmines pointed this out to the revising barrister at the court the householder and rightful voter's name would be struck out and he would lose his vote. Macartney and Ladd were sentenced to one month and three months in prison respectively, an outcome which the press hoped would put a stop to the hitherto widespread tampering with the register.[11]

As well as gaining the franchise, women could now stand for district council elections. One of the most important early successes in this regard in the Dublin townships was the election of Margaret Dockrell, a unionist, in Blackrock. Mrs Dockrell was regarded as the leader of the unionist grouping on the council, but was the object of anti-women bias in 1905. In that year's election the unionists won back control of the council from the nationalists. However, when it came to elect a chairman (a post Mrs Dockrell believed was her due) she was overlooked in favour of a man. Outraged, she declined the position of vice-chairman, a post she had held for the previous three years, as 'a protest against an act of flagrant injustice, not to herself alone, but through her to all women'.[12] For those who had voted against her, she had nothing but, 'infinite compassion'; she could only hope that 'their poor restricted outlook might be enlarged in the future'. Their action was castigated by her as a slur on the woman who bore them, their wives and their daughters. She praised those who had voted for her and saw that it did not detract from her womanliness for a woman to take part in public affairs.[13]

In Rathmines a two-ward system had been set up under the improvement act of 1885, when two districts of almost equal size replaced the old unequal Rathmines and Rathgar wards which had been created on the annexation of Rathgar. Twelve councillors for the east ward and nine for the west replaced the eighteen for Rathmines and three for Rathgar.[14] Nationalists in Rathmines believed that the two-ward system proved an obstacle to political advancement; areas likely to produce a nationalist majority like Harold's Cross had no separate political identity and were swamped by more conservative ratepayers in the rest of the large ward. The first decade of the new century saw a sustained attack on the system. Through a petition organized by a ratepayers' association over 600 nationalists called for an inquiry to look into the suggestion that five wards be created to replace the two. Dublin county council ordered the wards in Rathmines to be increased from two to five and the local government board confirmed this. The Rathmines council lodged an appeal and an inquiry was ordered. Witnesses claiming to represent over 3,000 electors against change appeared at the inquiry as did a solicitor on behalf of a committee in favour of retaining the two-ward arrangement. The Rathmines council objected to the petition got up by the ratepayers' association, stating that half of those who signed were not local government electors, as they claimed to be, and that there were other irregularities in the document. The council pointed out that not one person from the artisan class from Harold's Cross had signed the petition and that there had never been any complaint on the subject from that area. The council saw the 'real instigators of this agitation' as politically motivated and not really interested in Harold's Cross.[15] Those in favour of change had pointed to the fact that all the commissioners lived in the richer parts of the township. The council contended that this did not preclude such people from having the interests of the working class at heart; as evidence of this it was pointed out that they had already spent over £50,000 on artisans' dwellings, and had built a free public library, and a public park in Harold's Cross.[16]

The council went on to assert that if such a large working class existed in the township it would be easy to get one of its number elected. It went on to state patronizingly that working men did not have any real interest in the township, pointing to the fact that working men in general did not bother to vote. The petitioners contended that the town hall was not a suitable place for working men to vote, presumably meaning that it was not in their area, and that they would be overawed by its august surroundings.

The council went on to defend the monopoly of power by property owners. It suggested that the fact that working men did not vote might be evidence that they were satisfied with the management of the township. The proposal that men of certain political views should be represented was seen as mistaken; the business of the council was municipal affairs, it was argued, not to engage in political discussion. The best type of person to run the business affairs of the township was 'the man of education in business life, the person who from his property in the township had only one desire – to see it conducted on straight lines'.[17]

T.M. Healy and A.M. Sullivan acted on behalf of the petitioners. Healy, employing his ready wit and vitriol, attacked the opposing side. He claimed that Mr Seddal, the representative of the committee against change, arranged the 'ticket' of councillors in the Conservative Association rooms in Dawson Street. He went on to recall the time in 1895 when Sir Charles Dilke ordered a very slight extension of the franchise in a Rathmines local act. The consternation of the Rathmines men in the lobby of the house, he would never forget:

> He could only compare the confusion amongst a body of respectable and middle-aged gentlemen (laughter) to what would be witnessed if a big stone was lifted up on a green field, and the sunlight let in on the creature under the stone (laughter). What happened? Nothing happened; the franchise was extended, but all the prophesies as to the destruction of the township came to naught. 'Leave us alone in Lotus Land' was the cry of the commissioners.[18]

Healy went through the professions of the commissioners to point out that there was not one from the working class among them, and *Thom's directory* confirms that all of the commissioners resided in affluent streets in the township with valuations of between £30 and £50.[19] Claiming that three of the wards would remain with the conservatives, anyway, but that 'if they had more representatives of the poorer people on the board, instead of the electric pillars, three branches strong, in front of the door of every commissioner of Rathmines (laughter) there would be a little more light around the slums of Harold's Cross and other places where the poorer people lived and that 'after half a century of exclusion and boycotting, they might be entitled as a poor and feeble minority of the people to lift up their voices in the sacred temple of conservatism in Rathmines (applause)'.[20]

The case for change was supported by Daniel Tallon and Francis Adye-Curran. Adye-Curran, who had been active in the local branch of the Irish National Federation, stated that he and a colleague, Alfred Killingley, had contested township elections eight years previously. However, they had found that the wards were too big to canvass; when he attempted again about five years previously he had lost again. He had managed to obtain a place on the council however by joining the Conservative Association and 'paid fifteen pounds to a committee' of which Mr Russell was the chairman. He and three other liberals had been co-opted on the conservative ticket in this way.[21] This claim by Curran seems dubious, one would have thought that liberals, particularly one like Adye-Curran who had a high profile at the time, would have found it difficult to hide their true colours in such a small arena as the suburban townships.

The two sides threw accusations at each other. The conservatives were charged with running a Tammany Hall-type ward system, and they in their turn claimed that their opponents were operating under a number of front organizations and pointed out that the Rathmines Ratepayers' Association, the Rathmines Municipal Association and the Catholic Association all met at 75a Rathmines. It was eventually found that, as the 1885 act setting up the wards in Rathmines was a private act, Dublin county council had no jurisdiction in the matter and its order was *ultra vires*; neither had the local government board power to confirm the order. So Rathmines retained its two wards.[22]

In 1905, the Rathmines council was 'startled' to find that it was opposed 'based on no grounds that they were aware of' by a local chemist, T.J. English of Rathgar Road. The outgoing coterie of councillors regretted 'the expense and trouble of a contested election' and were gratified when English was not elected.[23] The only danger was that complacency would keep their potential voters at home. In the event English came last having polled 562 votes, with all of the unionist receiving over 800 votes each.[24] The fact that the outgoing councillors thought of themselves as being 'opposed' by anyone points to a common agreed agenda.

Co-operation however did exist between commissioners of different religious persuasions. When Thomas Edmundson was elected as chairman in 1905, Councillor Thomas Hewson was proposed as vice-chair. However, he refused to let his name go forward on the grounds that the council should be 'entirely unsectarian and non-political' and that someone 'of another sect' should be chosen; his wishes were then complied with and Francis McBride, a Roman catholic magistrate of Grosvenor Square, Rathmines was elected vice-chairman.[25] This is the only time that such a power-sharing arrangement is alluded to in the council minutes, the only other comparable plan being the ill-fated attempt to reserve one-third of the board's seats for Roman catholics in the early days of the township (see Chapter 2).

The co-opting of those favourable to the Rathmines board's views continued. For instance, when Robert Booth, a member of the council representing the east ward for over twenty years, died in 1913, a councillor for the west ward, H.J. McCormick resigned and was elected for Booth's seat in the east to make way for the co-option of Robert Benson of Orwell Park in the west ward.[26] In 1917, when a vacancy came up on the council the active Rathmines and Rathgar Ratepayers' Association suggested that Dr Jackson of Ranelagh Road be co-opted. However, the suggestion was ignored and a candidate of the board's choosing was picked.[27]

The council also took an active part in supporting unionist candidates in both the municipal and county council elections. The political complexion of such efforts can be seen in a motion passed without dissent in January 1914 at the close of municipal elections thanking the local unionist associations of the east and west wards and to their workers for 'the hearty support they accorded to us at the recent elections'.[28] Later that year the council passed with one dissenting voice a resolution that the council 'pledge themselves to support the candidature of Messrs Anderson and McBride for the position of county councillors and would earnestly appeal to the rate-payers, in their own interests, to vote solidly in their favour'.[29] Both Anderson and McBride were unionists.

Rathmines councillors had resisted giving themselves party labels, a practice which was nearly universal in local elections by then, the other Dublin urban districts included. In 1908 the outgoing Rathmines board decided to canvass on a party ticket; however it eschewed the label unionist, which, by politics, all its members were. They called themselves the 'commercial' candidates in deference to their business background and the business-like manner in which they liked to think they conducted township affairs.[30] All of the 'commercial' candidates were elected in the west ward; in the east ward an independent candidate, Thomas Saul, topped the poll with all the 'commercial' candidates taking the other seats.[31] In 1911 there was no contest at all and the old board was returned unopposed.[32]

In 1914, the old guard, described in the newspapers as the 'non-political ticket', was opposed by seventeen candidates on the 'political ticket' (nationalist).

Not one of the nationalists was elected in either ward. The nationalists put their defeat down to the short time they had in organizing themselves and to the fact that the nationalist vote was split. Michael Sullivan, one of the defeated nationalist candidates, asserted that a situation could not be allowed to continue where the large nationalist minority in the township was not represented. Referring to the recent Larne gun-running by loyalists, he pointed to the fact that in Ulster 'a sterner minority', fearing that they would not be represented, bought bayonets and guns. Nationalists in Rathmines, he announced, would not resort to such extreme tactics, but they would secure representation ultimately.[33]

The contrast with Pembroke could not be starker. From 1908, the conservative representation on the council began to decline and by 1913 there were only two unionist members left. The changing political complexion of the township was added to the opposition already there to the old order on the grounds of financial mismanagement. In August 1913, the council passed a motion, couched in very patriotic tones, congratulating John Redmond and his colleagues on 'the triumphant passage of the home rule bill through the House of Commons with such a splendid majority and thereby bringing the Irish nation, after a long night of oppression and misrule to an equality with all the self-governing nations of the world'. The motion ended proclaiming 'A Nation Once Again', with the two unionists voting against.[34]

A copy of the motion was sent to the Irish parliamentary party, and the reply of Patrick J. Brady, MP, gives us a further insight into the politics of the council. Referring to the two unionists who had dissented from the motion, he asserted his belief in free speech, especially at a time when so much was being heard of the persecution, civil and religious, which the opponents of home rule would be visited with under an Irish government. He pointed with pride to the record on this score of 'nationalist Dublin', of which, he claimed, the Pembroke township was a striking example. Three years previously unionists had contested all fifteen seats on the council, when for their part, the nationalists had only put up twelve candidates, although the state of the register 'made it certain' that all fifteen seats could be won by them. They had deliberately only contested twelve lest it be said that they wanted to exclude their opponents from their share in local government.[35]

The Pembroke council showed solidarity with workers in the poorer areas of the township during the great lock-out in 1913. It agreed to a request by thirty-two tenants of Pembroke Cottages, Ringsend, and nine in Donnybrook to withhold rent collection from them while they were out of work. All thirty-two were idle owing to the labour dispute and were unable to pay their rent. The workers came to an agreement with the council that as soon as the dispute was over they would resume payment plus 6d. per week until all arrears were paid.[36] The dispute came to the door of the council when the contractor building its working-class houses in Ballsbridge and Ringsend, Patrick Shortall, locked out his labourers. The council ordered an inquiry to see if the lock-out was justified, and if it was not, to take legal proceedings against the contractor.[37]

Loyal addresses to members of the royal family were a common feature of local government at this time. In unionist Rathmines there was never a question of a loyal address being opposed. However, this was not the case in other townships. The question of loyal addresses arose more often in the coastal townships of Kingstown and Blackrock as any visiting monarch or members of the royal family usually journeyed through them to the city. Five out of fourteen Blackrock councillors voted against presenting an address to Queen Victoria on her arrival in Ireland in 1900. A strong amendment to the address, moved by Councillor T.A. Byrne and seconded by Councillor L. Wickham, was ruled out of order. It stated

> that as representatives of nationalist opinions we cannot identify ourselves with any address of loyalty to Her Majesty the Queen on her coming visit to Ireland, and we consider the action of the loyal minority and their national associates in presenting such an address as unwarrantable and uncalled for, inasmuch as Her Majesty, through the lord lieutenant, expressed the wish and desire that her visit should bear no political significance whatever, and we are convinced that such exhibitions of so-called loyalty are from selfish and ulterior motives, at least on the part of so-called nationalists, and but tend to mislead Her Majesty and her ministers as to the real feeling that animates the majority of the Irish people, that will never be either loyal, content, prosperous or happy, so long as the just right to govern themselves is denied.[38]

A similar move was rejected in Blackrock in 1904 on the occasion of the imminent arrival of Edward VII and his queen. A proposal that 'no address be presented to the King and Queen until such time as home rule and a Catholic university be granted to Ireland' was defeated by eleven votes to three. By 1914, Kingstown was nationalist-controlled and protests such as that against the continuance of the arms' proclamation in Ireland and the killing of three people in Dublin by the King's Own Scottish Borderers were passed with a lone dissenting voice, that of the unionist, Robert Blood.[39]

DEMISE OF CLONTARF, DRUMCONDRA
& KILMAINHAM TOWNSHIPS, 1900

When the belated amendment of John Redmond for the extension of the city's boundary failed in 1898, Dublin corporation decided to introduce its own bill and the solicitor general ruled that it had full power to do so.[40] A report of the whole house of Dublin corporation recommended the promotion of a boundaries bill and this was unanimously adopted by the municipal council in October 1898. A meeting was held in the Mansion House the following February to obtain the necessary sanction of the burgesses to the promotion of the bill. At that meeting a poll of the burgesses was called for and the result showed a vote of 20,498 for the bill and 3,116 against, an overwhelming majority of 17,382. The corporation then invited representatives of the townships to a friendly conference to discuss the question of extending the city boundaries, but they all refused to accept.[41] The Rathmines council sanctioned its parliamentary committee to take all necessary steps to oppose the bill, and when the lord mayor and a deputation of members of the corporation were received by the first lord of the treasury, A.J. Balfour, Rathmines requested that it be received as well.[42]

In 1899 a select committee of the house of commons sat for seventeen days to take evidence on the bill and twenty-two witnesses appeared on behalf of the corporation. The preamble to the bill was passed, with modifications, including the area of the county that was to be included in the city. When the report of the select committee came before the house of commons it was opposed by the townships; but the decision of the committee was passed by a majority of 162 in a house of 420. John Redmond spoke in the house in favour of the bill. He claimed that Dublin was the only city in the United Kingdom whose boundaries had not been extended since 1840. The five townships ringing the city were seen as a liability to it. They had no notification of diseases act and there was no main drainage in three and a defective system in two. At present the corporation was installing a very costly main drainage system with no help from the townships. It was also erecting a fruit and vegetable market to serve the whole greater Dublin area at a cost of £150,000. He countered the argument that amalgamation would cause a rate increase by pointing to a provision in the bill that there would be no such increase in the suburbs for ten years.[43]

Edward Carson, opposing the bill, claimed that the suburbs annexed in English towns had wished to be taken over, and that this was not the case in Dublin. Despite a large increase in the electorate in Rathmines as a result of the local government act, all the candidates favouring amalgamation, including the lord mayor of Dublin, had been defeated in the most recent election in the township.

Three days later the bill was read for the third time by the house of commons without opposition. By this stage a number of amendments favourable to the townships had been inserted in the bill, and the corporation, hoping to avoiding the expense of a contest in the house of lords, renewed its efforts to negotiate with the suburban councils, but again without success.[44]

The bill duly came before the house of lords and was referred to a select committee there, which sat for fourteen days and examined numerous witnesses. The upshot was that the lords passed a watered down bill denying the corporation the townships of Rathmines, Pembroke, Clontarf and Drumcondra and two of the county districts. This would leave the corporation with only the township of Kilmainham and the districts of Crumlin, Chapelizod and Grangegorman. This amended bill was then rejected by the commons, which claimed that to accept such a drastic change to its original bill would deliver a very serious blow at the independence of the house.

The boundary bill was re-introduced in the following session of parliament and once again the corporation sought conferences with the townships. It soon arrived at a settlement with Drumcondra and Kilmainham. In Drumcondra the case against the corporation had been weakened by the fact that 500 ratepayers had petitioned in favour of the bill, and in Kilmainham 666 ratepayers out of 1,007 were also in favour of amalgamation. All of the townships contained people who were, for various reasons, in favour of amalgamation with the corporation. Many in Kilmainham and Drumcondra, working-class and lower middle-class townships respectively, were sympathetic to the dominant class in control of the corporation – the likes of shopkeepers, publicans and building contractors with a nationalist outlook. The more affluent Clontarf was divided on the issue of amalgamation and a plebiscite held there in May 1900 proved controversial. The local council claimed that there was a majority of one hundred and twenty against amalgamation. The corporation questioned the validity of the poll claiming that many papers had been spoiled or uncollected. It also claimed that the chairman of the council, Lord Ardilaun, who was against amalgamation, wielded huge 'personal and undue influence' in the area.[45]

The Rathmines councillors rejected once more the advances of the municipal representatives, more especially as they now felt that the city had obtained more than the space it needed from the modified bill of the last session, which it would be happy to see pass into law in this session. Stressing the prestige and importance of the township, the councillors claimed that among the cities and towns of Ireland, Rathmines was the fourth largest as regards valuation and the fifth as regards population. They regarded the present actions of the corporation as vexatious and warned that they would make the corporation pay all expenses they incurred in defending their independence.[46] To avoid a repetition of the logjam of the previous year the bill was referred to a joint committee of the lords and commons, and so another committee heard a succession of witnesses.

Apart from the township councils, their stockholders and property-owners, the bill was opposed by a range of interests including the earl of Pembroke, the Dublin United Tramway Company, the Dublin Districts Tramway Co., Dublin County Council, Trinity College, and the Dublin port and docks board. As we have seen, not everyone in the townships opposed amalgamation, however; even in Rathmines a ratepayers' association had been formed as a result of a steep rise in rates, which it put down to the high cost of maintaining the township's independence, and decided to support the corporation's case. The association requested the council to take a plebiscite in Rathmines as had been undertaken in other townships but it refused claiming that the last election had given the council a mandate for its actions.[47]

A number of Pembroke ratepayers felt that the township should be amalgamated with the city. A Pembroke ratepayers' association, headed by James Mahony, a city merchant and resident of Raglan Road, urged the Pembroke board to meet the corporation and when it refused to do so got up a petition signed by 950 of the 4,000 Pembroke electors. The association passed a resolution recognising that the claim of the corporation was just and indicating that its members were happy that amalgamation would not lead to a rate increase. A number of the residents acquainted with the poorer Ringsend and Sandymount part of the township spoke in favour of the bill on sanitary grounds, stating that many of these areas were neglected by the Pembroke commissioners. The corporation claimed that seventy-seven Rathmines ratepayers and property-owners had signed a petition in favour of amalgamation and that a request for a poll signed by 1,300 ratepayers had been sent to the Rathmines council.[48]

A powerful case in favour of amalgamation was made in an anonymous appeal in pamphlet form, addressed to the Rathmines ratepayers and published under the title *Boundaries or bankruptcy*. The oft-repeated claim of the township that the city was bankrupt and wished to acquire the suburban rates was refuted; it was pointed out that in fact the Rathmines debt per head of population was double that of the city; the corporation debt was £1,599,995 or £6.53 per head of population as against the Rathmines township debt of £336,122 or £12.09 per head. Looking at the debt on the basis of rateable valuation it was also shown that the city was again in a healthier state. The value of the city was £720,000 in 1898 as against £138,457 for Rathmines; this gave a proportion of debt to valuation per pound for Dublin of £2.22 as against £2.44 for Rathmines. It had also to be to borne in mind that Dublin city was notoriously undervalued.[49]

The administrative and sanitation record of Rathmines was attacked once more. It had been suggested that the building trade interest, always strong in Rathmines, was against amalgamation as it believed that the building bye-laws were more stringent in the city than in Rathmines. Some of the most wretched slums anywhere were to be found within the boundaries of the township, it was claimed; Harold's Cross road was fringed by a row of hovels. Although the council had ample space in the vicinity, the only dwellings for the working class built there had been erected by a private company – the Dublin Artisans' Dwelling Company. The houses that the council had built, at Gulistan, meant for the township employees, were largely tenanted by much better-off tenants than those originally intended.[50]

The 'improvements' of recent years were scoffed at, particularly the legal difficulties surrounding the building of the new waterworks. This referred to the scheme built under the supervision of Richard Hassard at Glenasmole, which had run into serious legal difficulties with the Dodder mill-owners. The anonymous pamphleteer outlined the history of the project in very negative terms, stating that when the township had been forced to give up the supply of dirty canal water, a waterworks bill was run through parliament. The reservoir was, by a costly error, positioned in the wrong place. Expensive litigation had ensued, followed by amending acts, and the ratepayers had been paying for it ever since. In the end the waterworks cost £220,000 for a population of at most 28,000 people, or an average of £8 per head, while Dublin had spent £730,000 on the Vartry scheme, giving better water to 245,000 people at a cost of £3 per head.[51]

The township's fire brigade was ridiculed. In recent years the Dublin brigade had been called to attend to twenty-three fires in the township saving £230,000 worth of property. An example of this had taken place the previous year when the large Pim linen factory at Harold's Cross had been saved by the Dublin brigade. It was asserted colourfully that if a fire were to break out in Harold's Cross in a westerly gale the exertions of 'the three or four nautically attired caryatids who polish the portals of the township fire station with their brawny shoulders' would hardly save the township.[52]

The corporation, in presenting its case to the joint committee of the houses of commons and lords, which got under way in May 1900, pleaded to be allowed follow its population as had been done in English cities. It pointed out that the population density of Dublin was extremely high at 64 persons per acre as compared to 25, 17 and 22 respectively in Hull, Shefffield and Bradford. The districts to be annexed were co-extensive with the urbanised area; this would amount to some 6,000 acres in the townships and 2,500 acres in the county area. The total population of the townships annexed would be 74,000.[53] This population was a natural part of it the city; it had grown as 'a swelling of city numbers'. There was nothing outside the city causing that growth.[54] The benefits of an extended boundary were explained by the medical officer of Liverpool. He asserted that the sanitary condition of that city had improved enormously from 1895 when four of its large townships had been incorporated into the city.[55]

The principle on which the corporation was working was that anyone who benefited from Dublin should contribute to the city. People living in the townships were of two kinds: firstly, those who had businesses in the city and lived in the townships; although these paid rates on their business properties in the city, the bulk of their rates was paid in the townships on their residential and rented out property; secondly, there was an army of professional men, government officials, highly-placed clerks and so on, who contributed absolutely nothing to the city.

The lord mayor of Dublin, Sir Thomas Pile, who lived in Rathmines, made use of the phrase 'community of interest' between city and suburb, which the corporation had first used at the Exham commission, and could be traced back as far as the English royal commission on boundaries in 1837. Pile explained what he meant by this relationship. Referring to Kenilworth Square, where he resided, he claimed that sixty-four heads of households were males and over twenty were female; sixty-two of the males did business in the city and seven of the ladies were widows of Dublin businessmen. He claimed that a like number of the residents of the other townships were similarly circumstanced.[56]

All of these suburban-dwellers enjoyed the facilities of the city, the law courts, educational establishments, markets, abattoirs, hospitals, poor houses, of which there were none in the townships, and they contributed nothing to their upkeep. As well as all these, the corporation kept a fire brigade which was often used by the townships. As an instance of the liability of the corporation for the upkeep of hospitals, he cited the annual grant of £5,825 made by the corporation to them. The Richmond Lunatic Asylum, which received patients from the townships, was maintained by the corporation at a total cost of £53,000.[57] Sir Charles Cameron, the Dublin city medical officer of health, pointed out that the amounts subscribed to the hospitals by Rathmines amounted to only £375, which came to 1¾d. per head of population compared to over 5d. contributed by those living in the city.[58]

The corporation admitted that it wished to gain ground in the county area to build on and also to prevent new townships from growing around the city boundary 'like ivy round a tree.' The new corporation would consist of 88 members of whom 28 would be elected by the townships; the corporation representatives pointed out that 17 of the city members of the corporation already lived in the suburbs, so adding these to the 28 would give the townships a representation of 45 out of 88.

The joint committee of the two houses recommended the absorption by the city of Clontarf, Drumcondra and Kilmainham and a section of County Dublin including rural parts which would give a margin for building land. These were mainly situated in the Grangegorman, Cabra, Chapelizod, Dolphin's Barn and Crumlin areas. The recommendations were acted on and in 1900 the townships of Clontarf, Drumcondra and Kilmainham were amalgamated with the city (see fig. 17) under an act of parliament.[59] The added area was 4,125 acres, the population 26,000 and the valuation nearly £100,000.[60] According to Joseph V. O'Brien, the financial obligations of the corporation in the new district in relation to sewerage and water supply were deemed to be more than the value received in rates.[61]

As regards Rathmines and Pembroke, the committee felt that they should be obliged to contribute to the city coffers, and an arrangement similar to the London equalisation of rates act of 1894 was recommended. Under such an arrangement the two townships would make a financial contribution to the city for matters which were regarded as a joint financial responsibility. This also was acted on and resulted in the Dublin, Rathmines and Rathgar and Pembroke (equalisation of rates) act, 1901 which regarded as one area the city of Dublin,

Figure 17: Local government units in County Dublin, 1900

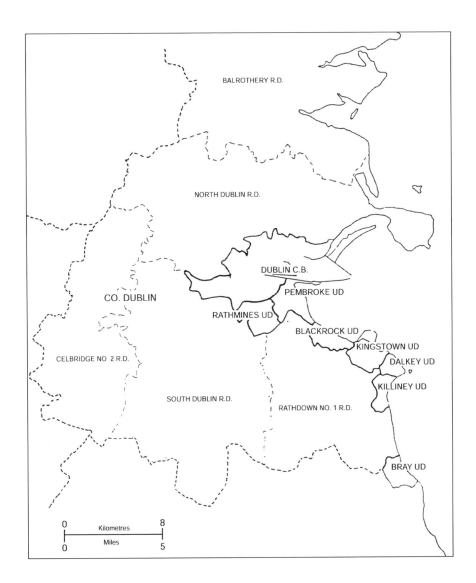

Source: Arnold Horner, 'The Dublin region, 1880–1982 an overview on its development and planning' in Michael J. Bannon (ed.), *The emergence of Irish planning 1880–1920* (Dublin, 1995), p. 45.

the Rathmines and Rathgar township and Pembroke township in respect of expenses incurred for the following purposes, sanitary matters under the public health acts (excluding main drainage and water works), public lighting, streets (including maintenance and cleansing), markets, reformatory and industrial schools, and lunatic asylums.

To ascertain the amount to be paid by each authority, the act provided for an inquiry to be held in 1902 and each succeeding tenth year to ascertain the average annual expenditure for the five immediately preceding years for the purpose of defraying the costs incurred under each heading above. The result of the first inquiry was that no equalization payment was to be made under the public health acts but that the townships would have to contribute substantially under the other heads (see fig. 18).

Figure 18: Liability of Rathmines & Pembroke townships under equalisation of rates inquiry, 1902

	Rathmines	Pembroke
Public lighting	£225	£10
Streets	£1,200	£50
Markets	£150	£100
Reformatory & industrial schools	£1,225	£860
Lunatic asylums	£1,740	£1,220

Source: Equalisation of rates inquiry 1911, D.C.A.

While the equalization of rates legislation deflated somewhat the demands for the absorption of Rathmines and Pembroke, the spectre continued to be occasionally raised. In 1917, the Dublin Citizens' Association invited the Rathmines and Pembroke councillors to a conference to discuss amalgamation with the city. The association had been set up some ten years previously by prominent ratepayers, mainly big businessmen and shopowners, to campaign against any increase in the rates. It had since extended its aims to include modest municipal reform.[62] The fact that the invitation was referred to the finance committee for discussion by a majority of one on the Rathmines council and not immediately rejected raised the ire of the strongly anti-amalgamation Rathmines and Rathgar Ratepayers' Association. It communicated to the council its 'strongest protest against the re-opening of the question of amalgamation with the Dublin corporation, this question having already cost the township many thousands of pounds'.[63]

Despite the constant threat to its independence, the Rathmines council still sought to extend its own jurisdiction. In 1902 the chairman proposed the annexation of the following areas which were contiguous to Rathmines: Terenure and Kimmage in the parish of Rathfarnham, and Tonguefield and Larkfield in the parish of Crumlin. However, it was not until 1905 that a bill was brought before parliament.[64] Steady growth had taken place in the Terenure district over many years. As early as 1879 an attempt had been made to constitute a township covering a wide area including Terenure and Rathfarnham. A bill to this effect was published in the *Dublin Gazette*.[65] When the proposed legislation failed to become law, the un-named promoters were, it was claimed in the press, liable to enormous costs. More recently, a prominent member of a local Terenure group now wishing to have the area annexed to Rathmines had attempted once again to have the area obtain urban district status, but once again the move was unsuccessful. Thomas Mayne, a former MP and ex-member of Dublin corporation, had employed a solicitor to prepare a case, but could not proceed as he was unable to obtain a guarantee as to costs.[66]

Terenure was in the control of the South Dublin Rural District Council, and Rathmines was very dissatisfied with the way in which the area was managed. Building had taken place to such an extent that the area was in a very insanitary condition owing to a lack of a proper sewerage system. Cottages bordering on Rathmines were regarded as a menace to the health of the township and were found to be so in a report to the district council. Overflow drainage increased to such an extent that Rathmines was obliged in self-defence to obtain an injunction against the rural district to prevent this. The injunction was not enforced for fear of making the public health situation much worse.[67]

Extra sewage from Terenure being discharged into Dublin bay through the Rathmines outfall sewer system led to objections by the Dublin port and docks board. This board had been established in 1869 as the authority for Dublin port, which included the lower Liffey Quays and Dublin Bay extending as far as Sutton on the north side and Dalkey on the south, but excluding Kingstown harbour.[68] The board believed that the annual contribution made by Rathmines towards dredging did not cover the increased work necessary. The matter came to a head when the port and docks board informed Rathmines that it would accept the increased discharge only for a further year. When Rathmines threatened the rural district with enforcing its injunction against accepting any more sewage from the Terenure area, a number of inhabitants from the district then approached the council, and after some discussion, agreed to be annexed, paying the same rates as other districts in the township.[69]

Dublin corporation, Dublin county council and the South Dublin Rural District Council all opposed the Terenure extension bill. The corporation wished in particular to protect its contract for the supply of water to the district. The county council saw Rathmines as wishing to gain an area of increasing valuation to the detriment of the county and with no compensation offered. Rathmines was aware of this aspect of the move and presented the proposal to its ratepayers as such. The port and docks board looked upon it as a way in which Rathmines could get around its veto on increased discharge by making the district part of the township. The only support for Rathmines came from Pembroke, as, of course, the problem was one for their joint drainage board. Pembroke saw the Rathmines action as obviating the need for the joint drainage board to enforce its injunction and regarded the move as 'necessary and right' and approved of it accordingly.[70]

The rural district council, in a circular sent to householders in the Terenure district, explained its objections to the proposed annexation. First and foremost, it appealed to the pockets of the ratepayers. It pointed out that, as a result of amendments inserted in the bill as it was passed by the house of commons, the Rathmines and Pembroke main drainage board would have to carry out works to purify the sewage before it entered the Liffey, This would cost anything from £112,000 to £200,000, which would have to be borne by the ratepayers of Rathmines and Pembroke, including the new district of Terenure.

As matters stood the rate in the Terenure district was 6s. 3½d., while that of the Rathmines township was 8s. and 9d. When the extra expense of rectifying the drainage was taken into account, it was clear that the residents of the new area would face a substantial new rates' bill. The rural district defended its record in attempting to supply a proper drainage system for the area. While its attempts to come to an agreement with Rathmines were frustrated by the Dublin port and docks board, it had also little success with Dublin corporation. The corporation was unable to take its drainage because of lack of a main drainage system. However, such a system would be complete within a year and the corporation came to an agreement with the rural district to have the sewerage of the Terenure area connected to it at a moderate levy on the rates of the area to be sewered. A further three pence would be levied on the whole of the rural district, including Terenure. This, it was claimed, would cover the entire cost of the scheme. Rathmines then dropped its extension plan.

CHAPTER SIX

Cultivating the civic arts:
expanded services

As the state more and more utilized local authorities to implement services, especially in the areas of health, education and leisure amenities, the townships increasingly accumulated new functions. As basic infrastructural needs such as a water supply and drainage were satisfied local authorities began to find the scope of their activities broadened, especially into cultural, educational and recreational spheres. However, we will begin by examining the role of the townships in the vital area of transport.

While neither Dublin city nor the townships ever initiated their own transport networks or took over existing systems as did Belfast its tramway in 1905, in their capacity as the roads' authorities in their respective districts, they had a vital influence on the development of transport. It is, perhaps, no coincidence that in the same year, 1834, which saw the opening of the Dublin and Kingstown Railway, the Kingstown township was founded. When the railway was later extended to Bray and beyond, it brought the further coastal area, Dalkey and Killiney, within commuting distance of Dublin. The high hopes of developers and investors for rapid suburbanization contributed to the establishment of local authorities there. The expected growth did not materialize, and development was sluggish and patchy. Rathmines and Pembroke were within walking distance of the city and reached in an even shorter time by those who could afford private carriages. The arrival of omnibuses in 1840 facilitated residence in the further reaches of these suburbs. However, with the coming of the trams in 1872, the suburbs came within the reach of large sections of the community.

Townships exercised control over those using their roads by laying down regulations regarding traffic and negotiating with car-owners and omnibus companies in order to keep down fares. Early in its existence, Rathmines concerned itself with the matter of transport between the city and the township and considered setting up its own onmibus system. In 1848 the chairman laid before the board a project for a system of omnibuses to ply between the city and the township. The board agreed 'individually and collectively' to support the undertaking for the benefit of the district and the comfort of themselves and their families and set up a sub-committee to deal with the matter.[1] It is not clear who

145

the instigator of the project was, or whether the chairman had a personal involvement in it, or what role the board would play in its development.

Nothing further was heard of this scheme but the public seemed to be unsure as to the nature of the involvement of the board in providing transport. The confusion stemmed from the fact that the board was renting out stabling in its own yard to a Mark Byrne for omnibus horses. The board had to point out to one complainant that its own officers had no connection with the omnibus service in the township. The omnibus service developed to such an extent that the Rathmines Conveyance Company proposed building stables in a key position at the corner of Rathmines Road and Castlewood Avenue. A memorial against this was addressed to the board, which replied that it did not uphold the objections and that interference was not in its provenance.

It has been shown that railways had a very limited impact on the development of suburbs.[2] During the period of railway mania in Ireland in the 1850s and after, numerous schemes for railways to cross the Rathmines township were placed before the board, with sometimes up to three projects lying on the boardroom table awaiting a decision. Many schemes were regarded by the board as being 'objectionable' or 'injurious' and some of the projects were regarded as not being genuine. In order to forestall this, guarantees were sought that projects would proceed as soon as possible after parliamentary approval had been granted.

Of all the proposals for railway schemes in the greater Dublin area only three lines were built which passed through the townships: the Dublin and Kingstown railway, which later became the Dublin and Wexford Railway; the inland line of the Dublin and Wexford from Harcourt Street to Bray, which went through part of the Rathmines township; and, on the north side of the city, the Dublin and Drogheda, which later became part of the Great Northern system which went through the Clontarf township. Mary E. Daly, citing British research on the very limited impact of railways on suburban expansion, shows that, although the Dublin and Kingstown Railway made efforts to keep fares low to attract commuters, when it was taken over by the Dublin, Wicklow and Wexford Railway, the policy was to serve the bigger towns rather than Dublin commuters. Frequent appeals were made by the coastal townships, especially Kingstown, for fares to be kept low. A glance at the history of the suburban railway stations indicates the sporadic nature of demand for a commuter service on these lines (fig. 19).

This shows that demand was not enough to sustain a station in much of Blackrock and Kingstown, but that Dalkey and Killiney had stations servicing commuters continuously. The evident neglect by the railway company of its suburban customers in preference to its favoured towns led Kingstown to seek lower fares. It succeeded in obtaining a reduction in 1865, which led Blackrock to send a deputation to the company to plead that the reductions be extended to the intermediate stations.[3] The Harcourt Street to Bray line through the Rathmines township had no impact on the growth of the district as no train

stopped there until the Rathmines and Ranelagh station was opened at Dunville
Avenue in 1896. A station existed at Clontarf on the Dublin to Drogheda line
from 1844, but closed in 1850 for weekday traffic. It was re-opened in 1898
shortly before the demise of the township.

**Figure 19: Suburban stations in townships on Dublin-Bray line
(line opened in 1834 to Kingstown and in 1854 to Bray)**

Station	Date open
Lansdowne Road	1870 on
Serpentine Avenue	2 months in 1835
Sandymount	1835–41; 1860–2; 1882–1901; 1928–60
Sydney Parade	1835–41; 1862–60
Merrion	1835–62; 1882–1901; 1928–9
Booterstown	1835–1960
Williamstown	1835–41
Blackrock	1834 on
Seapoint	1837–1960
Salthill & Monkstown	1837–1960
Kingstown (Dunleary)	1837–1960
Sandycove	1855 on
Glenageary	1867 on
Dalkey	1844 on
Killiney	1858 on
Ballybrack	1854–82

Source: Stephen Johnson, *Johnson's atlas and gazateer of the railways of Ireland*
(Leicester, 1977), p. 84

It has been argued that suburban growth did not need to wait on the provision of public transport to outlying areas.[4] The English experience is that seg-
regated suburbs developed before the arrival of cheap public transport.
Liverpool, Manchester, Birmingham, Leeds, Sheffield and London all had residential suburbs before the arrival of mass transit. There is no doubt but that the
arrival of the omnibus and the horse tram stimulated further colonization of the
outskirts of cities, particularly by the middle class who could not afford the private carriages of the villa-owners and inhabitants of the wealthier squares who
preceded them on the city's fringe. Rathmines, Pembroke and Drumcondra
could be regarded to a certain extent as 'walking suburbs' as they were within a
half hour walk of the city centre, and early photographs show large numbers of
pedestrians approaching the canal bridges, city bound, on the major thoroughfares. Until the electrification of the tramway system, transport, whether by train

to Blackrock, Kingstown, Dalkey and Killiney or horse tram to the other suburbs, was not cheap and was largely used by the middle classes. One effect the
arrival of a regular public transport system did have was that it was no longer
necessary for all homes to have carriage-houses attached to them; this made possible a greater density of housing.

As early as 1857 the promoters of the Dublin 'iron road or tramway' were
meeting the Rathmines board to discuss a link with the township. The well-
known American tramway promoter, G.T. Train, also made a proposal for a
tramway from the city through the township, the termini being St. Stephen's
Green and Roundtown (Terenure). The board was willing to negotiate with
these promoters and agree to the undertaking if it felt the terms were beneficial,
but was hostile to any attempt to rush a project through. As with railway proposals, the board was anxious to ensure that the tram schemes were serious. In
the case of one scheme a sum of £500 deposit was sought by the board, that
would be forfeit if the act were passed and the line not built 'forthwith'.[5]

The main purpose of the building of early tram lines was either to link the
main railway stations in the city or to provide a service to the rapidly expanding
suburbs. The importance of Rathmines was acknowledged when Dublin's first
tram line was laid down to connect the township to the city. Built by the Dublin
Tramways' Company, the service was inaugurated on 1 February 1872 and ran
from Garville Avenue, Rathgar to College Green. Success was immediate and
plans were laid for the opening of many other lines by the DTC and other companies. In October of the same year Pembroke was linked by a line running
from Nelson's Pillar to the tower at Sandymount. The following year Pembroke
was further penetrated by a line to Donnybrook. In 1874 Clontarf, then only
four years constituted as a township, was linked by a line to Dollymount.[6]

Figure 20: Dublin Tramways Company: passenger returns for 1878 (all routes to city centre)

Tenenure route	1,540,782
Sandymount route	1,175,896
Donnybrook route	780,077
Clontarf	790,514

Source: R.C. municipal boundaries, H.C. 1880, (2725), xxx, evidence of John Beverage,
para. 55

By this time it was felt that the wealthier citizens to the south of the city
were well catered for, while, apart from the Clontarf area, the north side had
been neglected by the DTC. For that reason, a director of that company
resigned from the board and set up the North Dublin Street Tramways'

Company to take advantage of the new opportunities opening up in the Drumcondra and Glasnevin areas. In 1875 the company laid down three lines to service these areas and also built a line to Kilmainham. The founders of the Drumcondra township admitted that the opening of the tramway gave a huge boost to the the area. Passenger returns for 1878 show how popular tram travel between the city and the townships was (fig. 20).

Electrification of tramways became a technological possibility in Dublin in the 1880s and when the three existing companies amalgamated in 1881 as the Dublin United Tramways' Company conditions of scale became favourable, and various schemes were submitted to the township boards for their consideration. Dublin corporation showed a distinct reluctance to allow electrification of the system in the city, while in contrast, the townships had a more progressive policy and co-operated readily with the tramway companies seeking to use the new source of power. In 1886 the tramway company was given permission by the Rathmines board for the experimental use of electricity in one of its cars for six months,[7] and the Kingstown surveyor was strongly in favour of a Dublin Southern Districts Tramway Company bill to introduce electricity on its system.[8] As an inducement, the tramway company offered Kingstown the use of the poles for electric lighting provided that the installation did not interfere with the running of the trams.[9] The first section of the Dublin United Tramway Company's system to be fully electrified was the line through the Clontarf township from the company's depot there to the city boundary at Annesley Bridge in November 1897.[10]

The provision of electricity opened up new opportunities for local authorities to engage in 'municipal trading' and Rathmines informed a deputation from its ratepayers' association that the council was considering purchasing the existing tram system in conjunction with the building of an electrical plant.[11] In 1896 a bill to this effect, the Rathmines and Rathgar township tramways and improvement bill, was drafted in the teeth of fierce opposition from the tramway company. Before the bill could be taken to parliament, a statutory meeting had to be called. The board gave special permission for this to be held in the supper room of the still-unfinished new town hall. At a heated meeting, which was packed with supporters of the newly amalgamated Dublin United Tramways' Company, a division was called and, by a majority of 108 to 61, the bill was rejected.[12] A poll of all ratepayers was then called for and it was decided to carry this out. William Anderson, the secretary of the tramway company and a ratepayer, took an injunction against the poll going ahead, but it was dismissed by the Master of the Rolls.[13]

The outcome of all this was an 1897 act to empower the Rathmines commissioners to purchase and work certain tramways of the Dublin United Tramways' Company.[14] These powers were never exercised but they gave the commissioners extra leverage in dealing with the tramway company. Agreement was reached after lengthy negotiations for the electrification by the tramway company of the system in the township.

The commissioners were very interested in promoting a tram line linking Rathmines, the Pembroke township and the coastal townships. Under the slogan 'Rathmines to the sea', a line was proposed from Palmerston Road to Sandymount. This would be one of the first cross lines in Dublin. Lines built previously had radiated from the city centre hub; the new line would cross a number of these spokes and avoid the city centre altogether. Both the Rathmines board and the DUTC drew up plans for the establishment of such a line. However, Pembroke did not look favourably on the idea of another township having rights over its roads. When an application from Rathmines to build the line was put before the Pembroke board it met with a hostile reception.[15] A joint meeting between the two boards was held on the issue and Pembroke reiterated its objection to ceding even limited powers on its roads to another township, and also to the proposed route.[16] Agreement was finally reached with both Rathmines and the DUTC, the latter consenting to pay Pembroke £200 per annum wayleave for every mile of electrically worked tramline in the township, and a line was built linking 'Rathmines to the sea'.[17]

While transport affected the daily lives, especially the working lives, of suburban dwellers, the question of housing went to the very heart of their well-being. The squares and terraces of large houses built by the middle-classes in the suburbs and the city tenements were, in a way, two sides of the one coin; the old houses deserted by the new suburbanites provided cramped accommodation for many poor families. However, the situation was not one of total contrast. Firstly, the townships were not established entirely on green-field sites; many areas had long-established settlements with comparatively sizable working-class populations, in particular the Ringsend and Irishtown areas of Pembroke, the Blackrock village and Williamstown village areas of Blackrock and the harbour area of Kingstown. Added to this was the population of labourers and craftsmen needed in the house-building industry, which was nearly always active in some part of the suburbs. This was partly a floating population, many of its members living in the city slums, but part of which undoubtedly began to reside in the back lanes of the suburbs close to the source of employment.

The political situation in the respective townships largely determined their response to the housing situation. A keen contest was taking place in the suburbs between unionists on the one hand, and supporters of the Irish parliamentary party, one of whose main planks at this time was urban housing. By an appeal to voters on the housing issue the nationalists began to court a lower middle-class and working class electorate. Pembroke, which was in the hands of a nationalist majority, was quite active in housebuilding, as were the coastal townships: a detailed list available for Blackrock, Kingstown, Dalkey and Killiney shows the pattern of this activity (fig. 21). Murray Fraser has estimated that, by 1914, the Dublin townships had housed over 6.5% of their populations in municipal dwellings, over three times the average in Ireland.[18]

The affluent appearance of the suburbs could deceive, as was pointed out by John Byrne Power, the energetic medical officer of health of Kingstown:

> On proceeding to examine the township with some care, the first thing which struck me was the number and wretchedness of what I may call the slums – miserable courts and rows of wretched hovels, in which a healthy or decent life is well-nigh impossible. These are, for the most part, hidden from view by dwellings of a more respectable character, being, in many cases, erected in what were formerly the yards or gardens belonging to the houses which conceal them, so that all seems prosperous enough to the casual observer. The number of such hovels and of their inhabitants indicates a proletariat out of all proportion to the possibility of employment in such a town.[19]

The record of the Dublin townships in the provision of houses for artisans and labourers is one of solid achievement. Their building programme far out-stripped other municipal authorities in Ireland in both the number and, espe-cially in the case of Pembroke, the quality of houses built. For long Dublin was notorious for its slums. The first intervention in the housing of the working class, or artisans, was by large employers, such as transport companies, from the 1850s.[20] In 1854 the Quaker textile firm of Pim built cottages for its employees at Harold's Cross in the Rathmines township.[21] The 1875 Artisans' dwellings act provided for slum clearance and building of dwellings in areas that were deemed to be unhealthy.[22] In 1876 the Dublin Artisans' Dwelling Company was formed by major business interests in the city. The earl of Pembroke subscribed £1,000 and the two Guinness brothers £5,000 each. By 1914 it had built a total of 3,081 houses.[23] The company built many of their cottages on open sites in the sub-urbs, including a site at Greenmount also in Harold's Cross. The choice of Harold's Cross may have been facilitated by Frederic Stokes, the Rathmines chairman, who was one of the founder members of the company. In all, the company built 318 cottages in the Rathmines township and also erected a scheme in Kingstown.[24] Dublin corporation's first venture into the provision of houses was the clearing of a four acre site on the Coombe in 1877 and leasing it to the Dublin Artisans' Dwelling Company.

The Victorians had a strong desire to reinforce middle-class values by social segregation and the creation of single-class, homogenous districts. From the inception of the Rathmines township, its board held the opinion that the pres-ence of inferior housing in the area would be a liability to it; indeed the presence of low value houses at Milltown had been a factor for not originally including it in the township. Developing Rathmines would, of course, need labourers, but the board did not appear to be prepared to have them living within its boundaries. This was an argument used by the corporation against Rathmines, claiming that

Figure 21: Houses built by coastal townships, 1880–1924

Blackrock			*Kingstown*		
1880	St Anne's Square	45	1904	Mills Street	16
1880	Temple Square	10	1904	Tivoli Tce. East	21
1908	Emmet Square	42	1904	Barrett Street	36
1908	George's Place	22	1904	Cumberland Street	20
1909	Rock Road	10	1904	Cross Avenue	12
1914	Brookfield Terrace	34	1904	Desmond Avenue	54
1914	Brookfield Place	69	1904	Dominick Street	56
			1904	Wolfe Tone Avenue	36
Dalkey			1904	Convent Road	9
1910	St Patrick's Square	24	1910	Convent Road	16
1910	St Patrick's Avenue	12	1912	Northcote Terrace	6
1910	St Patrick's Road	12	1912	Mary Street	26
1910	Beacon Hill	5	1912	Library Road	14
1919	Corrig Road	8	1924	Bentley Villas	10
1919	Carysfort Road	14	1924	Kelly Villas	5
1922	Carysford Road	10			
1922	Church Road	12	*Killiney*		
1923	Corrig Road	16	1900	Hill Cottages	10
			1913	Glenalua Terrace	10
			1913	Talbot Road	5

Source: Housing list, Dún Laoghaire/Rathdown archives

it was evading paying its fair share for housing the poor and that the whole burden was being shouldered by the city. While it is likely that some poor quality houses were swept away to make way for the squares and terraces, squalid abodes of the poor grew up unofficially in the back-lanes, alleys and courts of the township. Concerns were raised from time to time at the board about the need to restrict stables being turned into dwellings, but the general concensus seems to have been 'out of sight, out of mind'.

John Evans, the Rathmines township secretary, outlined to the Exham commission the situation as regards the dwellings of the poor in the township some twenty years before the council began any programme of building artisans' dwellings. The township contained some three hundred working-class dwellings; however, minimizing the extent of sub-standard housing in the area, he stated that 282 of these houses were for 'better class artisans' and were valued at close to £10 each.[25]

Blackrock, the first in the field, began to build artisans' dwellings with two early schemes, one in 1880 and one towards the end of that decade. A housing act 1885 (An act to amend the law relating to dwellings of the working classes 1885 48 & 49 Vict. c. 72) provided loans to local authorities, including the townships, to be repaid over sixty years at a rate of only 3.5%. This gave an incentive to the boards and the 1890s was a period of great house-building activity. This new sense of urgency was particularly strong in nationalist-controlled Pembroke. Its first scheme consisted of forty artisans' dwellings built in Ringsend in 1894. In 1912 eighty-eight houses were erected in Donnybrook, adjacent to Herbert Park. Seventy-seven of these, at Home Villas, were superbly designed. They were of two storeys and had baths, an unusual feature of artisans' dwellings at the time. The remainder, St Broc's Cottages, were one-storey. Pembroke later completed schemes in Clonskeagh, Donnybrook, Ballsbridge and Irishtown. Complementing the housing activity of the council in Pembroke was the erection of artisans' dwellings by the Pembroke estate. No such landlord interest was present to provide houses in Rathmines.

Pembroke proceeded with its building programme all through the first world war. Fear of large-scale unemployment, due to war-time retrenchment in the district, was in part the spur. However, increased costs during the war made the finishing of schemes planned before the outbreak very expensive, and in 1919 the council found that it had a shortfall of £20,000 in its housing account. To add to its problems, Pembroke had a rent strike in some of its smaller houses in 1920, organised by a tenants' association.[26]

Prior to 1908 the townships had built a comparatively large number of houses. Rathmines had a total of 355 dwellings built, Pembroke 269 and Kingstown 300, which as Fraser points out was up to a fifth of all houses built by local authorities at this time.[27] The housing act of 1908, promoted by the Irish parliamentary party and called after its original drafter, J.J. Clancy, an ex-Dublin corporation councillor, provided for a subsidy for municipal housing. The Dublin townships, especially Pembroke, availed extensively of its provisions, and built on an ambitious scale.

Kingstown, like Pembroke, was burdened with a large ill-housed working-class population. The survival of the reports of its medical superintendent officer of health and information on the leasing policy of Lords Longford and de Vesci make it possible to examine the housing situation in the township in some detail. Lords Longford and De Vesci had come into possession of their estate in 1797. They owned the land on which the town of Kingstown was built and the surrounding rural area. They claimed that up to the middle of the nineteenth century the estate had spent £50,000 on improvements in the rural area, including the building of a number of artisans' dwellings in the Sallynoggin area which were erected after 1900.[28]

The estate made much of its benefices to the township, including the granting free of rent or at a nominal sum sites for churches, schools, including the technical school, and the Carnegie library. It had also contributed £200 towards the setting up of the technical school and offered to pay for the purchase of the site for a park from the Board of Works but the offer was refused.[29]

The town of Kingstown had been leased out for ninety-nine years in 1804 in long strips running from Tivoli Road to George's Street and from George's Street to the sea road. The leaseholds in the eastern end were well developed and streets such as Clarinda Park, Corrig Avenue and Northumberland Avenue were built, but the western end did not fare so well. Mulgrave Steet, Patrick Street, Paradise Row and York Street contained poor classes of houses, and when the harbour was being built cabins were erected in their gardens which developed into slums.[30]

As a result the medical officer of health was eager to point out the disadvantages the township laboured under compared to some of its wealthier counterparts. Reporting the death rate for 1886 as 22.5 per 1,000 in Kingstown, 30.1 in Dublin and 20.5 in Rathmines, he went on to state:

> This death rate seems, no doubt, high for a town enjoying so many natural advantages as Kingstown. The physical conditions of life in Kingstown are certainly not such as would account for this comparatively high death-rate, and I fear that the principal cause is to be found in the privations the poor are subject to from want of means of subsistence. From careful investigations which I have made, I believe that the proportion of poor in the entire population of Kingstown township amounts to one third, while in the wealthier township of Rathmines the proportion amounts to only one seventh. The influence of poverty upon our population is shown by our comparatively high death rate and remarkably low birth rate.[31]

As much as to bad diet and inadequate health care, he attributed this regrettable situation to poor housing. Being also port medical officer, he expressed concern about the susceptibility of Kingstown to the importation of disease, having one of the busiest harbours in the country. In 1901 the danger of bubonic plague spreading from Glasgow was a particular concern. However, the type of housing which the poor inhabited in the area, one-roomed cabins, was not seen as the same hot-beds of disease that the city tenements were. The housing situation was a particular embarrassment to an area that wished to promote itself as one of the best health resorts in the United Kingdom.[32]

By 1903 Kingstown felt obliged to build artisans' dwellings costing £58,000, quite a burden to the ratepayers.[33] The Kingstown council showed concern for those who might be displaced by the removal of insanitary dwellings and have nowhere to live before replacements were built. A projected scheme of artisans' dwellings would have displaced 139 persons from miserable dwellings with nowhere to go; however the plans were changed so that only eight families –

thirty-two people in all – would be dispersed, and the others would have houses built and ready to be occupied before they were asked to leave their old
dwellings.[34]

Kingstown was openly critical of the housing policy of landlords in its area.
In contrast to the Pembroke estate, the admittedly more modest estate owners
in the district were, it was claimed, more akin to slum landlords. Kingstown
public health committee reported the situation to the board:

> As you are aware the heaviest and most tedious portion of the labours of
> the public health committee is the supervision of the inspection of the
> dwellings of the poorer classes, and the directions of the efforts made in
> various ways to compel Lords Longford and De Vesci and Lord
> Carysfort to keep their cottages and cabin property in a sanitary condi-
> tion. Our efforts have never been received in that spirit we should expect.
> It takes legal proceedings in the majority of cases to effect passing reme-
> dies, and when our medical officers of health certify that certain premis-
> es are unfit for human habitation, or when our sub-sanitary officers get
> orders in the magistrates court to compel the owners to effect certain
> necessary and urgent improvements under the public health acts, the
> owners evict the unfortunate occupiers and dismantle the premises.

According to the report the displaced occupiers were then forced into small
insanitary tenements. The report went on to cite the eviction of a mother and five
children from Paradise Row. Out of common Christian charity she was housed
by a neighbour, who also had five children. The two families – twelve people in
all – were now occupying a small house, the room occupied by the dispossesed
family measuring 14 feet by 7 feet and seven high, allowing the air space for six
human beings that the local government board recommended for a cow.[35]

The Rathmines board set about purchasing land with the intention both of
building a large town hall for themselves and also providing artisans' dwellings
for the workers of the area. In 1887 the board applied for a number of loans
amounting to £40,000 under the 1885 housing act. These were to defray the cost
of the purchase of lands at an area known as 'The Chains' and at Streamville,
both at Upper Rathmines Road.[36] There was some opposition to the proposal
that these sites be used to house the poor, and local inhabitants met the commissioners to make their feelings known. The commissioners then decided to
consult with Lord Meath about the suitability of using land at Gulistan, which
they were renting from him, for cottages.[37] They considered selling their interest
in it to the Artisans' Dwelling Company for the erection of houses, and applying
for a grant from the recently-formed Guinness Trust (later the Iveagh Trust) for
the building of such houses.[38] The trust was responsible for the slum clearance
of the Bull Alley area of the city, but was unlikely to give grants to other bodies.

Plate 7: Flats at Mountpleasant shortly before demolition

The matter dragged on for so long however that the local government board urged the commissioners to take the matter more seriously and put the housing acts into force.

As in the case of Kingstown, the Rathmines experience of large landowners and housing was not a happy one. Lord Meath, who had objected to the building of cholera sheds by the Rathmines board on the land at Gulistan, of which he was the ground landlord, now objected to the building of artisans' houses there. On taking legal advice, the commissioners believed that they had a right to carry on such an undertaking, the only worry being the shortness of the lease, which was for only thirty-eight years at £40 per year.[39] A more satisfactory arrangement was arrived at some years later when the commissioners threatened to obtain powers of compulsory purchase, and as a consequence, a lease for 300 years at £100 a year was negotiated with Lord Meath.[40] A contract was drawn up for the erection of twenty-eight houses by a local builder, a Mr Pemberton, for £250. On their completion in 1895 the smaller cottages were rented for 4s. a week and the larger ones for 4s. 6d.[41] In 1898 it was decided to build another thirty cottages, which were to be cheaper than the original twenty-eight. When this scheme was completed, the council then felt it needed to build cheaper accommodation for workmen. The rent of the small houses at Gulistan was beyond the pocket of the ordinary working man, as the council itself admitted. It now began to draw up plans for the building of blocks of flats 'to suit the wants of the working classes'.[42] Block dwellings had been built by Dublin corporation since 1887 and were not very popular with tenants or many social reformers as they were seen to perpetuate ghetto-like conditions rather than eliminate them.[43] Two pieces of land were bought; one on which stood houses known as Plunkett's cottages, off Mount Pleasant Avenue, between Rathmines and Ranelagh, and another known as Hollyfield in Upper Rathmines. While the original idea had been to build cottages on these sites, the council soon accepted plans for blocks of flats. A competition for the new buildings was held and the entry of F.G. Hickson was accepted. Beckett and Metcalfe, later well-known Rathmines councillors, were to be the building surveyors.[44]

The lord lieutenant opened the new buildings at the end of 1903. In its address the council pointed out that 291 dwellings had been completed and were let at the following prices; a dwelling with three rooms and its own sanitary accommodation 4s. 6d. per week, one with two rooms and its own sanitary accomodation 3s. 6d. per week, and one-room dwellings with joint sanitary accommodation 1s. 9d. and 1s. 6d. per week. It was pointed out proudly that as far as possible all classes had been provided for. The lord lieutenant expressed the hope the new accommodation would raise the status of the worker and still further reduce the already low death rate in the district. He pointed out that Rathmines now compared favourably with the most enlightened towns in other parts of the United Kingdom in its provision of housing for the working class.[45]

This rosy picture can be set into context by comments of a resident of Ranelagh speaking of the 'buildings' in both Ranelagh and Upper Rathmines twenty years later. By then the 'barrack system' they represented had become a blight on the good name of the township: 'it should be a lesson to the council not to erect such "shanties" in the future, because they are only a slight elevation above the slum tenements'.[46] However, at the start of 1930, the last year of the council's existence, a loan of £20,000 was obtained for the building of more flats on vacant land at Mount Pleasant and Hollyfield buildings.[47] The record of the Rathmines council in housing up to 1908 can be seen in fig. 22.

Figure 22: Rathmines township: early housing schemes

Date built	Site	No. & type	Valuation
1895/98	Gulistan	63 cottages	£4 5s.–£6
1903	Hollyfield	120 flats	£2–£5.10s.
1903	Mount Pleasant	249 flats	£1 15s.–£5

Source: Rathmines Township minutes 1894–1903

An area of tenements and slum dwellings at Church Place, behind shops and houses at the junction of Rathmines Road and Castlewood Avenue was an embarrassment to the council for many years. A provisional order for slum clearance was acquired from the local government board in 1914, and plans were drawn up for the building of a small scheme of houses; however, the outbreak of war halted any progress. In 1919 when the council returned to the matter the provisional order had to be altered as new housing legislation restricted the number of houses which could be built to the acre.

Buying out the current owners and occupiers at Church Place proved costly. The council began to baulk at the scheme and sought legal advice as to whether it could take control of the area as a 'model slum landlord' (its own term). It was advised that such a move would be neither 'politic or economic', as the area was unfit for human habitation and a very large sum would have to be expended on it to meet current sanitary requirements.[48] Arbitration was carried out to compensate the owners of property on the site and this cost the council almost £5,000. It was at the end of 1921 that Rathmines began to renew its building programme, which had been on hold since the outbreak of the war. The Church Place scheme was completed, and a compulsory purchase order was obtained from the local government board, shortly before the demise of that body, for land in Kimmage for house building purposes.

Announcing what became known as the 'million pound programme' for housing, a 1922 circular from the minister of local government in Saorstát Éireann to the Rathmines council cautioned that it could not enter into any financial arrangements that would involve any future government in financial commitments extending over a long period of time.[49] This communication encapsulated the dilemma facing the new government. The priority given to housing matters by nationalist politicians under the British administration and the expectations raised became increasingly difficult to maintain and deliver on, now that they were in power and faced civil war and a severe post-war economic depression. Consequently the injection of funds for housing was short-lived. The 1922 measure did, however, envisage over 2,000 urban houses being built and once again the Dublin townships in general were quick to avail of its funding, while it lasted.[50]

Rathmines dragged its heels however. The minister of local government expressed his anxiety that 'no delay which can be avoided should occur in the commencement of work on the Kimmage Road site which your council has been authorised to acquire' and enquired what steps had been taken to secure entry on to the land and in what manner the work was to be carried on. In the meantime, the council also made land in its possession on the south side of Kimmage Road available under a new 1925 Saorstát Éireann housing act (1925/12 [I.F.S.]) to members of public utilities societies for the building of seventy-eight houses.[51] The Saorstát Civil Service Public Utility Society and the Irish Sailors' and Soldiers' Trust acquired developed land from the council for building. In the late 1920s the council gave grants of £75 per house to private house-builders and £100 to members of public utility societies.[52] Building was eventually begun in Kimmage (see fig. 23) and the Church Avenue scheme of slum clearance and house-building was also completed before the abolition of the council in 1930.

Figure 23: Houses built by Rathmines Urban District Council at Kimmage

Site	No.	Valuation
Kimmage Road	20	£9 & £10
Larkfield Avenue	51	£8 10s.
The Square	29	£8 10s.
Priory Road	24	£7 10s. & £8 10s.

Source: Dublin City Archives

In the late 1920s two unusual arrangements were entered into by the Pembroke council. In 1927 it negotiated the acquisition of Beggars' Bush barracks for housing as the army were about to quit 'in view of the very large number of slum houses urgently required to be closed', that is detenanted, as they were unfit for habitation.[53] The council was in the process of taking possession of the barracks, including a football pitch, which was to be used by the youth of the area when the district was amalgamated with the city. An interesting attempt was made to preserve denominational communities in the district when Pembroke expressed a willingness to agree to let the Dublin Methodist Housing Committee nominate the tenants for a certain number of houses in return for the committee purchasing Pembroke debenture stock to the amount of the cost of ten houses of the four- to five-room type being built by the council.[54]

By this time those inhabiting artisans' dwellings were not necessarily totally dependent on such housing, and Pembroke resolved to proceed against those tenants who were living in accommodation elsewhere and letting out their council cottages to others, the cottages being 'required for those for whom they were originally intended'.[55] Adapting to changed circumstances the council drew up a scheme allowing tenants to purchase their houses over a twenty five-year period, seemingly the only council to enter into such arrangements at this time.[56]

Another major achievement of the townships was the building of impressive town halls. The building of town halls served the dual purpose of providing a township administrative centre and a venue for large meetings and concerts. They were also impressive manifestations of civic pride and symbols of the independence of the local boards.

In the 1840s, the Rathmines commissioners obtained a house in a central position on Rathmines Road from which to administer their affairs. In 1867 a modest

Plate 8: The original Rathmines Town Hall

Source: Watercolour in album presented to Frederick Stokes, 1878, NLI, MS. 7994.

town hall was erected attached to this house. The commissioners stated that it would fill a long-felt want for a meeting place in the area, and it was hoped that a registry court and polling station would be based there. The commissioners with their usual anxiety not to exceed their fixed rate, contented themselves with a room of moderate size, and of the plainest description. The designs were prepared by Henry Johnston, the township surveyor, and the building was described as comprising 'a room 52 by 22 ft. and 18 ft. high, a gallery 25 by 10 ft. There is a platform 10 ft. wide at the upper end, and the whole is well lighted and conveniently arranged'.[57] There was also a committee room and a chairman's room. The building work was carried out by John Brady of Camden Street. The *Irish*

Plate 9: Rathmines Town Hall, opened 1898

Source: Photograph (1997) courtesy of Rathmines Senior College

Builder outlined the commissioners' hope for the new facility: 'it is intended, we understand, to permit the use of the room for any purpose of an unobjectionable character, of interest to the neighbourhood, at a merely nominal charge'.[58]

While Rathmines was content with its modest edifice, perfectly in keeping with its policy of strict economy, Blackrock took the initiative in building a town hall on a grand scale. The need for a hall was felt most acutely in the outlying coastal townships. Rathmines and Pembroke were close to the city, with its relative abundance of venues for large gatherings. Shortly after the passing of the Blackrock township bill in 1863, a proposal that a hall be built was agreed on by the board. Work began soon afterwards and the town hall was opened in 1866.[59]

The Pembroke township built a fine town hall in the Ruskinian gothic style. It was designed by Edward H. Carson and his pupil J.L. Robinson and opened in 1880 with the generous assistance of the Pembroke estate. Robinson also designed the Kingstown town hall in the Italian palazzo style complete with bell tower. These monuments to the wealth and self-confidence of the bodies that built them provided an example for Rathmines when it decided to replace its modest house and added hall.

Having spent much time investigating the suitability of many sites in Rathmines for a new town hall, the board decided to build on the site of the old township house and added hall. This was adjacent to the township works' yard and land that was being leased from the earl of Meath, on which eventually artisans' dwellings and an electricity plant would be built. There was some disagreement on the board as to whether a new town hall should be built at all as long as the township lacked dwellings for the poorer classes. Powers to build a town hall were obtained by act of parliament in 1893.[60] Work began on the new building on 1 January 1895. The building erected was a fine red Dumfries sandstone and brick edifice designed by Sir Thomas Drew. Its most prominent feature was a clock tower standing 128 feet.

Chancellor and Son, clockmakers of Lower Sackville Street, Dublin, wrote to the local newspaper appealing to the Rathmines board to support one of their clocks for installation in the tower against foreign competition. The firm had been fifty years in business and claimed that it could compete with any English or Scottish house. As a local example of its work, it pointed to the newly-erected clock over Findlater's shop in Rathmines, which it believed was an ornament to Rathmines.[61] Chancellor's tender was accepted and a clock with four dials, each ten feet in diameter, was installed at a cost of £130. The clock chimes were also made in Dublin; Matthew Byrne of James's Street supplied them at a cost of £264.

An oriel window was placed projecting four feet above the main entrance of the building supported by a figurehead which acts as a keystone for the entrance porch. The interior included an assembly hall to accommodate 2,000 people with a horseshoe gallery for 500 at one end and a platform and orchestral gallery at the other. There was also a supper room which could be hired for banquets and semi-private events. Under the hall there was a gymnasium and under this again a kitchen and lift. On the first floor overlooking Rathmines Road was a board room where the council meetings would take place (the township had become an urban district council at the time the new town hall was built, see Chapter 6). The principal staircase was built of Portland stone with a massive newel at the bottom. The builder was John Good of Great Brunswick Street. The entire building was to be heated by hot air.[62] The interior fittings, including a magnificent wood carved fireplace in the board room, were by Carlo Cambi of Siena, who was also responsible for the doors and panelling in the National Library and National Museum of Ireland. The total cost of building and furnishing the town hall was estimated near its completion at £18,000; this represented a halfpenny in the pound on the valuation of the township.[63]

The first meeting in the new town hall took place on Wednesday 17 November 1897. It had been decided that there would be no special opening ceremony. Fottrell, who had now been in the chair for twenty years, saw the occasion as a suitable opportunity to retire, the great work now completed.[64] The first public event in the new town hall took place when on the following Wednesday when a recital of Handel's *Messiah* was performed.[65] The Rathmines town hall became a venue for frequent concerts, including those of Percy French, lectures and some of the earliest picture shows in Ireland.

Clontarf built a modest hall fronting the sea wall close to St Lawrence Road. The hall was roofed with pitch pine and could accommodate 600 people. Accommodation at the rere and overhead was provided for a board room and offices. The building was of red brick and the plans and specification were by William G. Perrott, the township surveyor.[66] In Dalkey the medieval building, known as 'Goat's castle' was converted into a town hall by the architect J.S. Fuller in 1872 at a cost of £500.[67]

Electric lighting began in an experimental way in Ireland with the erection of an arc lamp outside the offices of the *Freeman's Journal*, in 1880.[68] An electricity mania followed resulting in some spectacular company collapses. This led the government to introduce legislation to allow local authorities enter the field, a move felt necessary to restrict private companies from exploiting their position as had happened earlier in the supply of gas. By 1882, when a new electricity act was passed (Electric lighting act 1882, 45 & 46 Vict. c. 56), the two interests competing for supplying the service were the corporation and the Alliance Gas Company.[69] The corporation built a power station at Fleet Street and the gas company a much smaller undertaking at Hawkins' Street.

Municipal authorities were being advised to establish their own supplies. An engineer, who had experience in setting up electricity supplies for many English municipal authorities, was retained by Kingstown to direct them on the question. He advised the council to establish its own generating station, claiming that few private companies were in operation outside London. He claimed that those

Plate 10: Blackrock Town Hall

Plate 11: Pembroke Town Hall

Plate 12: Kingstown Town Hall

authorities that had established their own gas supplies, including Belfast, found it advantagous and made a profit from which they were able to erect public buildings and keep down rates. Dublin corporation, he claimed, had made a profit, which, had it been a private company, could pay a dividend of 4.5% at the end of its first year. Never before in the history of local government were so many authorities undertaking works at the same time. He went on to claim that the provision of public lighting stimulated a great demand for lighting in private homes. Despite these claims, the experience of many municipal bodies with supplying their own gas and water, including Rathmines under the latter head, had been far from satisfactory and many bodies now hesitated about electricity.

To avoid monopolies, the government, under the 1882 act, gave private companies control of their undertakings for only twenty-one years, after which time the local authority would have an option of buying them out. This meant that

Plate 13: Pembroke Council Chamber

many who were convinced of the value of electric lighting hesitated to invest, as they feared that they might not have recouped their outlay within that period of time. With both the municipalities and private investors now holding back, electricity was slow to develop for six years. Many authorities that had obtained provisional orders were tardy acting on them and some orders were revoked due to lapse of time. In 1888 an amendment was passed extending the period of initial control by companies to forty-two years; from the date of this amended legislation on, electricity stations began to be established in increasing numbers.[70]

In 1890, Rathmines, having first sounded out the gas company's intentions regarding electricity, set up a committee to look into the question.[71] A number of private companies began to apply for the franchise to light the area, including the Electric Engineering Company of Ireland, the Irish House to House Electric Company, and Porte, Sykes and Company.[72] However, as a result of the deliberations of the new electric light committee, it was decided that the township itself would apply to the board of trade for a provisional order to construct works to 'produce, store, supply and sell electricity' for public and private lighting in the township under the 1882 and 1888 lighting acts.[73] Approval was acquired in 1896 and a loan of £50,000 sought for the scheme; but the matter of raising funds for electric lighting and obtaining tenders dragged on for a number of years and it was 1900 before it was reported that the electrical works for the district were near completion. A resident engineer was employed and a canvessor to afford information to consumers about the advantages of the new source of power; advertisements were also placed in the newspapers.

The Rathmines plant was built on a part of the council's land behind the town hall close to its Gulistan artisans' dwellings. The capital cost of the undertaking was £71,00. It was carried out under the supervision of Mr Pilditch, who was clerk of the works, and Mr Hammond, the first engineer. At the Rathmines plant steam was supplied from three Lancashire boilers, each capable of evaporating 7,000 lb. of steam per hour at a pressure of 160 lb. The electricity supply was three-wire DC capable of energizing 22,500 lamps in consumers' premises. By the aid of a battery, this could be increased to 30,000. Altogether 45 miles of cable were laid. Public lighting consisted of 108 arc lamps in the principal thoroughfares spaced 65 yards apart and 18 feet high. There were a further 230 shorter posts in the quieter streets. For domestic use the charges were 6d. per unit for light and three pence per unit for heat and power. A 'free' wiring scheme was in practice which consisted of a charge of 1d. per unit on the bill. A technical consequence of the still-fragmented local administration in the Dublin area was that while the city adopted an alternative current system of electricity the townships installed a direct current network, an arrangement which would cause problems if the individual systems were to be integrated.[74]

George Henry Cadogan, the lord lieutenant, opened the electricity station in August 1900 and switched on the power in the township.[75] Success was swift

Plate 14: Lamp-post on Palmerstown Road inscribed '1900 Rathmines Urban District Council', the year the township opened its electricity power station

and it was reported as early as October that two-thirds of the area had its public lighting powered by electricity. By the end of 1900, owing to the huge demand, specifications for additional plant at a cost of £7,500 were being prepared. A number of reductions in the cost of electricity were offered to customers and by mid-1901 terms of 4½d. per unit for private dwellings and 3d. for power for heating were being offered.[76] When fully operational, the works had a salaried staff of nine men, including engineers, office staff and collectors. The waged staff, such as fitters, stokers, swichboard attendants etc. numbered fourteen; casual labourers were also employed.[77] By the early 1920s there was a need to supplement the council's output and a loan of £10,000 was sought to obtain a bulk supply from Dublin corporation – up to 200 KW annually for five years at a price not exceeding 2d. per unit.[78] Domestic electricity supply was not spread over the township evenly and in 1917 it had not arrived in Harold's Cross, and houses were still lighted by gas.

Pembroke and Kingstown also built their own power stations. The Pembroke station was at South Lotts, and Rathmines and Pembroke co-operated later when a cable was laid from the Pembroke plant to Gulistan to enable Rathmines avail of surplus Pembroke power.

As the amount of domestic refuse collected by the corporation and townships increased, it became difficult to find landfill sites for its disposal. Disused quarries, a favourite dumping area for refuse, were gradually filled and more and more waste land was needed for building. By the turn of the century, the problem of the disposal of rubbish became acute. By 1895 Kingstown was collecting 8,000 tons of domestic refuse a year, both from bin-rounds, and from ashpits emptied on request. This amounted to 1,035 pounds per head of population, an amount which was regarded as excessive. Dublin partially solved the problem by bringing the refuse to the sea in its barge, the *Eblana*. The remainder was brought to the corporation's depot, where some was sold to farmers as fertiliser and some burnt in furnaces of a primitive type. A major problem arose when the *Eblana* was prevented from going to sea by bad weather or had to wait for a build-up of sufficient refuse on George's Quay, where it was scattered and blown around, causing a nuisance. The problem did not end when this waste was dumped; there was a build-up of material on the sea-bed which caused mud banks to silt-up the channel.

The corporation contracted with Goddard, Massey and Werner of Nottingham for the erection of a refuse destructor in Stanley Street. Refuse destructors were in use in nearly all the larger British cities at this time. They were extra-efficient incinerators in which waste material, including infected clothing and faecal matter, was burnt. As a spin-off from this, the heat generated was sometimes used to make steam to drive machinery, such as hay-cutters for feeding horses. Another by-product was clinker created by the incineration process which had some market value as building material, and was often used by local authorities for making footpaths and concrete slabs and flags.[79]

Kingstown, having the marine facilities at its disposal, also looked at the possibility of dumping refuse in the sea. Its surveyor reported that the best site for a barge to transport waste would be at the disused bathing place at the back of the west pier. Drawbacks were that a large and expensive barge would need to be employed, and as in Dublin bay, there was a real danger of the build-up of mud banks. This, clearly, was a prospect not in the best interests of a major port, and not likely to be looked on favourably by the harbour commissioners. Land dumping or the erection of a destructor were the options recommended.[80]

Rathmines began to look into the effectiveness of refuse destructors in 1902 and sought a loan of £8,000 from the local government board to build one.[81] Pembroke began to erect a destructor shortly afterwards. It was of the type designed by Horsfall of Leeds and was erected at Londonbridge Road.[82] The Rathmines facility, of a similar type, was built adjacent to its electricity plant behind the town hall. The chief benefit of the destructor was that of waste disposal. Steam was sold to the electrical plant for £450 a year and so its coal bill was reduced, but whether it was reduced by that amount is doubtful. The clinker produced as a by-product was used in the council's footpaths and even in some walls of the artisans' dwellings, but was difficult to dispose of to outside customers.[83]

From the 1860s there was a growing interest in cities in opening up parks and green spaces to the public. This was regarded as being of particular benefit to the lower classes. The *Dublin Builder* put it to its readers that it was 'well to consider the peculiar necessity, in this age of progress, for promoting the education of our working classes in refinement and artistic taste, through the medium of public parks, gardens, and pleasure grounds', and went on to wage a campaign for the opening of Dublin's squares to the public.[84]

Indeed Kingstown, as far back as 1834, had the aim of opening up a green space as an amenity inserted in its founding act of parliament. It obtained power to establish Victoria Square as a 'public park'; this was to be an open space surrounded by terraces of houses that were already being built. This would not be what later would become known as a public park – the residents of the square were to pay a rate for the establishment of the green space and all others would pay a pound a year for using it.

While the people of Dublin had the fine amenity of the Phoenix Park for their enjoyment, there was a lack of small green spaces open to the poor adjacent to where they lived. Phoenix Park was under the control of the Office of Public Works, and when a proposal was made in 1864 to put St Stephen's Green under the control of the office also and open it to the public, it was opposed by the corporation because it would not be under its own management. This dog-in-the-manger attitude of the municipal authority delayed the opening of the Green for some years; public access was not obtained until 1880.

While suburban dwellers with their terraces of houses having large back and front gardens and access to private squares were less in need of open spaces than the crowded denizens of the city's tenements, the townships became active in acquiring and laying out public parks for the recreation of their residents (fig. 24).

In Rathmines the possiblity of obtaining Kenilworth Square as a public pleasure ground on very favourable terms arose under the enabling legislation, the Public parks (Ireland) act of 1869, (32 & 33 Vic. c. 28). This act gave power to towns and townships to establish parks by borrowing money and levying a rate for the purpose and to make bye-laws to regulate them. A majority of the residents of Kenilworth Square agreed to the admission of the public to the square, with only a small but vocal number objecting. Among the issues that arose was the question of opening the park on the sabbath, which was allowed under the act, and the matter of erecting buildings on it.[85] The issue was debated frequently at board meetings in the 1870s but nothing ever came of it.

Parts of the coastal townships were areas of great natural beauty, and the fact that pressure on open spaces for building there was not as great, meant that there was more willingness to set aside land for recreation. Much of this land was in the hands of large landlords, and this facilitated the creation of parks.

The fact that the Pembroke estate had so much land in its gift worked to the benefit of that township. The low-lying, waterlogged sloblands at Booterstown and Blackrock were a great nuisance to the Blackrock township. A deputation from the Blackrock board took the opportunity of the coming of age of the earl of Pembroke to wait on him and present its plan for this area to him. It pointed out that the board's current expenses left it with only two pence on the rates to spare to drain the area and open it to the public. It requested £5,000 from Pembroke to achieve this object, proposing to call the new amenity 'Pembroke Park' as an inducement.[86] He eventually agreed to provide £1,500 and this was accepted. The park was laid out and eventually opened in 1873, complete with artificial lake and bandstand.

Figure 24: Public parks created by Dublin townships

	Acreage	Dates
Blackrock People's Park	13.2	1873
Kingstown People's Park	5	1890
Victoria Park	110.7	1891 (taken over)
Palmerstown Park	6	1894
Harold's Cross Park	3	1894
Sandymount Green	.75	1900
Herbert Park	32	1911

Source: Various townships' minutes 1873–1911

In the early 1890s the Pembroke estate offered land at Ringsend, in the poorer part of the township, to the Pembroke board for use as a public park. Pembroke later agreed to a request by the board that part of this land be used for the building of houses for the working class. In 1876 the estate expressed its impatience with the inactivity of the township in relation to the laying out of a park on this land, and, as a result, the work was completed shortly afterwards.[87] In 1900 the township took over Sandymount Green.[88] The granting of land in Ballsbridge by Lord Pembroke to the urban district council, to be used as a public amenity, led to the only open rift between the council and the Pembroke estate. Shortly after the land was granted, the council let it out to a committee planning an industrial exhibition, resulting in the successful Irish international exhibition of 1907. Arising from the success of the exhibition, the council was approached by a new committee which was hoping to hold another exhibition in 1908. Lord Pembroke let the council know that he was against this, as the intention was that the land should be used as a public park open free of charge to all inhabitants of the area. When a vote was taken on the matter, the council was

Plate 15: Building work at Blackrock Park

split down the middle as to whether to let the land for a further year and it was then passed on the casting vote of the chairman. Pembroke then personally wrote to the council expressing his outrage at its decision. This is the first and only time that Lord Pembroke appears to have personally communicated with the township, in every other case it had been through his agent. He was compelled to write, he said, because 'the council and some of the ratepayers, do not seem to desire to have a public park and do not appreciate the gift'. He angrily pointed out that he had not offered the land to them for money-making purposes. He considered resuming possession and instructed his agent to list all the structures erected on the land and to have them removed.[89]

Victoria Park in Killiney was laid out on the fiftieth anniversary of the accession of Queen Victoria in 1887 and opened by Prince Albert Victor. It was maintained by commissioners, including Lord Ardilaun who funded the landscaping of St Stephen's Green, the earl of Meath, and others. It was taken over by the Killiney and Ballybrack commissioners in 1891. At this time also Kingstown acquired the site of a quarry and Martello tower for conversion to

Plate 16: People's Park, Kingstown, *c.*1910

People's Gardens, Kingstown.

a People's Park. The grounds were landscaped and opened in 1890 and two fine ornamental cast-iron fountains erected. In the summer of 1895 Dalkey drew up bye-laws for its new public park at Coliemore Road.[90]

The act of parliament obtained to legalize the Rathmines waterworks included a section giving the board powers to turn Harold's Cross Green into a public park. This entailed railing its three acres, one rood and four perches, thereby extinguishing its rights of way, a move that entailed a lengthy legal struggle. The 1869 parks' act and an amendment of 1872 were the legislative powers availed of.[91] William Shepherd, a landscape gardener who had previously laid out St Stephen's Green, was employed in Harold's Cross Park, and he brought the same blend of formal and informal design to bear on the the new park. Harold's Cross Park was opened to the public in early September 1894.

The granting of a piece of private land as a public park by its owners should have been a much more straightforward matter than that experienced at Harold's Cross, but in fact that was not the case. In 1881 the agents for Lord and Lady Mount Temple offered six acres of land to the board to be used as a public park, to be known as Palmerston Park. The board agreed to this if the Mount Temples undertook to pay an annual sum of £70 towards its maintenance. They offered to pay £40 per annum and the board accepted this and preparations were made for taking over the ground. In the meantime Lord

Plate 17: People's Park, Kingstown/Dún Laoghaire

Peoples Park, Dun Laoghaire, Co. Dublin.

Mount Temple died and the matter came to an abrupt hiatus. Complaints began to be received by the board about the state of the neglected land. Enquiries to Lady Mount Temple in 1891 elecited the information that she was unable to pay the promised annual sum. Pressure was brought to bear on the board by deputations from local residents demanding that the ground be taken over, and it agreed to do so if the residents would contribute the sum of £600.

The delay in acting was further compounded by a disagreement among the residents about building a public road through the park, and as to whether it should be open at night time. In 1893 agreement was finally reached and the ground was handed over by Lady Mount Temple as a gift, the leaseholders and residents in the area contibuting their £600 towards its enclosure. The ground was laid out by William Shepherd and the board obtained agreement to lay out a pedestrian throughroad from Palmerston Road to Orchard Road.

By the last quarter of the nineteenth century, British manufactures were being overtaken by foreign competition. Concern over this led to the setting up of the royal commission on technical education in Britain which sat from 1881 to 1884. An Irish report was drawn up for the commission by William Kirby Sullivan, a prominent proponent of technical education.[92] There was also a growing awareness in Ireland that industrial training had been neglected in an economy that had hitherto been dominated by the agricultural sector. In par-

Plate 18: Dripping well, Palmerstown Park

ticular, it was felt that the age-old apprentice system was totally inadequate for modern industries. The royal commission led to the passing of a technical instruction act in 1889 (Technical instruction act 1889, 52 & 53 Vict. c. 76) but it was not until the department of agriculture and technical instruction was set up under the 1898 Local government act that progress was made in this matter in Ireland.[93]

The act sanctioned one penny in the pound on the rates for the establishment of schools. While this was generally regarded as inadequate, the establishment of technical schools began. Dublin corporation opened technical schools in Kevin Street and Bolton Street and, in the townships, Pembroke proved to be the pioneer in technical education, as it had been in housing. The council decided to open a technical school to cater for the working-class population of Ringsend and Irishtown. Responding to the local needs of the community with its long sea-faring tradition, a fishery school was included in the Ringsend college, only the second such school in Ireland. This initiative by Pembroke opened a decade of education achievement by the Dublin townships when between 1893 and 1903 five very progressive schools were established (fig. 25). In 1903 Pembroke

opened its second school. It was situated at Shelbourne Road and taught commerce and domestic science.

Figure 25: Dublin townships' technical schools: dates of establishment

Pembroke Technical & Ringsend Fishery School	1893
Rathmines Technical Institute	1901
Kingstown Municipal Technical School	1901
Blackrock Municipal Technical School	1901
Pembroke Technical School (Shelbourne Rd.)	1903

Source: Various township minutes 1893–1903

Rathmines regarded the limited rate for technical education as totally inadequate for the establishment and maintenance of a school and sought the support
of the other townships in appealing to the treasury to defray half the cost of
administering the technical instruction acts. With the improved situation after
1898, Rathmines began to act. A technical instruction committee was formed in
1901, and in 1902 set about renting premises for the formation of a school.[94] The

Plate 19: Harold's Cross Green, opened as a public park 1894

Plate 20: Pembroke Technical School commemorative brochure
1893–1978

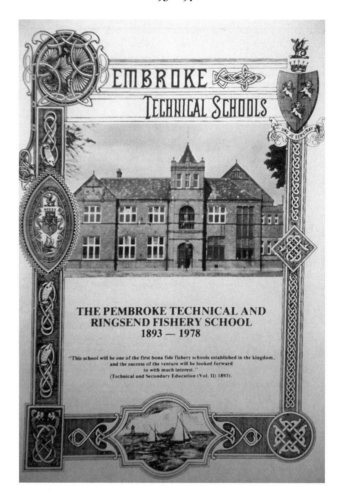

premises acquired on Rathmines Road had a long history of involvement in education as it had been at one time the well-known Rathmines School of Dr Charles
Benson. Founded in 1856 and recently closed, it included among its past-pupils
the writer, George Russell (Æ), Robert Macalister, the archaeologist and eleven
bishops. The technical school opened on the premises in 1901. Horace Plunkett
took a keen interest in the Rathmines technical college and was invited to give a
series of lectures in the town hall by the technical instruction committee. Plunkett
was the effective head of the department of agriculture and technical instruction
at the time.[95] While 'technical education' was catered for in the city and parts of

Pembroke, the Rathmines council felt that from its opening in 1901 its school should cater for the particular social and occupational structure of the area; those entering commerce, especially accountancy, banking and insurance. It was even hoped that the school would be in a position to provide candidates to fill all the commercial posts in Ireland.[96] As Sir Horace Plunkett put it, Rathmines wished to enter the 'industrial movement', but few industries were to be found within the boundaries of the township. However, for technical purposes, Rathmines saw itself as part of the capital of the country, and, in exchange for the services Dublin was providing for Rathmines, Rathmines would offer a service to Dublin, and indeed the whole country, by providing a school entirely devoted to commercial education. Indeed the township prided itself on the claim, whether true or false, that Rathmines had the only commercial college run by a local authority in the whole of the United Kingdom. Its principal took great satisfaction in the seriousness and dedication in his students, linking this to their age. He pointed out that the majority of students in the school were over twenty five-years of age, many were over forty and indeed some over fifty. Most of them were already engaged in commerce before enrolling in the college, demonstrating the need for such instruction.

In 1902 Charles Oldham, later to become a distinguished economist and professor of economics at University College, Dublin, was appointed principal of the school. Oldham was in favour of the teaching of Irish and clashed with the council on this matter. When he sought permission to have a number of special subjects, including Irish, taught in the school, the council agreed to all the subjects, except Irish, by a vote of eight to five. Voting was very much on unionist/nationalist lines. In fairness to the unionists, many of them claimed not to be against Irish *per se*, but did not see it as a commercial subject. The argument of those in favour was that its use was increasing and that it would be of benefit to their students to have a knowledge of it.[97] Horace Plunkett, who had a very high regard for the work of Oldham in Rathmines, requested him to send him a memorandum of reasons for including Irish on the Rathmines school curriculum. Oldham's arguments were not based on strictly nationalist grounds, but, he claimed, were purely commercial and practical. Pointing to the insularity of the English and the 'poverty of English speech', he claimed that Irish 'endows us with the vocal and aural capacities that makes the learning of any other language come easy'. To promote his views, he had the memorandum published with the permission of Horace Plunkett.[98]

In 1912, the Rathmines council caused controversy when it dismissed Hanna Sheehy-Skeffington from her teaching post in the Rathmines Technical Institute. Sheehy-Skeffington was a radical campaigner on behalf of the rights of women and had been one of the founders of the Irish Women's Franchise League (1908). She had been teaching part-time in the college for three years and was ostensibly let go owing to falling numbers in her class. However, it was widely believed that the true cause was her militant activities on behalf of the

Figure 26: Plan of Rathmines Technical Institute, 1912–13

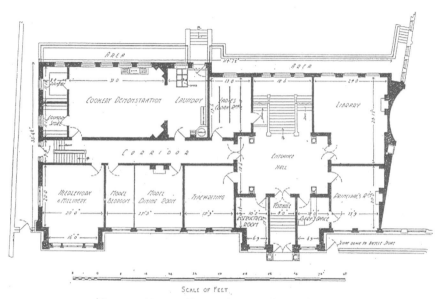

Rathmines Municipal Technical Institute – Ground Floor.

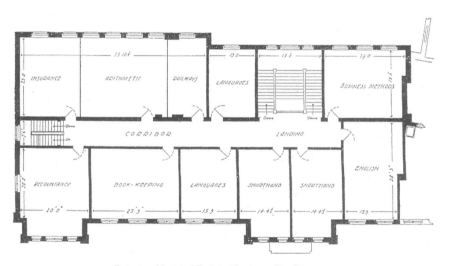

Rathmines Municipal Technical Institute – First Floor.

Source: Rathmines Technical Institute prospectus 1912–13 (Dublin, 1912)

women's suffrage movement and in particular her stint in Mountjoy jail. Strong support from the women's and nationalist movements and the teaching profession failed to have her re-instated.[99]

Rathmines and Rathgar always had a large army of domestic servants and the council felt that vocational training for this sector should not be overlooked. In 1908 a school of cookery and domestic economy was opened at 52A Carlton Terrace, Upper Rathmines, with Miss Lizzie R. Proctor as instructress. Both these schools and the school of commerce were brought together in a fine new college premises also housing a Carnegie library (discussed below) erected opposite the town hall in 1913 (fig. 26).

The new college, known as the Rathmines Technical Institute, prospered as its enrolment figures for its first twenty-five years show (fig. 27). While the institute may not have come close to providing canditates for positions covering all of the country, it did draw students from all over Dublin and townships (fig. 28). On the demise of the township, the institute came under the control of the City of Dublin Vocational Education Committee, and shorty afterwards was extended to cater for increasing numbers. The School of Domestic Economy transferred to the new Cathal Brugha Street College of Domestic Science in 1942.

Figure 27: Numbers of students attending Rathmines technical Institute, 1902–26

Session	Men	Women	Total
1902–3	222	111	333
1907–8	254	105	359
1913–14	345	582	927
1919–20	416	779	1,195
1925–26	612	1,008	1,620

Source: Technical Instruction Commission 1922–27

Kingstown struck a penny on the rates and opened a technical institute in 1901. It offered a wide curriculum, including a course in navigation to cater for the needs of the port. Scholarships were funded by Lords Longford, De Vesci and Carysfort. Also in 1901 a Blackrock technical school opened in temporary premises. A large new school, attached to the town hall, was built between 1904 and 1907, and by the 1930s up to 640 students were being taught there.

A major contention in city/township relations was the lack of hospitals in the townships. The Exham commission had pointed this out, and since then the townships had grudgingly made annual contributions to the city hospitals. When the Cork Street Fever Hospital asked Rathmines for a contribution in 1901, the council requested a return of the number of Rathmines patients treated there in the previous year before considering the request.[100] Also, on the matter of the spread of disease, a major complaint made by the corporation was that the townships, despite the urgings of the loal government board, delayed for years adopting the Notification of diseases act.

Figure 28: Catchment area of Rathmines Technical Institute, 1902–26

District	Commerce	D. Economy	Total	Percentage
Rathimes	440	249	689	42.5
Dublin	337	179	516	31.8
Townships	321	94	415	25.7

Source: Technical Instruction Commission 1922–27

The danger of admitting fever patients to general hospitals posed an increasing health problem in the Dublin area towards the end of the nineteenth century. Some hospitals began to refuse such patients; the Rathdown board of guardians, for instance, refused to take cholera patients from Kingstown, which forced the township to resolve to buy land compulsorily at Carriglea for the erection of cholera sheds.[101] In January 1895 a meeting was held in Dublin under the auspices of the public health committee of the corporation to consider this urgent matter. Representatives of the North and South Dublin Unions, the township authorities and the city public health committee attended. It was recommended that one or two isolation hospitals be set up in rural areas, remote from places of high population, and that no further patients with infectious diseases be sent to the Dublin hospitals. While a draft plan of action was outlined, no joint effort involving the townships resulted, and each individual authority was left to take action as it felt obliged.[102]

The survival of full reports of the Kingstown medical officer of health provides an insight into the problem facing local authorities in general and that of a major port in particular. The medical officer called the attention of the council, as the sanitary authority, to the fact that Rathdown board of guardians, as the port sanitary authority for Kingstown harbour, had passed a resolution to remove the already existing intercepting hospital, sited in a number of sheds on the East Pier. He went on to contend that

> though this hospital could not have been made available for any but seaborne cases of infectious disease, yet, for this purpose alone, in the absence of any other such hospital, it was well to have it, and at least it was a standing protest against a sanitary defect such as does not exist, I believe, in any other district of the United Kingdom. The facts I allude to are as

follows: extending along the coast from Merrion to Killiney bay are the three townships of Blackrock, Kingstown and Dalkey. The total population of these townships is over 30,000 persons, with a valuation of £140,000 and yet, for all this populous and comparatively wealthy district, there is no hospital for the treatment of infectious diseases, nor is there one within reasonable distance. No doubt, here in Kingstown of late years we have had a low zymotic death-rate, but we enjoy no immunity; and even during the last five years I have reported on many distressing cases where the patients have been removed to hospitals in Dublin, a distance of eight miles by road. It is strange that we should have been for three years in possession of a site for an hospital for infectious diseases within the township, and as yet no step has been taken either to erect one for Kingstown, or to combine with the adjoining township for the purpose.[103]

The results of this neglect were seen when diptheria broke out in an orphanage in the township in March, 1899. Twenty-one children were removed to hospital, eight to Loughlinstown and thirteen all the way to Cork Street Fever Hospital. Two of the children moved to the latter, poor house hospital, died. Byrne Power used this tragic event to press on his board the urgency of adopting the Notification of diseases act, something he appealed for, to no avail, on almost an annual basis. If the act were in force, he would have been notified immediately and been able to take action sooner. He received a letter from the resident medical officer in Cork Street complaining that the children had arrived 'blue with cold' and in a state of collapse. He went on to comment: 'I consider it pitiable that these poor children had to be taken out of their beds in high fever to undergo such a journey. Had either of the little creatures removed to Cork Street on the twenty-fourth, whose lives must have been in danger, been found dead in the ambulance, the question of providing an infectious diseases hospital for the district would have come to a crisis.'[104] He recommended that hot water jars and blankets be made available for the ambulance. He again appealed for the notification act to be brought in and that an isolation hospital be built as there was little he could do to isolate patients in the dwellings of the poor.[105]

While there was a scare of bubonic plague in the city in 1900, which caused the Rathmines medical officer of health to order dwellings to be white-washed, w.c.s to be kept in regular order and ashpits cleaned, the major health problem still to be tackled was tuberculosis. When a royal commission found that the disease was spread by contaminated milk, the district council urged the government to put the distribution of milk under the control of a state department as the existing system of regulation was a failure, especially in country districts where there was practically no supervision at all.[106] Rathmines claimed that it was the first local authority in Ireland to seek to make TB compulsorily notifiable under the terms of a bill covering a number of matters it presented to parliament in

1905, but that the city members and the corporation 'talked it out' – that is, killed it by time-wasting.

Co-operation between townships eventually came about with the setting up of a joint hospital board between Rathmines and Pembroke, with equal representation from each council, for the erection of an isolation facility to deal primarily with smallpox. This resulted in the proposal to erect chalets with sixty beds at Clonskeagh. Local residents went to court to prevent the erection of the Clonskeagh hospital. The opposition was led by a Mrs Boswell, who owned St James' Terrace, adjacent to the site of the proposed site. She claimed that if the hospital was built it would be a source of infection for herself and her family, who lived in one of the houses, and to her tenants, who lived in the eleven others. The court held that it was not proved that smallpox was spread by 'aerial convection' and Mrs Boswell lost her case, and the building of the hospital went ahead.[107] The links already forged between Rathmines and Pembroke were now strengthened by the joint hospital board (fig. 29).

Clonskeagh hospital was set up outside the urban district in order to minimise the type of major objections which arose when the Royal Hospital for Incurables in Donnybrook decided to build a new unit at Leeson Park for advanced tuberculosis patients. Rathmines council itself supported a deputation from the area protesting about it, and stated that it was injurious to the health of the neighbourhood and likely to seriously deplete the value of property in the area near it. It granted the use of the town hall free to Councillor Sibthorpe for

Figure 29: Rathmines & Pembroke joint boards

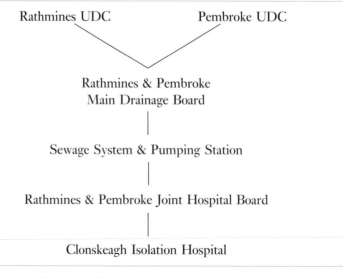

Rathmines UDC   Pembroke UDC

Rathmines & Pembroke
Main Drainage Board

Sewage System & Pumping Station

Rathmines & Pembroke Joint Hospital Board

Clonskeagh Isolation Hospital

Source: Rathmines & Pembroke Townships' minutes

a public meeting of protest.[108] Clonskeagh hospital was later the subject of a different kind of controversy when nationalist ratepayers expressed a wish that Roman catholics have a representation on the hospital board, pointing out that while most of the patients in the hospital were catholics, there was never a member of that persuasion on the board.[109]

The Public libraries and museums (England & Wales) act 1850 was extended to Ireland in 1853. Its inappropriateness to Ireland can be seen in the fact that it allowed only municipal authorities with a population of 10,000 and over to strike a rate to support a library. Very few urban centres in Ireland had such populations.[110]

The Public libraries (Ireland) act 1855 was more suited to Irish conditions. It allowed local authorities with populations of 5,000 and upwards to strike a rate of one penny to establish libraries. Progress was slow as the one penny rate was too low for most authorities to erect and maintain libraries. It was nearly thirty years before Dublin availed of the act, and the first free public libraries in the city were opened by the corporation in 1884 in Capel Street and Thomas Street. The first purpose-built library was erected on the North Strand in 1900.[111]

Lack of recreational and educational facilities in the Rathmines area was noted in the local press as early as 1868:

> It is singular that in the great township of Rathmines there is neither a hotel, clubhouse, public library, or concert room. Would it not be wise to induce the young people to take amusement near home, and save journeys to and from the city.[112]

At around the same time the Dublin townships, with their relatively large rate bases, began to avail of the act also and by the time of their abolition the townships would boast five fine public libraries (see figs. 30 and 31). Rathmines adopted the public libraries act in 1887, as many local bodies in Britain did, to mark the diamond jubilee of Queen Victoria. Rathmines was the only authority in Ireland to do so, and lost no time in establishing a library committee. A library was then opened at 53, Rathmines Road in June of that year. Parliamentary approval for the building of a purpose-built library was obtained in 1893, but by 1899, when no move had been made to build, the library moved to more extensive premises at 67, Rathmines Road as demand for its services increased.[113]

Impetus was given to the erection of large purpose-built libraries when generous grants became available in Ireland through the generosity of Andrew Carnegie. The first application by Rathmines to the Carnegie Trust was refused on the grounds that the township already had a library. In 1903 another application was made and, having convinced the trust that the present premises were inadequate, a grant of £7,500 was offered. The trust gave substantial grants towards the building of libraries, provided a site was obtained by the recipient body. A suitable site was difficult to find in Rathmines, but after a number of years, a very prestigious location was obtained. It was directly opposite the town hall on the corner of Rathmines Road and Leinster Road, on the site of a house called Leinster Lodge. It was large enough to accomodate both a technical school and a library. Correspondence with the Carnegie Trust was carried on for a number of years before any work was carried out and at one stage its offer was almost withdrawn because the conditions laid down could not be met. However, in 1911 a successful conclusion was reached with the grant being increased from £7,500 to £8,500 and a library built.[114]

Figure 30: Carnegie libraries built by Dublin townships

Year	Built	Cost
Dalkey	1900	£592
Blackrock	1906	£3,000
Kingstown	1912	£3,784
Rathmines	1913	£8,500
Pembroke	1929	£5,000

Source: Township minutes 1902–30

The caution with which both the trust and the Rathmines council proceeded was perhaps as a result of the less than happy experience of Blackrock in library building. Almost a decade previously the Blackrock board had applied to the trust, stating that it was about to build a technical school and that a new library at the same time was desirable. The first set of plans submitted were not accepted, as it was felt that there was not enough room set aside for the library, but in 1903 a grant of £3,000 was promised by the trust and work began in 1905. The building, like its technical school, was attached to the town hall and was built with a sand-cement facade done in the classical manner.[115] By the end of 1906 there was a shortage of funds to finish the building, and the trust was appealed to again, this time without success. Adverse comments made to the Carnegie Trust about the library and ill-kept, soiled books, caused a representative of the trust to investigate the matter with the council, and a number of what were seen as malpractices by the trust were noted – for example, the fact that the upper part of the building was being used for public meetings.

The impressive Rathmines library, designed by the firm of Batchelor and Hicks, integrated a library and technical school, each with its own seperate entrance. The library contained a reading room, reference rooms and newspaper room. The style was mock Tudor with terracotta finish designed to enhance the town hall. In a spirit of frugality and serious-mindedness, it was proposed by the council that there be no ceremony for the opening of the library and technical school. The library committee and the technical instruction committee asked the

Figure 31: Kingstown and Pembroke libraries

council to reconsider the matter, feeling that all their hard work and achievement should be marked in some way. The original decision was overturned and the opening ceremony for both buildings was set for 24 October 1913.

Those gathered in the town hall for the occasion were addressed by Justice Barton, Fr Thomas Finlay, SJ, professor of moral theology at the Catholic University and a strong supporter of Horace Plunkett's agricultural co-opera-tion, and Mr Forte of the Belfast Technical Institution. The chairman of the council then declared the new buildings open and asked those present to cross the road to inspect them.[116] The old library building, across Rathmines Road from the new one, was used for the erection of a proper fire brigade headquar-ters for the township. John Roy was appointed librarian in 1911, when the library had 225 borrowers and 3,000 volumes on its shelves. The magnificent new building did much to increase readership, and by 1930 it had 7,000 bor-rowers and 30,000 books. In 1929 195,000 books were issued for home read-ing.[117] The Public libraries (Ireland) act, 1920, permitted authorities to raise up to three pence in the pound on the rates and Rathmines immediately imposed this. A children's section of the library was opened in 1923 and the Carnegie Trust granted £450 towards the purchase of books.[118]

Under the acts it was not necessary for members of library committees to be councillors and such bodies in Ireland were noted for their clerical representation. This was the case in Rathmines where local clergymen were seldom absent from the library committee. Reading material was closely vetted and the committee felt obliged occasionally to censor the material made available to its readers, even newspapers. It instructed the librarian 'to expunge as far as possible all sporting news relating to horse racing from the newspapers provided for the public in the library'.[119] In 1905 Councillor Carruthers objected to an attempt by the council to give a second seat to a Roman catholic clergyman on the library committee, stating that the committee had 'too much of the theological about it'. His inter-vention was successful and the second priest was not accepted.[120]

Dalkey was unusual in that its library building was erected partly by public subscription, with funds for the site being provided by the Carnegie Trust. Township residents topped up the £224 already provided by the rates by sub-scribing £245 and pledging £34 a year for the following six years. The rates would yield a further £50 per annum. As no landowner was prepared to donate a site, the council appealed to the Carnegie Trust which, impressed with the commitment of the township ratepayers, broke the usual rule of only contribut-ing for the building by granting £592 in all, £400 covering the purchase of the site. The building, erected in Castle Street, cost £925, and had a reading room and newspaper room.[121]

Kingstown was more fortunate as the site for its library was donated by Lords Longford and De Vesci. The architects, O'Callaghan and Webb, designed an impressive classical facade on a corner site. Like Rathmines, its first appli-

Figure 32: Rathmines administrative nucleus including town hall, public library, fire station, refuse destructor, morgue, electricity works, artisans' dwellings (Gulistan cottages); a technical institute was later built opposite the town hall

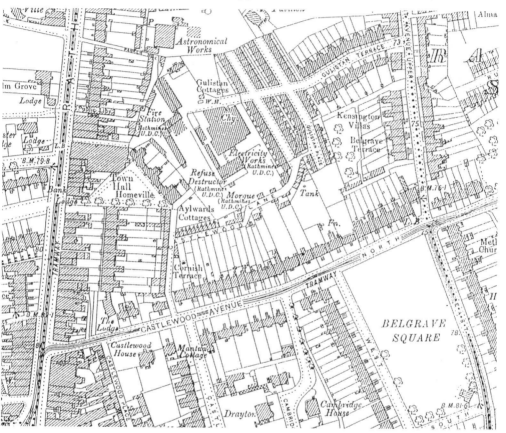

Source: O.S. 6 inch map 1908 (Map Library, Trinity College, Dublin)

cation to the Carnegie Trust was rejected as it already had a library. In 1909 a fresh application was made and £3,784 was granted. The library was opened in 1912 and had the usual reading and newspaper rooms.[122]

In 1912 the Carnegie Trust promised a grant of £5,000 to the Pembroke township for a library in Ballsbridge and £2,000 for one in Ringsend. However, the great war intervened before anything was done. Defence of the realm regulations, which prohibited expenditure on public buildings of more than £500 without special license, caused the project to be shelved. £7,700 was eventually granted in 1925 to build both libraries but the council decided to build only one, which was opened adjacent to the town hall in Ballsbridge in 1929.[123] The writer

Plate 21: Rathmines Library and Technical Institute

Frank O'Connor was its distinguished first librarian. Killiney failed to avail of a Carnegie grant; the problems of a low population and consequent low rate base prevented it from taking up £900 offered to it in 1911.[124]

While national schools in Ireland came under state supervision as a result of the Stanley act of 1831, attendance at school was not compulsory. This was seen as a defect in the system and a new Irish education act, the Irish education act 1892 (55 and 56 Victoria, c. 42) introduced an element of compulsion. Children between the ages of six and fourteen were required henceforth to attend school. Local committees, half of whose members were nominated by the local authority and half by the commissioners of national education, were entrusted with the task of carrying out the legislation. By 1908 only ten councils throughout the country had failed to enforce the act.[125] Attendance officers were appointed, and they presented quarterly reports on the numbers enrolled and attending schools in the townships.

In Kingstown, the legisation was first acted on in the last quarter of 1896. Twelve schools were visited in that period and a total of 2,256 pupils were found to be on the rolls, 1,090 boys and 1,166 girls. There was an average attendance daily of 1719 pupils. Two hundred and sixty children were found to be irregular attenders, ninety of whose parents were warned and seventy-six houses visited.[126] Authorities had power to prosecute and fine parents up to five shillings plus costs. Kingstown fined regularly and sought power for magistrates

to send children to industrial schools.[127] A more comprehensive school attendance act was passed in 1926.

In the 1920s a number of groups, including the Irish Women's Franchise
League, had taken up the issue of school meals, perceiving that children were
being prevented from taking full advantage of the provision of education because
of lack of food during the day. When a number of prominent members of the
league gained influential positions on the Rathmines council it is not surprising
that they began to vigorously pursue this matter. Pembroke, which had not got
the same representation of campaigning women, considered that the number of
children coming to its schools without breakfast was too small for it to set up
a public kitchen and recommended that the matter be dealt with by the St
Vincent de Paul Society through the issuing of vouchers for food which could
be eaten at home.[128]

The women councillors in Rathmines, in particular Dr Kathleen Lynn,
strongly advocated the adoption of any legislation furthering the welfare of the
poor and, in particular, children. In 1923 when the public health committee recommended that the provision of meals act be adopted, Councillor Sibthorpe and
the unionists recommended that it be sent back, and the number of children
likely to be involved calculated and the cost per child estimated at the rate used
by Dublin corporation.[129] The result of this estimate was that the cost of 1,000
school meals per day for 40 weeks would be £1,666 13s. 4d., with a further £182
for administration; transport and other costs would amount to a further £300.
Councillors Kettle and Lynn moved that the schools' meals act be adopted, and
this was done, with the unionists objecting.[130] The statement drawn up by the
council introducing the measure to its ratepayers shows a high level of concern
for the educational welfare of the children. It states that

> the council is satisfied that children attending national schools in the dis-
> trict are unable by reason of lack of food to take full advantage of the
> education provided for them and that the council have ascertained that
> funds other than public funds are not available or insufficient to defray
> the cost of meals furnished under the act and that application be made to
> the minister for authority to expend out of the rates such sum as may be
> requisite to meet the cost.[131]

The townships saw the establishment of baths and wash-houses both as a public health measure and as a recreational facility. The enabling act was the Baths
and wash-houses act of 1846. This act allowed baths to be taken over or new ones
erected, and the expense taken from the rates. A clause in the act stated that the
number of baths for the 'labouring classes' was to be not less than twice the number of baths 'of any higher class'. A schedule laid down the charges for use of the
baths; for one person above eight years of age the charge was 1d. for a cold bath,
including the use of a clean towel, and 2d. for a hot one. Several children bathing

together could have a cold bath for 2d. and a hot one for 4d. The Dublin and Wicklow Railway Company had established sea-bathing places at a number of places along the coast to encourage business. At Salthill an oval-shaped pool was built and a gents', and separate ladies', bathing place near the station at Blackrock. Blackrock township's first concern about these was that public decency be preserved and it made sure that breaches were prosecuted by the police. It had screens placed around the bathing place adjacent to the railway station.

The on-going problem of the discharge of raw sewage into the sea by the townships' sewers and the inactivity of the various boards in the matter of the provision of a main drainage system endangered bathers using traditional bathing places along the coast. It was to counteract this that the policy of taking over or building baths, where the intake of water could be controlled, arose. While the laying of intercepting sewers in Blackrock and Kingstown no doubt improved the quality of water for bathing, the work involved could also affect bathing facilities. The main drainage tank put an end to the free bathing place for females at Kingstown. To offset this, the boards included in the Blackrock and Kingstown drainage and improvement act of 1893 powers to establish and maintain sea baths. Kingstown adopted the 1846 act,[132] and took over the old baths at Salthill from the Blackrock council as a bathing place for children in 1905.[133] Kingstown also took over Victoria baths, which dated from the 1840s, and after renovations re-opened them in 1908. At the same time the working classes who, it was felt, were more in need of baths for washing than recreation, were seperately catered for and hot water was provided for them by steam from the refuse destructor. A ceiling of £1,000 was to be spent on this project, compared to over £9,000 santioned to be borrowed for the Victoria baths.[134] In 1928 a controversy arose in Blackrock over the council's plan to buy the existing public baths. The council hoped to hold international swimming events there during the upcoming Tailteann Games. The baths were eventually bought by the council for £2,000 and a further sum of around £3,000 was borrowed to restore them for the games.

Kingstown was anxious to promote itself as a health resort and the provision of bathing facilities was seen as a necessity for this also. Despite its sewage problems, its medical officer of health constantly compared its death rate with coastal towns on the south coast of England and encouraged bathing and other amenities associated with a seaside town. The board was vigilant to ensure that the cross-channel ferry business was facilitated and made efforts to attract the Isle of Man ferry to its harbour. It also petitioned the lord lieutenant to be allowed to levy a rate to advertise the district.[135]

Pembroke investigated the possibility of taking over the private Merrion Baths but nothing came of it. The provision of baths and wash-houses arose frequently at meetings of the Rathmines council. Land was acquired for the purpose on Rathmines Road but no funds were ever allocated for the project before the demise of the council.

Figure 33: Rathmines urban district council, administrative structure in early twentieth century

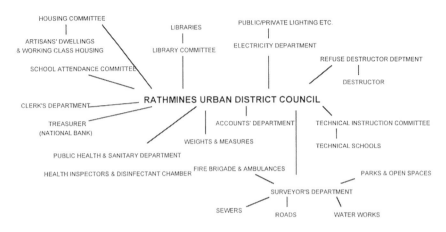

Source: Compiled from various Rathmines UDC minutes

A practice that grew increasingly unpopular was that of holding dead bodies in public houses until an inquest was conducted. Public houses were increasingly regarded as inappropiate for such a purpose, even by publicans. They saw the use of public houses as coroner's courts and temporary morgues more as a disruption to trade than an opportunity to increase business. In 1905 the Licensed Vintners and Grocers Association attacked the Rathmines council for not moving to provide a morgue. It decried the fact that an area of 33,000 people had to use licensed premises for such business. It saw the coroner's court as an 'invasion' and the whole procedure a great indignity to the dead, a body often having to be held in a stable or outhouse until the inquest was held.[136] Eventually morgues were built, the Rathmines facility being at the back of the town hall yard. The Pembroke morgue was erected on the opposite bank of the Dodder to the main drainage pumping station. The four coastal townships also had responsibility for the burial of the dead. From 1899 on, they together with Rathdown no. 1 rural district, jointly managed Dean's Grange cemetery.[137]

The widening powers of the councils can be seen in the appointment of a pensions' committee in Rathmines in 1908 under the Old age pensions act of that year.[138] The township inspector of weights and measures was made also an inspector under the Shops' act of 1912 and the board undertook the inspection of picture theatres in early 1914.[139] Urban district councils were given the power to grant licenses for the showing of films in 1909, the year that James Joyce opened the Volta, Ireland's first cinema in Mary Street, Dublin. The Princess cinema in Rathmines was the first purpose-built picture house in the country and was opened in 1912. By the time another cinema, The Stella, opened in 1923 the township had been given supervision of cinemas in its area under the censorship of films act. The new cinema applied for and was granted a license. Three township censors had the task of passing or rejecting films shown in the area.[140] but new legislation passed by Saorstát Éireann later the same year took away the power of censorship from urban district councils and granted it to the newly appointed official censor.

By the time of their demise as part of the major restructuring of local government in 1930, a wide spectrum of services devolved on urban district councils, encompassing the provision of water and electricity, preventative measures as regards public health, care of the sick, housing, infrastructure and transport, social welfare and leisure, death and burial. In response to these demands, Rathmines and the other townships developed a highly complex administrative structure and large staffs. An outline of the Rathmines structure can be seen in fig. 33.

To conclude, the period from the 1880s saw the township boards involved in the provision of services and amenities never envisaged by their founders. While the impetus for much of this stemmed from central government, the responsibility for the implementation of aspects of social policy was placed on local bodies. Internal forces were also at work. J.A. Hassan, in his study of the growth of the water industry in England in the nineteenth century pointed out that 'civic pride' was often regarded as an important influence in overcoming the economical attitude and zeal for retrenchment manifested by the shopocracy that increasingly dominated councils like Manchester during the second half of the nineteenth century.[141]

While an 'economy party' was always strong in Rathmines and had its adherents in other townships, the withdrawal of Frederick Stokes in 1878 paved the way for a less restrictive view of spending ratepayers' money, leading eventually to the building of impressive civic buildings such as a town hall, library and technical college.

The creation of an environment conducive to the building of middle-class housing by the provision of such services as water and public lighting was the *raison d'être* of the foundation of the townships. However, as an era of more social responsibility dawned, the boards found themselves involved in house-building for a different class. The inception of state loans and grants and a greater amount of centralised control, epitomised by the local government board, allowed townships to juggle on the one hand the provision of services, and low rates on the other. Rathmines township, dominated by an economy party, built a relatively small amount of artisans' dwellings and sub-standard workers' accommodation, while the coastal townships and Pembroke had a fine record in this regard. In the area of public health a rather belated move was made by

Pembroke and Rathmines to address jointly the question of the cure of disease by the establishment of a fever hospital, despite opposition by some ratepayers.

While transport was vital to the development of the townships, the huge capital cost of providing their own systems made such a venture non-viable for such under-funded entities as the corporation and the satellite bodies. However, the provision of electricity, refuse disposal systems, technical schools and libraries show that the larger townships were capable of a dynamic response to modern requirements. The schools responded to the needs of local areas with Pembroke more concerned for the advancement of the less well-off, and Rathmines responding to more middle-class aspirations.

CHAPTER SEVEN

In time of international and domestic war, 1914–23

The period under review in this chapter led to political independence for the greater part of Ireland. The prelude to this was international war and both it and the conflict which led to political independence for the greater part of Ireland had repercussions at local level. The Great War impinged on the work of the townships, and events in Ireland and in particular in Dublin from 1916 to 1923 had a more profound effect. Attempts to establish local government by the counter-administration to British rule set up by the illegal Dáil Éireann have been characterized as the 'most adventurous experiment' conducted by that body.[1] Two able administrators, William T. Cosgrave and Kevin O'Higgins, walked the tightrope of ensuring that local bodies transfered their allegiance to Dáil Éireann without provoking the British authorities to cut off the funding necessary to carry out their administration and supply their services.

On 2 September 1914 in the town hall in Rathmines Councillor R.D. Bolton moved a resolution (carried unanimously by the unionist-dominated board) 'that the chairman be requested to call a public meeting in the town hall, Rathmines, to encourage recruiting for Kitchener's army'.[2] The 'international crisis' under which the above motion was recorded in the minutes, known now as the first world war, inaugurated a spell when international conflict and domestic unrest were to influence greatly the working of Rathmines and the other councils, and eventually find them serving in a new state.

Rathmines immediately looked to practical matters such as the protection of the waterworks and encouraging recruiting for the army. It was believed that public utilities such as the waterworks at Glenasmole were vulnerable to attack from the air or sabotage, and measures were taken to make them more secure. The town hall, as indicated above, was put to use for recruiting. The war office wrote asking the council to encourage recruiting among its employees. Some had already enlisted; for instance, the council's 'horse-keeper' was allowed half wages during his absence, a portion paid to his wife and the balance lodged to his credit in the bank.[3]

Intensified efforts to enlist Irishmen voluntarily in the British army, arising from the failure of the authorities to impose conscription on Ireland, led to the first voice raised against recruiting in the Rathmines council chamber. In August

1918, when Sergeant Sullivan and a deputation from the recruiting council, set up the year previously in an effort to reverse falling enlistment in the army, were granted a hearing by the councillors, Councillor Thomas Kennedy protested, claiming that it was an infringement of the standing rules forbidding the discussion of politics. The chairman, George Metcalfe, ruled that the matter was not political and the deputation's request that the urban district form a recruiting committee was agreed to.[4] Kennedy was honorary secretary of the Rathmines and Harold's Cross branch of the Irish National Federation. He had stood on the conservative ticket, but on his election he stated that he was in fact 'non-party', and he now appeared to be revealing nationalist sympathies.[5] Space was granted for the recruiting campaign in the town hall free of charge. Kennedy, a maverick who was the lone nationalist voice on the council for the duration of the war, kept up his opposition until the cessation of hostilities. He dissented when a resolution of congratulations at victory in the war was passed immediately after the armistice in November 1918. However, he resigned in July 1919 and his place on the council was taken by Capt. W. Lombard Murphy, son of William Martin Murphy, the industrialist, who had just died.[6]

As well as workers joining the ranks there were recruits to the officer corps among the councillors. Gerard Plunkett's resignation from the council was announced at a meeting on 2 June 1915, as he was being posted to the Dardanelles; his death in action was reported at the very next meeting of the council on 18 June. His brother, Oliver Plunkett, was co-opted to the board but he subsequently resigned when he joined the Army Horse Transport Service Corps.[7]

In Rathmines, loss of personnel was accompanied by financial retrenchment as government grants and loans became scarce. The question of building further artisans' dwellings was shelved, and, as further expense was incurred by the need to replace horses acquired by the war office, it was decided to put off the laying of a new water main from Glenasmole to Ballyboden until hostilities ceased. Matters became so serious that just before the end of the war the council considered selling off the electrical plant, probably as a result of the difficulty of obtaining coal.[8] When Frederick Fawcett, the clerk of the council for twenty-six years, died in 1914, the salary offered to his successor was £300, a reduction of £100.[9] However, a war gratuity of 1s. was given to each man earning less than 25s. per week, to terminate at the end of the war.[10]

The urban districts responded to the appeal for an increase in food production and the 'digging for victory' campaign. On a request from the Vacant Lands' Cultivation Society councils sought land in their areas for allotments which were to be granted to residents to grow food.[11] A series of talks on the cultivation of gardens was held in Rathmines Technical School and 5,000 leaflets on the same topic were printed. A request to landowners for land for allotments in the township resulted in the offer of four acres on an unbuilt area in Rathmines known as the Thacker estate and ten on the estate of Sir Frederick Shaw in Terenure. Four pounds an acre was paid to the Thacker estate for its land and twenty-five plots were rented to residents at 10s. each for eleven months. Seven acres of the Shaw land was taken up at £5 an acre. There were seventy-eight applications for allotments on this land at Bushy Park and the demand was satisfied by dividing it up into 100 allotments.[12]

While resolutions of a political complexion did not arise in Rathmines, things were different in nationalist Pembroke. Support for the Irish Volunteers went so far as to acceding to the force's request for the use of ground at Riverview for drilling and in early August a resolution was passed agreeing with John Redmond, in his 'brilliant and memorable statement' that the British government could take its troops from Ireland, and its shores would be defended by the Irish National Volunteers and the Ulster Volunteers.[13]

While the Easter rising of 1916 took its heaviest toll on the city of Dublin, the townships did not escape unscathed. Pembroke was closest to the conflict and Boland's mills, on the outskirts of the township, were occupied by the rebels. On Wednesday of Easter week the town hall was occupied by the British military and became the headquarters of the 58th (north midland) division. The council chamber was turned into an officers' sleeping quarters and offices. The council met in the technical school on Shelbourne Road and for three weeks an attempt was made to conduct township business from there. Movement was strictly curtailed in the district, and those on official business for the council were issued with passes. J.C. Manly, the township secretary, in a report to the commissioners after the rebellion, stated that fighting took place in many parts of the district; the electricity works were fired at and a number of places were shelled by the military. Ballsbridge was on the route of troops arriving from Kingstown heading for the city and they met stiff resistance at Mount Street bridge on the city/township boundary. The technical school in Ringsend found itself in a dangerous situation. The caretaker of the school, fearing it might be shelled, phoned the military to inform them that a suspicion on the north side of the Liffey that firing was emanating from the school was mistaken.

A public health hazard in Pembroke had to be dealt with at the cessation of hostilities. It was known that a number of bodies were buried in the district and these had to be located and removed by the township authorities. Three, two soldiers and a civilian, were removed from the grounds of the parochial hall in Northumberland Road and one from a garden on the same road. The local government board granted the council £100 for relief of urgent cases that arose as a result of scarcity of food and difficulty in the distribution of separation allowances and old age pensions.[14]

Large numbers of troops came into Ireland through Kingstown and newly-built council houses at Sandycove were taken over as billets, trees were damaged and the baths and wash-houses were used. After the rebellion the damage was assessed by the council at £347 12s. Food scarcity was also a problem in Kingstown as it was cut off from Dublin, showing, incidentally, how heavily it depended on the city. A.V. McCormick, a local coal merchant and shipbroker put the S.S. *Dunleary* at the disposal of traders for the transport of supplies from Liverpool.[15]

The presence of a large army barracks in Rathmines gave rise to a number of tragic events during the 1916 Rising. There were exchanges of fire between the garrison in Portobello barracks and members of the Irish Citizen Army on the city side of the canal and the tower of the town hall was used as a observation post by the military. The action of Captain Riversdale Bowen-Colthurst in murdering five people in cold blood, some in Portobello Barracks and some on Rathmines Road, stunned the township; the victims were Francis Sheehy-Skeffington and two journalists, a young boy and Richard O'Carroll, a member of Dublin corporation; all were unconnected with the rebellion. The council's ambulance corps, which had already been used for transporting wounded soldiers from the front as they embarked from hospital ships to city hospitals, was pressed into service in the city during the rising, for which it was thanked by Sir John Maxwell, commander of the British forces in Ireland.[16]

In the council chambers, reaction to the rebellion varied. Dublin corporation sent a copy of a resolution in relation to the rising to Rathmines, but in time-honoured fashion it was just noted as 'read'.[17] Kingstown passed a motion deploring the loss of life and destruction of property but condemned no one.[18] Nationalist-controlled Pembroke condemned the 'recent outbreak, which we believe to be gravely detrimental to the real political and industrial interests of Ireland'. The unionists were prepared to support this motion, however an addendum calling on all nationalist Irishmen to support John Redmond's constitutional policy, including home rule, of course, resulted in their withdrawal of support.[19] On the question of those imprisoned after the rising, a letter to Rathmines from Madame O'Rahilly, widow of The O'Rahilly, killed in the fighting, in relation to the prison conditions of Countess Markievicz, a future member of the council, was 'read', while Pembroke adopted a Dublin corporation motion demanding the release of the prisoners from English jails and, pending that, the granting to them of political prisoner status.[20]

Blackrock's condemnation of the rising was quite strong; its members expressed their 'heartful reprobation of the mad and mischievous revolt which has taken place in our midst'. Similar to the position taken in Pembroke an approval of the attitude taken by John Redmond was part of the motion and because of this the unionists, including Lady Dockrell, voted against and the motion only passed by five votes to four, with two councillors abstaining.[21]

The local government elections, due to take place in 1917, were postponed until 1920.[22] There was unease among local authorities when under the Representation of the people bill (1917), it was proposed to take away from the secretaries of county councils and clerks of borough and urban district councils the duty of preparing the registry of parliamentary and local government electors; this was regarded as an injustice to those officials whose salaries, Rathmines claimed, were to a large extent made up of the fees they earned under the franchise acts.[23]

Shortly after the establishment of the first Dáil Éireann in January 1919, the rejuvenated Sinn Féin party, now the political embodiment of militant republicanism, began communicating with the urban district councils. When a vacancy arose on the Pembroke council, the Sinn Féin director of elections, Diarmuid O'Leary requested that Batt O'Connor of Brendan Road, Donnybrook, a supporter of the party, be co-opted; the councillors, however, ignored the request and chose a magistrate from Sandymount.[24] In Rathmines Joseph MacDonagh, secretary of the Ranelagh Sinn Féin club, wrote to the council querying the appointment of officials.[25]

After the capture of the national stage by Sinn Féin in 1918, when it won 73 of the 104 Irish seats at Westminster, the government knew that it was only a matter time before this was mirrored at local level. In anticipation of a strong nationalist and republican showing in the 1920 local elections the British government introduced proportional representation, to be applicable to Ireland only. The intention was to assist political minorities keep a foothold in areas where they were in danger of being overwhelmed – in effect, the unionists in most of Ireland. Furthermore, republicans claimed that it would lessen the impact of Sinn Féin owing to the large number of spoiled votes expected as a result of the intricacies of the new system.[26] There was much concern on both sides of the political divide that the proportional representation system was not understood; Rathmines requested the local government board to organize lectures in the town hall to explain the new system.[27] In order to ensure representation to minorities the government also divided many areas into smaller wards. In particular this would isolate unionist areas and provide them with council seats in local districts dominated by nationalists. The local government board stipulated how many wards there were to be and the number of seats in each.[28] For the 1920 election Rathmines was divided into four wards for the first time.

Amid much political turmoil preparations began for the local government elections of January 1920. The lead-up to the elections saw Wexford, Waterford and Kilkenny put under martial law and the arrest of Sinn Féin candidates and agents.[29] In Rathmines the electioneering by the outgoing unionist members and like-minded new candidates was much more restrained than the open appeal on party lines in some of the other townships. Sinn Féin sought to allay ratepayers' fears of extravagant expenditure by candidates new to local politics and asked them to see through attempts by unionists to mask themselves as 'ratepayers' candidates' and label republicans as 'political'.[30] Eleven outgoing members and five new candidates made an appeal based on the solid achievement of the old

Figure 34: 1920 election results in Rathmines Township

E = elected

East Ward 1

4 seats

William W. Carruthers (U)	494 E		William Sears (S.F.)	678 E

West Ward 1

5 seats

William W. Carruthers (U)	494 E	William Sears (S.F.)	678 E
Kathleen Lynn (S.F.)	427 E	George Metcalf (U)	502 E
James Dwyer (S.F)	382 E	J.J. McKensie (U)	297 E
John Russel (U)	221 E	John Doyle (S.F.)	245 E
Patrick Moore (N)	202	J.J. Kiernan (N)	180
William M. Hatte (U)	117	M. Ffrench-Mullen (S.F.)	133 E
Thomas O'Connor (S.F.)	83	A.A. O'Malley (U)	111
		George Irvine (S.F.)	93

East Ward 2

7 seats

West Ward 2

5 seats

Joseph McDonagh (S.F.)	549 E		
J. Sibthorpe (U)	456 E	Robert Benson (U)	508 E
J.C. Anderson (U)	422 E	Robert Brennan (S.F.)	499 E
Frances Kent (S.F.)	363 E	Margaret K. Dixon (U)	392 E
Mrs. T.M. Kettle (N)	361 E	William Ireland (U)	258 E
Dr D. Jackson (U)	367 E	P.J. Munden	244
Thomas Saul (Ind.)	260	C.B. Boyle (Ind.)	226
Dr H.B. Goulding (U)	235 E	M.J. Mulcahy (S.F.)	205 E
T. Cullen (S.F.)	127	S.G. Slater (U)	130
R.D. Bolton (U)	103	A. Nicholls (S.F.)	116
George Daly (S.F.)	52	F.W. Giddings (U)	78

Out of a total number on the register of 13,801, 10,014 valid votes were polled, which broke down as follows:

Unionist	4,589	Nationalist	987
Sinn Féin	3,952	Independent	486

Source: *Irish Independent*, 19 Jan. 1920

council. They pointed to progress in the sanitary condition of the township, the state of the roads and footpaths, and achievements made in the water supply, electric lighting, technical education and library facilities.[31]

The only allusion to the current political upheaval was a commitment to uphold the traditional focus of the council on the business at hand: 'we are convinced that it is only by rigidly excluding from the discussions of the council all

political or sectarian subjects, as has been our invariable practice, that the important affairs of the township can receive the attention they require and which we
have always endeavoured to give them'.[32]

In Rathmines thirty-six candidates had been nominated for the twenty-one
seats on the council. Sixteen were unionist, eleven of whom were outgoing councillors; fourteen were nominated by Sinn Féin; four were nationalists and two
were independents. Seven women stood: five for Sinn Féin, one unionist and
one nationalist. Of the three Sinn Féin women, one, Dr Kathleen Lynn, had
fought in the 1916 rising. Many of the Sinn Féin candidates were proposed by
catholic clergymen, including Archdeacon Mark Anthony Fricker, parish priest
of Rathmines and the Revd Cornelius O'Shea, superior of St Mary's College,
Rathmines Road. Archdeacon Fricker proposed among others, Kathleen Lynn,
who was a member of the Church of Ireland.

In 1920 Sinn Féin captured 72 out of 127 urban councils and county boroughs in the country, including narrow control of Dublin corporation. Fig. 34
shows the result in Dublin. Sinn Féin controlled Dublin corporation and together with a strong nationalist representation brought an end to effective unionist
power in Blackrock.[33] The parties were evenly balanced in Pembroke and
Rathmines, with the unionists in the latter township having a majority of one
over Sinn Féin and one nationalist. The smaller coastal townships had a remarkably strong representation by labour, especially Dalkey. New members on the
Rathmines council included, Dr Kathleen Lynn, James Dwyer, Mrs Mary
Mulcahy, Mrs Frances Ceannt, James Doyle, Miss Madeline Ffrench-Mullen,
Mrs Mary Kettle and Joseph MacDonagh.[34]

Joseph McDonagh was a brother of the executed 1916 leader, Thomas
McDonagh, and had himself taken part in the rising and been interned. Owing
to his political involvement, he had to give up his position in the inland revenue
department. He was president of Pearse's school, St Enda's, and had written
some plays. In the general election of 1918 he was elected for North Tipperary.
As well as being elected to the Rathmines council he was elected as alderman to
represent Merchant's Quay ward in the municipal corporation.[35]

Dr Kathleen Lynn stood as a member of Sinn Féin. She was born in the west
of Ireland of a well-to-do family, and became one of the first women doctors in
Ireland. She had a passionate interest in social justice and the rights of the
oppressed. She was a strong supporter of James Connolly and became chief medical officer of the Irish Citizen Army. She had tended the wounded at City Hall
during the Easter Rising and been imprisoned. Her great concern for the health
of children had led to the founding of St Ultan's hospital in Charlemont Street,
on the edge of the township and she lived at 9, Belgrave Road, Rathmines, where
she also had her surgery, which was always crowded by the poor and needy.[36]

At the first meeting of the newly elected council on 30 January 1920, the
unionists made the first move with Councillor William Carruthers proposing

that Councillor Benson be elected chairman. An amendment was proposed by MacDonagh, seconded by Mrs Ceannt on behalf of Sinn Féin that Councillor Sears be elected chairman but this was defeated by eleven votes to eight, with Mrs Kettle, the nationalist, abstaining. Mrs Ceannt was proposed for the vice-chair but was defeated by Councillor William Ireland by the even narrower margin of eleven votes to ten. The nationalists then tried to get all the ordinary business of the council adjourned until the next meeting, but this was lost. They then tried unsuccessfully to have standing orders suspended. A long wrangle then ensued over the membership of committees.

The enmity between the two parties is evident in the attempt by the unionists to lessen the complement of their Sinn Féin opponents. Bankrupts were debarred from becoming councillors. The unionists sent a letter to the secretary of the council asserting that James Dwyer of 5, Rathmines Terrace, who had been recently elected a member of the council, had 'carried an arrangement with his creditors' in 1917 and so was disqualified to act as councillor. His election was declared null and void on the casting vote of the chairman. When it came to fill the vacancy the unionists proposed William Hatte and Sinn Féin Thomas O'Connor; after much wrangling and many names being proposed by the republicans, including that of Mrs Burgess, the wife of Cathal Brugha, the meeting had to re-assemble in the afternoon before Hatte was eventually co-opted.[37] In 1921 Sinn Féin was still being outvoted and cross-party co-operation not much in evidence. The unionist, Councillor Ireland, was elected chairman and when the nationalists proposed Dr Kathleen Lynn as vice-chairman, she was opposed by the unionists who voted in their candidate, Councillor McKensie.[38]

In Kingstown one of the first moves of the Sinn Féin and nationalist members was to have the name of the district changed to Dún Laoghaire. Kingstown, and the other townships had come under pressure for some years from the Gaelic League to do their part in furthering the cultural revival. In 1902 the league had begun a campaign to have the name changed and to call all the streets, avenues, roads, etc. within the township after Irishmen and Irishwomen, whether saints, scholars or patriots and erect bilingual nameplates. This and an attempt to have the crown on the township flag replaced by a harp failed however.[39]

In 1920 the name-change move was proposed by Councillor Seán Ó hUadhaigh and seconded by Councillor Edward Kelly and was carried by ten votes to eight. The Royal Victoria baths were changed to Dún Laoghaire baths and all letter-heads were ordered to be bilingual in the future and the council cheques to be in Irish only.[40] Acceptance of the new name took time and repeated requests were made to the postal authorities to recognize it; a letter from the painters' union in Dublin addressed to the Kingstown Urban District Council was returned to it with the observation that no such place as Kingstown existed.

A further name-change proved to be unsuccessful. Patrick Moran was hanged in Mountjoy jail for the assassination of a British officer on Bloody Sunday,

1920. He had lived in the George's Street area of Kingstown. When it was decided at the council to change the name of Lower George's Street to Moran Street the requisite number of names was obtained but they did not hold property amounting to the required two-third's valuation necessary for a change.[41]

In early 1919, when Dáil Éireann set up its own department of local government with William T. Cosgrave acting as minister and Kevin O'Higgins as his deputy, it competed with the British local government board for the allegiance of Irish local authorities. It should be noted that for much of the period from the elections of 1920 to the end of 1921 no clear policy on how local bodies should act was being followed by the Dáil. This was partly owing to uncertainty as to how to proceed without putting central funds to local bodies in jeopardy, and to the disruption following the jailing of key personnel on the republican side, including Cosgrave and O'Higgins. The matter was exacerbated by the fact the Cosgrave was ill during a crucial period in 1920.[42]

By mid-1920 all county councils and most borough councils in the 26 county area had come to recognise Cosgrave's department.[43] Pressure was put on local authorities to maintain their allegiance by the local government board, which announced in July 1920 that all financial assistance would be withdrawn from authorities which did not recognise it nor accept the authority of the British government. The problem for Sinn Féin-dominated boards was attempting to withdraw allegiance from the local government board but avoiding treasury grants being cut off. Kevin O'Higgins, in particular, did not wish to see local bodies precipitate a withdrawal of funding and the question of allegiance to the Dáil was not demanded of authorities at this time. Most of the councils delayed biting the bullet for as long as they could, reading both local government board and Dáil Éireann circulars as they received them. The Kingstown minutes are quite clear on this matter, and it did not, in fact, pledge its allegiance to the Dáil and agree 'to function under the control and supervision of the department of local government' until the truce and the start of the peace conference in the autumn of 1921. It also resolved to recognize the 'Dáil, parish or district courts' on the same occasion.[44]

After much evasion, Pembroke eventually agreed to continue to send its audits to the local government board when requested by ultimatum to do so. The fine balance between the unionists and Sinn Féin on the Rathmines board is highlighted by their reaction to this measure – in this case bringing about a republican victory. When, in pursuance of its directive, the local government board sought from the Rathmines council an assurance that grants from the local taxation of Ireland account would be used for the purposes assigned by statute and that the council's accounts be submitted to the board's audit, Councillor MacDonagh moved that the letter be assigned to the waste paper basket and the local government board be informed of the council's action. The motion was carried on a show of hands six to five, owing to the absence of some unionist councillors.[45] Blackrock was giving recognition to the local government board as late as the close of 1921, previous correspondence from Dáil Éireann being ruled out of order. However, the council did protest strongly at the arrest of republican councillors at a meeting of the council in January 1921, expressing particular outrage at the fact that the arrests were made at a meeting to fill the various offices on the council.[46] To set this in context, by August 1921 only forty-one local bodies, outside the six northern counties, including twenty-six urban district councils and two town commissions still recognized the local government board.[47]

Violent incidents in the Anglo-Irish war shocked representatives of all shades of political opinion. The killing of two policemen, Assistant Commissioner W. C. Redmond at Harcourt Street, Dublin, and Constable Luke Finnegan at Thurles, in January 1920 was condemned by the Sinn Féin-controlled Kingstown council.[48] A number of Sinn Féin members of various councils were unable to attend council meeting regularly because they were in prison. As they had to resign, a standard £1 fee was imposed on them. This was not always collected, or it was greatly reduced, as in the case of Councillor Ó hUadhaigh in Kingstown, whose fine was cut to 1s.; 'his resignation being due to no whim of his, but to his imprisonment in Kilmainham, where his only outing is on a military lorry as a hostage.'[49] The ordinary business of the townships became difficult under war conditions especially when curfew was introduced. The Kingstown surveyor applied for permits for two water inspectors and three firemen to be about at night, although the republicans inserted an addendum that no such permits would be sought in future.[50]

Of particular concern was the attempt by the government to impose 'political tests' as a condition of employment in local authorities. Such tests sought declarations by prospective employees that they would be loyal to the government. When the republicans on the Rathmines board tried to raise this matter, they were ruled out of order. Those adhering to the republic tried to have recognition granted to its institutions in other ways; when the tramway company raised the matter of increasing fares they tried unsuccessfully to have the matter put before arbitration of Dáil Éireann.[51] Kingstown was strongly against such tests and was even willing to withdraw business from banks which victimised their employees in this way.[52]

For many years nationalists had sought to use local bodies for the airing of political grievances while unionists claimed that such forums were not the place for this type of discussion and that they should confine themselves to the business in hand. Anti-Treaty nationalists very promptly reverted to the position of their erstwhile unionist opponents when it suited them. This can be seen from the reaction of anti-Treaty members of Kingstown council to discussion on the Anglo-Irish agreement. When it was proposed by Councillors Devitt and O'Brien that the council endorse the action of George Gavan Duffy TD in signing the peace treaty and call on the Dáil to ratify it, Ó hUadhaigh proposed an unsuccessful amendment stating that 'since the establishment of our national leg-islature, namely Dáil Éireann, the function of local government bodies as a forum for the discussion of political questions, which was inevitable while the people had no other organs of expression, have ceased, and we therefore decline to express any opinion on the question of the arrangement with Great Britain now before the Dáil, which is exclusively one for the Teachtaí and the sovereign people of Ireland'.[53]

Elections were due to take place in January 1923 and their postponement by the department of local government led to some disquiet. It was nearly three years since elections had been held and some people were not impressed by the representatives that the troubled times had thrown up. A letter-writer to a local Rathmines newspaper stated:

> Owing to the political situation a number of makeshifts were elected three years ago, and it is now time to give some of these the 'push'. They have succeeded admirably in proving their incapacity for public life – especially some of the lady members. It is practical work that is wanted on public boards and not emotional and hysterical partisans – of either sex.[54]

During the civil war, councillors and public alike were shocked by the brutal killing as he served a customer in his shop in the centre of Rathmines of James Dwyer, president of the Sinn Féin Club in Rathmines and former councillor. The violence continued with attacks on the homes of many pro-Treaty sup-porters including those of Councillors Sears and Lombard Murphy, and on Sunday morning 29 April the premises of the assassinated James Dwyer and Lee's department store in the centre of Rathmines were blown up.[55]

The council voted in favour of a motion sent to them by the Cork Harbour Board calling on the Free State government to appoint three members of the Dáil to act in conjunction with the Seanad peace committee and meet three neu-tral Irishmen, acceptable to the forces in opposition to the government, to dis-cuss the best means to bring about a cessation of hostilities and establish peace on a firm basis.[56]

When a meeting to set up Cumann na nGaedheal was called in Rathmines in April 1923, two leading Rathmines council members took a prominent part; M.W. O'Reilly chaired the meeting and Liam Hayes acted as secretary.[57]

In conclusion, the Dublin townships showed unanimity in their support for the war effort at the outbreak of hostilities in 1914. Nuances are evident: in Rathmines emphasis is on recruitment for the army and in Pembroke for support of the Irish Volunteers. The war took a toll on the resources of the townships such as manpower, both at board and staff levels, and finances, resulting in a scaling down of capital-intensive projects like house-building. The war effort was supported by practical measures such as the digging for victory campaign.

While the international war impinged on the townships at a certain remove, the 1916 rising had a more immediate impact resulting in death and destruction and the disruption of council business especially in Pembroke and Kingstown. Politically the ground shifted, culminating in the victory on the national stage of Sinn Féin in 1918. At local level the new order was reflected in the election results of 1920. These elections proved to be less than decisive, however, and Rathmines and Pembroke were finely balanced. The election, did bring on to the councils a group of dynamic and talented individuals, especially women with a revolutionary background, who brought a radical flavour to council meetings.

CHAPTER EIGHT

In a free state, 1922–30

After almost three years of political turmoil and violence the Dublin townships found themselves in a new state. While the new state proved conservative in many aspects of public administration, it instigated sweeping changes in local government. Some of the most fundamental changes took place in the Dublin area.

It was generally felt that major measures to deal with the problems of Dublin needed to be taken by the new Free State government after it assumed power in 1922 and survived a civil war. The most pressing need was for re-construction of the inner city destroyed in that conflict and the 1916 rising. At the end of 1922 a greater Dublin reconstruction fund was set up and, although it was not envisaged that its area of operation would extend to Rathmines, the Rathmines council agreed to appoint representatives to confer informally with the body set up to administer it.[1] This was followed by the Dublin reconstruction (emergency provisions) act, 1924 (1924/24 [I.F.S.]). This act, together with an earlier act of 1916, the implementation of which was delayed because of the civil war, provided loan capital and gave the corporation a veto over the type of development which was to take place and power to acquire derelict sites.[2] The Rathmines council waited until 1928 before it requested that the 1924 act apply to the district, too late to have any effect.[3] The request was unlikely to succeed in any case as no structural damage had been suffered in Rathmines in the conflict.

The new department of local government and public health received the powers it needed to effect change at local level in the Local government act of 1925 (1925/5 [I.F.S.]). Despite a threat over its continued existence, Rathmines moved to amalgamate part of the rural district surrounding it as it became clear that the days of rural districts were numbered and the two rural council areas contiguous to the township, South Dublin rural district and Rathdown no. 1 rural district, faced abolition under the provisions of the 1924 act. An 'outer area' annexation motion, to include the rapidly growing areas of Rathfarnham, part of Harold's Cross, Terenure and Milltown was discussed by the council and a committee set up to consider the move. South Dublin Rural District Council asserted that it would prefer to be amalgamated with the city than be taken over by Rathmines.[4] With the building of houses in Kimmage the last large unbuilt area of the township was being used up and many felt that expansion was desirable – the creation of a 'greater Rathmines', as the local press called it; however, no further moves were made to expand Rathmines.[5]

With the approach of the local government elections in June 1925, the voters would have a chance for the first time since the heady days of 1920 to elect
new urban district councils. The run-up to the election was notable in
Rathmines for the establishment of the Rathmines and Rathgar Municipal
Progressive Association. It would appear that many shared the view that the
political activists who had come onto the board in 1920 were not suitable material for local representatives now that peace had arrived. At its inaugural meeting the association stated that its object was to put forward non-political
candidates in the coming election and 'to promote municipal welfare on business lines without introducing politics'.[6]

Candidates of the association, known as 'progressives' swept to power in the
election, taking fourteen of the twenty-one seats. Labour won four, with Sinn
Féin holding three; four of the pre-independence unionists were also returned.
The press hailed the victory of the non-political candidates in Rathmines and in
other townships. It was recorded that the 'ratepayers and business' candidates
were in the majority not only in Rathmines but in Pembroke, Blackrock, Dún
Laoghaire and Dalkey. The *South Dublin Chronicle* saw the result as a sign that
the electorate was 'sick of politics' and wished that such matters should be left
to Merrion Street (where the government offices were situated).

While they did not label themselves as such, and no numbers are available,
it appears that a majority of the 'progressives' were either members of, or sympathetic to Cumann na nGaedheal, the pro-treaty party. Some evidence of the
council's leanings can be seen in an unsuccessful attempt by republican (anti-
Treaty) councillors Lynn and Ffrench-Mullen to have a vacancy on the council in 1924 filled by Hanna Sheehy Skeffington; instead William (Liam) Hayes,
a member of Cumann na nGaedheal, was co-opted.[7]

The new Rathmines councillors included Sir Simon Maddock, secretary of
the Cemetery Company of Ireland, who was knighted in 1922 and a leading
member of the Progressive Association. Others included Marie Johnston and
William Norton of the Labour Party (Norton would later become a leader of
that party); and Countess Markievicz and Seán Lemass of Sinn Féin. Liam
Hayes, who had chaired the inaugural meeting of the progressive association,
was also a member of Cumann na nGaedheal. He was described in the election
results in the press as a 'progressive'. It would appear that those representing
the new establishment wished to eschew party labels as the old establishment,
the unionists, had done in the past. The reasoning behind such a tactic was
much the same – to disarm opposition from those opposed to such parties on
ideological or political grounds. Much wrangling between republicans and the
'progressives' became a feature of debate in the council chamber in these years.
A controversial section of the local government act, section 71, obliged those
seeking a post or a promotion in local authorities to take an oath of allegiance to
the new state. Seán Lemass moved a motion protesting against this section,

claiming that it 'introduces a political test interfering with the efficient administration and rights of public bodies to elect and promote officials strictly
according to merit and length of service, and in the interests of efficiency in the
public service we demand the abolition of such tests'. This was ruled out of
order and Lemass then proposed, and Countess Markievicz seconded, a motion
that standing orders be suspended, but this was defeated.[8]

The motion of Lemass had been ruled out of order under a long-standing
section of the standing orders ruling out discussion of political matters. In an
attempt to clarify matters Councillor Mrs Kettle proposed that the township
clerk be asked for a definition of 'politics'.[9] Her further motion that they send
a deputation to the minister for local government to urge on him that section
71 be rescinded was ruled out of order, and so were further attempts to raise
the matter.[10] In the following year, when the department of local government
informed the council that the clerk of works on the Church Place house-building scheme was obliged to subscribe to the declaration of allegiance under the
act, the council decided to seek legal advice to avoid further controversy.[11]

The republican and labour councillors made their influence felt in a number
of moves considered radical for Rathmines; feeling that the morning meetings of
the council only suited those with enough leisure or wealth to take time off to
attend, they called for evening meetings. A motion to this effect from Norton
and Lemass was carried, but the evening experiment did not appear to have been
successful, and morning meetings were resumed after five months.[12] Sinn Féin
representatives were particularly concerned that local labour should be used as
much as possible in all works in which the council was involved. When an agreement was made with the corporation for the supply of electricity, the engineer
was asked to consider the employment of Rathmines labour as much as possible for the laying of the cable from the sub-station to the Rathmines works.[13]

When house-building was resumed in 1923, it was proposed by Mrs Ceannt
and Dr Lynn that the contractor be empowered to employ outside labour only
when all available suitable local labour had been taken up, and that he was to
notify the council when it was necessary to bring in outsiders.[14] The council
was against having to use the labour exchange to enlist workers as there was no
local office of the exchange in Rathmines and so using the system would bring
in outsiders. A fair wages clause was demanded on all contracts signed with the
council from 1927 on.

The 1920s was a period of much unemployment and hardship for the less
well-off in Dublin, exacerbated by the general strike in Britain in 1926 which
cut off supplies of coal. Reports of great distress and even starvation were
reported in the suburbs.[15] Meetings of the Rathdown board of guardians and
the Pembroke council were besieged by the unemployed. The Pembroke inci-
dent had a political complexion. About fifty of the unemployed invaded the
council chamber in December 1926. They were mainly ex-army men who

clamed that the council was not abiding by the wishes of the government to give priority of employment to ex-soldiers. The council responded by stating that those with no army record were employed because they were starving.[16] In 1929 a meeting of Dún Laoghaire council was invaded by a group of the unemployed and the councillors held captive in the council chamber for over an hour, with one of the unemployed commandeering the chair.[17]

As the country grew less disturbed politically, the continued presence of the radical women and labour councillors such as William Norton on Rathmines council ensured that social welfare issues became prominent on the agenda in this distressing period. In the difficult year of 1926 Rathmines obtained a grant of £6,786 from the department of local government for road improvement. Councillors Kettle and Norton had a motion carried to the effect that, in view of the continuance of widespread unemployment amongst all sections in the district, a condition attached to the grant that preference had to be given to ex-national army men, should be withdrawn so as to enable the council to give priority to local unemployed men whether or not they had served in the army.[18]

With the onset of the winter of 1926–7, the plight of the unemployed in the district became acute, and a special meeting was called by Labour and Sinn Féin to deal with the fuel emergency. Countess Markievicz and Madeline Ffrench-Mullen suggested two shiploads of coal from America or elsewhere, and a supply of turf, be brought in for sale to the poor of Rathmines, and that the yard of the council be used as a depot. This was rejected, but it was agreed to send a deputation to the minister for industry and commerce and to the Dublin city commissioners to see if some of the supplies already available could be procured, and a public meeting was convened to consider the emergency.[19] With the approach of Christmas, the council appealed to the department of local government for a grant for public work to alleviate distress and promised to supplement any grant by an equal amount. A sum of £1,000 was obtained from the department and a scheme of road widening and cleaning of lanes, mainly in Upper Rathmines, was started on 13 December, just in time to be of benefit for Christmas.[20] This Christmas relief work was repeated in subsequent years.

A number of important changes regarding infrastructure and services came about in the last years of the councils. In Rathmines a dispute arose between the council and the tramway company. In 1926 there were twelve years to run before the council could take up their right to purchase the system from the company. Negotiations were entered into to extend this. The council proposed allowing the company a further thirty years provided it was paid wayleave fees of £50 per mile. This the company refused to do but settled for a scheme under which it would co-operate with the council in undertaking road improvements and keep its fares down on routes in the township.

Much more far-reaching was the loss of the electricity works by Rathmines and Pembroke, a move which had a seriously demoralising effect on both urban districts. With the establishment of the Electricity Supply Board in 1927 the state gained a monopoly in the production and supply of electricity. The small producers of electricity, such as the Rathmines and Pembroke townships, were to be acquired either by agreement or compulsory purchase. The council objected to the bill for the 'confiscation' of the electrical undertaking, and the fact that it was being rushed through the Oireachtas without time for amendments.[21] A public meeting was called, although Councillor Norton, who was in favour of public ownership, voted against holding it. Opposition was to no avail, and in 1929, when the ESB made its formal request for the handing over of the works, the council could only enter a protest at the property of the ratepayers being taken over. It made an appeal for the officials' jobs to be safeguarded and that the price of electricity to consumers be kept as low as possible.[22] The ESB investigated the possibility of buying steam power from the council's refuse destructor but decided not to do so.

Expected changes in the policy on local government under the new administration were first seen in 1923 when the poor law unions were swept out of existence. These unpopular institutions were regarded as symbols of an outdated morality that saw the poor as deserving meagre and begrudging support under harsh conditions. The Cumann na nGaedheal government's attitude was largely one of achieving economy and minimizing political dissent from troublesome local bodies. There was a trend towards centralization and a distinctly cavalier attitude was taken to local institutions. The Ministries and secretaries act of 1924 (1924/16 [I.F.S.]) had set up the new ministry of local government and public health. In 1925 rural districts outside County Dublin were abolished, as it was believed that they were uneconomic and not capable of fulfilling the task of providing the services, such as housing, required of them.[23] The Dublin bodies received a stay of execution as the whole structure of local government in the city and county came under review.

Section twelve of the Local government (temporary provisions) act 1923 empowered the minister for local government and public health to hold a local inquiry into the performances of any local authority, and, where satisfied that the duties of such local authority were not being effectively discharged, had power to dissolve the authority and transfer its property, powers and duties to any body or persons he thought fit.[24] By 1931 a total of thirty-one local bodies, including Dublin corporation, had been dissolved as a result of political dissent or financial difficulties. An inquiry into the administration of the affairs of Dublin corporation had been held and, as a result of the report of the inspector, the minister dissolved the corporation and transferred its powers to three commissioners, Séamus Murphy, Patrick J. Hernon and Dr William C. Joyce. It was intended that an elected body would be restored, however before that was done, it was considered opportune that the whole problem of the boundaries of Dublin should be re-opened and examined.[25]

Utterances from those in authority did not bode well for the future of the urban districts under the free state government and the annexation of those closest to the city became a probability rather than a possibility. The governor general and the president of the Dáil expressed their wish to see a capital 'appropriate' to a self-governing Ireland.[26] The corporation, not surprisingly, moved to capitalize on this mood and arranged a conference on extension to be held in the Mansion House in January 1924, inviting representatives from the urban and rural districts to attend. Reaction in Rathmines and Pembroke varied, with the former agreeing to send representatives and the latter refusing.[27] Blackrock, Dún Laoghaire and Dalkey jointly agreed to oppose the corporation's moves to take over any part of their area and, if pressed to a vote on such a matter, to leave the conference.

The worst fears of the townships were exceeded by the ambitious scheme drawn up in a bill by the corporation's law agent. This proposed extending the boundaries to include all urban districts in the county from Howth to Killiney, also taking in Bray, Co. Wicklow, and large tracts of the adjoining countryside. Ernest Blythe, the minister for local government and public health, informed the executive council that as Dublin was now the seat of government, its boundaries were 'no longer merely a matter for the corporation'. Charles O'Connor, a former local government board inspector, was commissioned to prepare a memorandum on the matter. O'Connor rejected the corporation's proposals and recommended a much reduced area, taking in Rathmines and Pembroke and some adjoining land. A rate in aid towards city expenses was proposed for a further area along the lines of the equalization of rates scheme imposed on Rathmines and Pembroke in 1900.[28]

In 1925, in response to these proposals, the government recommended the setting up of a commission, known as the Greater Dublin Enquiry, under the chairmanship of William Magennis, professor of metaphysics in University College Dublin. Other members included Alasdair MacCabe, Siobhán Bean an Phaoraigh, Patrick MacKenna, Ernest H. Alton, H.S. Guinness, J.T. Farrell, Oliver St John Gogarty, Alfred Byrne, Richard Corish, P.J. Egan and Richard H. Beamish. The inquiry was given the wide brief of examining how an efficient and economical local government structure could be drawn up for Dublin and its environs. The Rathmines council, having discussed the matter agreed to have its chairman give evidence to the inquiry in opposition to the corporation.[29] Blackrock and Dún Laoghaire, moving towards amalgamation themselves, made a joint submission to it. A wide variety of evidence was heard from witnesses from the urban and rural district councils, and representatives attended from the port and docks board, the Dublin Chamber of Commerce, the Dublin United Tramway Company, the Civic Survey, the Institute of Architects and other interested bodies.

The report, drawn up in 1926, recommended sweeping changes for Dublin. It proposed the incorporation of the contiguous urbanised areas with the city to form a greater Dublin. This would include the former Rathmines and Rathgar and Pembroke townships. The area would also include parts of the county outside the existing townships, defined as an area 'wherein the municipal and industrial welfare of the population was bound up with interests identical to, and indissolubly connected with the interests of Dublin City proper'.[30] It was regarded as an area which had become decidedly urban in character or would become urbanised in the immediate future. It pointed out that similar measures had been adopted in cities like London, Bristol and Birmingham, which had 'with notable advantage' assimilated their surrounding townships.

The government of this greater Dublin would be carried out by one elective central authority, a great council, headed by a city manager. The office of the lord mayor would be abolished. The great council would have two subordinate councils, the Dublin council and the coastal borough council. The report made some concessions to the larger townships in that it proposed that within the Dublin council representatives from Rathmines and Rathgar and Pembroke might function as an advisory committee in regard to certain services in their respective localities.

As it became clear to the coastal townships that amalgamation of some sort would be imposed, they made efforts to take matters into their own hands. A voluntary amalgamation of Kingstown, Blackrock, Dalkey, and, on occasions, Killiney, had often been proposed. The matter had been given serious consideration in 1903. The general picture now was that Dún Laoghaire was very much in favour of the move, not surprisingly, as it was the largest township and would be in a commanding position in an expanded area. Blackrock delayed making a decision, and was in favour of including a greater area than that comprising the established township, so that it would act as a balance to Dún Laoghaire. Dalkey was against the plan, as it felt that it would be swamped by its more powerful neighbours and Killiney was ignored by the other three, being regarded as too rural and underdeveloped. As the abolition of the smaller bodies by the government to form one large one became almost certain, Dún Laoghaire appealed for the postponement of the 1925 elections in Dalkey, Blackrock and Dún Laoghaire itself as it regarded the expense involved as a waste of money.[31]

In early 1924, as a response to moves by the corporation to enter into negotiations with them, the coastal townships held a conference on the question of amalgamation with each other. As it was clear that the inexorable trend was towards the amalgamation of smaller units it was felt that the best defence the coastal townships could offer was to unite voluntarily on their own terms. Three options were considered: firstly that of simply creating a united urban district having extended powers for public health and other services; secondly, establishing a borough with the right of electing a mayor and having other powers and privileges it thought advisable to obtain; or, finally, establishing a county borough with the full status of a city like Dublin or Limerick and other cities. It was felt that the latter option would be strenuously opposed by the county council as it would infringe on the finances of the area and fragment its administrative structure. Also, opposition would be expected from the gas, tramway and railway companies. The formation of a simple borough was considered the best option. The conference, attended by representatives from Dún Laoghaire, Dalkey and Blackrock, but not Killiney, recommended that a joint committee be established to formulate a scheme for amalgamation.[32] Dalkey, however demurred, fearing it would lose all identity in the enlarged district. It agreed, however, to join with the other townships to oppose the movement for a greater Dublin.

Over the course of many meetings attempts were made to prepare a bill consistent with the interests of Dún Laoghaire, Blackrock and Dalkey. Dún Laoghaire favoured a simple amalgamation of the existing townships, while Blackrock proposed an extended area to include Killiney, Foxrock, Newtown Park and Stillorgan. A deputation to the minister for local government was appointed. The minister, in his reply to the townships' representations, stated that the proposals could be carried out under the Borough funds act of 1880, but that he would only give his approval to the amalgamation provided it had ratepayers' support, and that all expenses incurred were met by the rates. However, he felt that it would not be proper for him to be for or against the proposal. The borough proposal had to have the support of the ratepayers. The South County Dublin Ratepayers' Association held a public meeting in favour of a borough made up of the coastal townships and part of the rural district of the barony of Rathdown, and set up a borough promotion committee.[33]

Negotiations over the details of amalgamation dragged on for some time. Eventually it was proposed that Dún Laoghaire be assigned three aldermen and eight councillors, Blackrock two aldermen and seven councillors and Dalkey one alderman and three councillors. This was regarded as being very favourable to Blackrock, taking into account its population and valuation. Two conditions were laid down by Dún Laoghaire. One was that Killiney and any rural district were not to be included and the other was that any profitable undertakings (electricity generation for example) would have their profits used only in their own district. The immediate advantages seen in the scheme were that administration would be less costly and there would be more to be spent on services. At a special meeting of Dún Laoghaire councillors held in April 1924, the proposed voluntary amalgamation of the three townships was carried by a large majority, with only two councillors voting against. It was decided that, with the agreement of the two other townships, a bill for the uniting of the three would be promoted in the next session of the oireachtas.[34] By June 1924, the three townships had largely agreed on these proposals and to promote a bill for amalgamation. However, a year and a half later, it was reported that the bill had been held up as the government wished to await the report of the Greater Dublin Commission.[35]

The government's proposals were that all four coastal townships were to be amalgamated and a borough created. At a conference of the four townships the borough proposal was accepted. However, the conference was not in favour of the proposed managerial system for the new authority, and if there was to be a manager, believed that powers should be sought for the new council to be able to remove, reinstate, and suspend the manager and officers constituting the executive, and of fixing their salaries. The conference also sought to increase the proposed eleven members of the borough council to fifteen. A deputation went to the minister for local government and public health to discuss these matters.[36]

From the time of the publication of the report of the Greater Dublin Commission, it was clear that the townships were doomed. Together with the taking over by the Electricity Supply Board of the power supplies the situation induced a kind of paralysis in the various council chambers, knowing their fate was sealed, and many schemes were delayed until the new structure revealed itself. The report made some concessions to the larger townships in that it proposed that within the Dublin council representatives from Rathmines and Rathgar and Pembroke might function as an advisory committee in regard to certain services in their respective localities.

The long-awaited Local government (Dublin) bill was published in 1929. The bill proposed the extension of the municipal boundaries and the amalgamation of the coastal townships entailing the abolition of the urban district councils of Rathmines and Rathgar, Pembroke, Blackrock, Dún Laoghaire, Dalkey and Killiney. This would also entail the dissolution of the joint hospital board of Rathmines and Pembroke, the joint drainage board of Rathmines and Pembroke and the joint drainage board of Dún Laoghaire and Blackrock.

A special meeting was held by the Rathmines council to consider the matter. As it turned out not much discussion took place. It appears that the matter was considered a foregone conclusion and any position the council might take on the issue would be irrelevant. Two motions were before the council in relation to the bill. The first one, proposed by Councillors John G. Gogan and John Healy, simply stated that the council approved of the principle embodied in the bill, that is, that the city boundary be extended to include Rathmines. This was withdrawn and a motion by Councillor Byrne and others was put forward. This favoured the proposals of the Greater Dublin Commission and instructed the council's solicitor to bring in amendments to bring the bill into closer conformity with the recommendations of that commission. This was also withdrawn and the motion which was eventually passed, by seven votes to five, stated that the council disapproved of the bill and called for its rejection. A committee was set up to protect the interests of the council.[37] A copy was sent to the area's Dáil representatives and the former Rathmines councillor, Seán Lemass, now a Fianna Fáil member of the Dáil.

The Local government (Dublin) bill came before the Dáil for its second reading in 1930, moved by General Richard Mulcahy, a resident of Rathmines. He informed the house that within the land and sea boundaries of County Dublin there were no fewer than twenty-five bodies dealing with local government matters. He went on to outline the history of the townships, especially Rathmines and Pembroke, and the numerous attempts by the corporation to annex them. He recounted how the Exham commission had recommended annexation to the city and a majority of three to one in the house of commons had voted likewise. He outlined the arguments for annexation put forward by the corporation over the years, based on the findings of the Exham commission. These included the contention that an artificial boundary divided the townships from the city, and that in effect the residents of the suburbs were citizens of the city. The existence of the townships was seen as a device by which wealthy businessmen avoided paying their fair share of local taxation, especially for services not provided by the townships such as a cattle market, abattoirs and health services. The city was hemmed in by a 'ring fence' and could not grow although the townships formed a continuous built-up area contiguous with the city. In England the fact that cities (or towns) and their suburbs were a continuous built-up area was a criterion for the extension of boundaries.[38]

Attempts by Rathmines to thwart or change the legislation were unavailing, despite the holding of a public meeting on the matter in the township in March 1930. Amendments in the Dáil were ruled out of order. An order was received from the department of local government informing the council that 14 October would be the appointed day for the termination of council business. The last meeting of the council was held on 8 October 1930. Having passed a vote of thanks to the council workers, the last action of the council was to sanction the outlay of £1,860 for the site of public baths at William's Park.

Less than two years previously the council had, rather belatedly, and perhaps in a attempt to protect its identity, applied for and was granted a coat of arms and flag by the chief herald of the free state. As early as 1916, nationalists in Kingstown had attempted to have its old coat of arms with its crown representing the British monarchy replaced by a new device on a green background.[39] The new Rathmines flag had been flown over the town hall as meetings of the council took place in the last few months of its existence. Mary Kettle commented that 'as they had been told that their days were numbered it would be as well if they went down with their flag flying'.[40] At the last meeting of the council Madeline Ffrench-Mullen requested that the council flag be placed in city hall.[41]

Summing up the post-independence era, with the establishment of the Irish Free State government, the wheels were set in motion that eventually saw the demise of the remaining Dublin townships. However, it was to take seven years before this was accomplished. The fate of the townships was tied to plans for

the complete re-organization of local government in the country and in particular the future of Dublin corporation.

With the re-emergence of a strong economy party in 1925, the Rathmines
council shows a certain continuity with the nineteenth century. It is possible
perhaps to see the disturbed years of 1920–5 as an interruption of normal business. This development came about as a reaction to arid party politics of a
strongly ideological nature seen as not suitable for the local scene; still, the ide-
ologues hung on, and their contribution to local politics is noteworthy for their
commitment to social change. Sinn Féin councillors, particularly the women,
with the help of labour councillors, pressed for measures in relation to the
unemployed and child welfare.

The morale of the council was gradually sapped however by the Damocles'
sword of amalgamation with the city hanging over it. Demoralization was further deepened, both in Rathmines and Pembroke, by the loss of local electricity undertakings. It is difficult to avoid the feeling that opposition to
amalgamation in the townships was less than vehement. When the extension of
boundaries came about, despite protests, the overall mood was that of bowing
to the inevitable.

Notes

INTRODUCTION

1   Mary Daly, *Dublin; the deposed capital* (Cork, 1984), p. 324.
2   J.H. Dyos & M. Wolff (eds), *The Victorian city; images and reality*, 2 vols (London, 1973); J.H. Dyos, *Victorian suburb: a study of Camberwell* (London, 1975).
3   F.M.L. Thompson (ed.), *The rise of suburbia* (Leicester, 1982).
4   H.B. Clarke, *Dublin c. 840 to c. 1540: the medieval town in the modern city* (Dublin, 1978).
5   Mary E. Daly, 'Irish urban history: a survey' in *Urban History Yearbook* 1986, pp 61–72.
6   Mary E. Daly, op. cit. (Cork 1984); J.V. O'Brien, *'Dear dirty Dublin'; a city in distress, 1899–1916* (Berkeley, 1982).
7   Anngret Simms & J.H. Andrews (eds), *Irish country towns* (Cork, 1994); Anngret Simms & J.H. Andrews (eds), *More Irish towns* (Cork, 1995); H.B. Clarke (ed.), *Irish cities* (Cork, 1995).
8   Tom Kennedy (ed.), *Victorian Dublin* (Dublin, 1980); Peter Pearson, *Dún Laoghaire / Kingstown* (Dublin, 1981) & *Between the mountains and the sea: Dún Laoghaire-Rathdown county* (Dublin, 1998); Mary E. Daly, Mona Hearn, Peter Pearson, *Dublin's Victorian houses* (Dublin, 1998).
9   Susan Roundtree, 'Mountpleasant Square', unpublished Master of urban and building construction thesis (NUI, UCD, 1991); Anne Lavin, 'Leinster Square (with Prince Arthur Terrace), Rathmines, Dublin: an early suburban speculative terraced housing development 1830–52', unpublished Master of urban and building conservation thesis (UCD, 1995).
10 Deirdre Kelly, *Four roads to Dublin, the history of Ranelagh, Rathmines & Leeson street* (Dublin, 1995); Pearson, Peter, *Dún Laoghaire/ Kingstown* (Dublin, 1981).
11 Ruth McManus, *Dublin: building the suburbs, 1910–1940* (Dublin, 2002).
12 K. Theodore Hoppen, *Ireland since 1800; conflict and conformity* (second edition, London & New York, 1999) p. 25.
13 Derek Fraser, *Urban politics in Victorian England* (Leicester, 1976), p. 9.
14 L.P. Curtis, Jr., *Coercion and conciliation in Ireland, 1880–92* (Princeton, 1963), p. 381.
15 For example, Dónal A. Murphy, *Blazing tar barrels and standing orders: North Tipperary's first county and district councils 1899–1902* (Nenagh, 1999); Brian Donnelly, *For the betterment of the people: a history of Wicklow County Council* (Wicklow, 1999); Gabriel O'Connor, *A history of Galway County Council, Stair Chomhairle Chontae na Gaillimhe* (Galway, 1999).
16 Jacinta Prunty, 'From city slums to city sprawl: Dublin from 1800 to the present' in Howard B. Clarke (ed.), *Irish cities* (Cork & Dublin, 1995).
17 R. Muir, *A history of Liverpool* (first published 1907, reprinted Wakefield, 1970), p. 337; quoted in Derek Fraser, *Power and authority in the Victorian city* (Oxford, 1979) pp 49–50.
18 Tom Garvin, *1922, the birth of Irish democracy* (Dublin, 1996); Arthur Mitchell, *Revolutionary*

government in Ireland: Dáil Éireann 1919–22 (Dublin, 1995); Russell Rees, *Ireland 1905–25: vol. 1, text and historiography* (Newtownards, 1998).

19 David Fitzpatrick, *Politics and Irish life 1913–22: provincial experience of war and revolution* (Dublin, 1977).

CHAPTER ONE: ESTABLISHING TOWNSHIPS

1 F.L.M. Thompson, 'The rise of suburbia', in R.J. Morris & Richard Rodger (eds), *The Victorian city, a reader in British urban history 1820–1914* (London, 1993), p. 150.

2 Donald J. Olson, *The growth of Victorian London* (2nd edition, London, 1979), p. 18.

3 Maurice Craig, *Dublin 1660–1860* (Dublin, 1969), p. 101.

4 Anon., *Gardiners' Dublin: a history and topography of Mountjoy Square and environs* (Dublin, 1991), pp 23–7.

5 L.M. Cullen, *Princes and pirates: the Dublin Chamber of Commerce 1783–1983* (Dublin, 1983).

6 L.M. Cullen, 'The growth of Dublin 1600–1900: character and heritage', in F.H.A. Aalen & Kevin Whelan (eds), *Dublin: from prehistory to present* (Dublin, 1992), pp 254–67.

7 Anne Lavin, 'Leinster Square (with Prince Arthur Terrace), Rathmines, Dublin: an early suburban speculative terraced housing development 1830–52', unpublished Master of urban and building conservation thesis (UCD, 1995), p. 2.

8 Jacqueline Hill, *From patriots to unionists* (Oxford, 1997), p. 197.

9 *Thom's directory* (Dublin, 1853), p. 961.

10 Ibid., pp 961; 989; 991–2; 1018.

11 Ibid., p. 973.

12 Ibid., pp 1006; 1012; 1013–4.

13 Ibid., p. 986.

14 Ibid., pp 971; 978–9.

15 *FJ*, 26 July 1900.

16 J.H. Martin, 'The social geography of mid-nineteenth century Dublin' in William J. Smyth & Kevin Whelan (eds), *Common ground: essays on the historical geography of Ireland presented to T. Jones Hughes* (Cork, 1988), p. 179.

17 Francis Elrington Ball, *A history of County Dublin; second part* (Dublin, 1903), p. 100; Deirdre Kelly, *Four roads to Dublin: the history of Ranelagh, Rathmines & Leeson street* (Dublin, 1995), pp 20–1.

18 Brian Donnelly, 'An overview of the development of local government in Ireland' in *Irish Archives*, iii, no. 2 new series (autumn, 1996).

19 Helen Burke, *The people and the poor law in nineteenth century Ireland* (Littlehampton, 1987), p. 63.

20 Geoffrey Best, *Mid-Victorian Britain, 1851–1875* (London, 1979) pp 53–57.

21 An act to make provision for the lighting, cleansing, and watching of cities, towns corporate, and market towns in Ireland, in certain cases 1828, 9 Geo. IV, c. 82.

22 Virginia Crossman, *Local government in nineteenth-century Ireland* (Belfast, 1994).

23 An act for paving, watching, lighting, regulating, and otherwise improving the town of Kingstown in the county of Dublin 1834, 4 & 5 William IV, c. 90.

24 For example, Gunson to Hall, lib. 3 p. 88, no. 691; Hammond to King, lib. 19, p. 455, no. 10557; Cormick to Woodcock, lib. 36, p. 26, no. 21025, Registry of Deeds, Dublin, Dublin register 1708–38.

25 *FJ*, 20 Feb. 1845.

26 *Inquiry into the collection of rates in the city of Dublin*, [C 2062], H.C & H.L, 1878, xxiii, evid. Frederick Stokes, para. 5264.

27 *Report of royal commission appointed to inquire into the boundaries and municipal areas of certain cities and towns in Ireland*, pt. 1, H.C.1881 (2725) xxx, evid. Evans para. 2518 (hereafter *R.C. municipal boundaries* 1).

28 David Dickson, 'Second city syndrome: reflections on three Irish cases' in S.J. Connolly (ed.), *Kingdoms united? Great Britain and Ireland since 1500: integration and diversity* (Dublin, 1999).

29 Hill, *Patriots*, pp 209–10.

30 Ibid., pp 283–4.

31 Jacqueline R. Hill, 'The role of Dublin in the Irish national movement, 1840–48', unpublished PhD thesis (University of Leeds, 1973), p. 171.

32 Ibid., p. 194.

33 Derek Fraser 'Urban elites in Victorian Britain' in *Urban History Yearbook*, 1985, p. 3.

34 Inscription on Stokes family tomb, Mount Jerome Cemetery, Dublin.

35 *Thom's directory* (Dublin, 1847), p. 582.

36 Helen Burke, *The Royal Hospital Donnybrook, a heritage of caring 1745–1993* (Dublin, 1993), pp 93; 107;148.

37 Letter of Frederick Jackson to chief secretary, N.A.I., Chief Secretary's Office Registered Papers (hereafter CSORP), 1848 A 11623.

38 *Royal commission to inquire into municipal corporations (Ireland)*, pt. 1 1835 (23) xxvii, p. 260.

39 *FJ*, 20 Feb. 1845.

40 Ibid.

41 Crossman, *Local government*, pp 66–7.

42 *SN*, 27 Jan. 1847.

43 Ibid., 14 Feb. 1847.

44 Ibid.

45 Ibid.

46 *R.C. municipal boundaries* 1, para. 2386.

47 Minutes of the commissioners of the Rathmines township, 7 Nov. 1855, DCA, UDC/1/Min 1/2.

48 Ibid.

49 *RC municipal boundaries* 1, Stokes, para. 7575.

50 Ibid., para. 7477

51 Crossman, *Local government*, p. 72.

52 Best, *Mid-Victorian Britain*, pp 57–9.

53 Mary Daly, *Dublin: the deposed capital* (Cork, 1984), pp 162–3.

54 An act to make better provision for the paving, lighting, draining, cleansing, supplying with water, and regulation of towns in Ireland 1854, 17 & 18 Vict. c. 103.

55 *Thom's directory* (Dublin, 1913), p. 768.

56 An act for transferring from the grand jury of the county of Dublin to the Commissioners of Kingstown the management of the roads and bridges in the said town, and for better improving the same 1861, 24 & 25 Vict., c. 118.

57 Daly, *Dublin*, p. 199.

58 Rathmines mins., 14 Nov. 1849, DCA, UDC/1/Min 1/1 (no page numbers were available for consultation for the first two volumes of the Rathmines township minutes, UDC/1/Min 1/1 [1847–53] and UDC/1/Min 1/2 [1853–61]).

59   *R.C. Municipal boundaries* 1, evid. Vernon para. 4762.

60   *IB*, 1 July 1860.

61   Ibid., 1 Oct. 1863.

62   An act for the improvement of the township and district of Dalkey in the barony of Rathdown and county of Dublin 1867, 30 & 31 Vict. c. 134.

63   *FJ*, 17 Oct. 1870.

64   *DB*, 15 Mar. 1864.

65   *Thom's directory* (Dublin, 1867), p. 1561.

66   *FJ*, 17 Oct. 1870.

67   Colum Kenny, *Kilmainham; the history of a settlement older than Dublin* (Dublin, 1995), p.7.

68   *IB*, 1 June 1867.

69   Ibid.

70   *RC municipal boundaries* 1, evid. Alexander McDonnell, paras. 6130–31.

71   An act for the improvement of Kilmainham in the barony of Upper Cross and county of Dublin 1868, 31 & 32 Vict. c. 110.

72   *RC municipal boundaries* 1, para. 5966.

73   Daly, *Dublin*, p. 166.

74   *FJ*, 4 Oct. 1893; Stephen Johnson, *Johnson's atlas and gazetteer of the railways of Ireland* (Leicester, 1997), p. 96.

75   *DB*, I Aug. 1862.

76   *RC municipal boundaries* 1, evid. Vernon para. 6251.

77   Dublin corporation mins., 6 Feb.1865, C2/A1/25, pp 424–6. DCA, Sth. William St, Dublin.

78   *RC municipal boundaries* 1, evidence George Tickell, para. 6409.

79   Ibid., evid. Vernon, para. 6252.

80   Ibid., evid. Vernon, para. 5413.

81   An act for the formation and improvement of Clontarf township, comprising the districts of Clontarf, Dollymount and Ballybough in the barony of Coolock and county of Dublin 32 & 33 Vict., c. 85, 1869.

82   Daly, *Dublin*, pp 168–9.

83   An act for the formation and improvement of Drumcondra, Clonliffe and Glasnevin, in the barony of Coolock and county of Dublin; and for other purposes 1878, 41 & 42 Vict. c. 157.

84   *RC municipal boundaries* 1, Evid. Michael Petit, p. 280.

85   Dublin corporation mins., 17 Aug. 1863, DCA, C2/A1/23, p. 450.

86   *RC municipal boundaries*, 4, evid. Samuel Black, Belfast evid., para. 121.

87   Ibid., evid. 125.

CHAPTER TWO: TOWNSHIP ADMINISTRATION

1   Rathmines minutes, 8 Dec. 1847, DCA, UDC/1/Min 1/1.

2   Ibid.

3   *RC municipal boundaries* 1, evid. Edward Fottrell, paras. 4035 and 4036.

4   Daly *Dublin*, p. 228.

5   *RC municipal boundaries* 1, evid. Mark Bentley, para. 4162.

6   *FJ*, 13 Nov. 1847.

7   Jacqueline Hill, *From patriots to unionists: Dublin civic politics and Irish protestant patriotism, 1660–1840* (Oxford, 1997), p. 382.

8   Ibid., p. 197.

9   Patrick Fagan, 'The population of Dublin in the 18th century with particular reference to the proportions of protestants and catholics', *Eighteenth-century Ireland*, vi (1991), p. 149.

10 Ibid., p. 147.

11 W.E. Vaughan and A.J. Fitzpatrick (eds), *Irish historical statistics: population, 1821–1971* (Dublin, 1978), pp 51–62.

12 *General report, census of Ireland 1891* (Dublin, 1892), p. 461.

13 Mona Hearn, *Below stairs: domestic service remembered in Dublin and beyond, 1880–1922.* (Dublin, 1993), pp 6–8.

14 Rathmines mins., 30 Jun. 1849, DCA, UDC/1/Min 1/1.

15 Daly, *Dublin*, pp 199–200.

16 *RC municipal boundaries* 1, evid. R.J. Ennis clerk of Kingstown, given at Kingstown, paras. 1–14.

17 *Report of the select committee local government and taxation of cities and towns in Ireland*, H.C. 1878 (262) xvi, paras. 2895–2898.

18 *RC municipal boundaries* 1, evid. of Michael Murphy, para. 3216.

19 Ibid., para. 4150.

20 Ibid., para. 4150.

21 Ibid., evid. Mark Bentley paras. 4258–4292.

22 *FJ*, 23 Oct. 1869.

23 An illuminated address to Frederick Stokes, 1876, NLI, MS 7994.

24 Helen Burke, *The Royal Hospital Donnybrook: a heritage of caring, 1745–1993* (Dublin, 1993), p. 121.

25 Ibid., p. 115.

26 *RNDL*, 25 Jun. 1898.

27 *DB*, 15 Oct. 1862.

28 *RC municipal boundaries* 1, evid. John M'Evoy at Kingstown, para. 191.

29 Rathmines mins., 25 Oct. 1848, DCA, UDC/1/Min 1.

30 Ibid., 25 Oct. 1848,

31 Ibid., 26 July 1848.

32 Cormac Ó Gráda. *Black forty-seven and beyond* (Princeton, 1999), p. 44.

33 Rathmines mins., 28 Feb. 1849, DCA, UDC/1/Min 1/1.

34 Ibid., 12 Mar. 1851.

35 Ibid., 18 Feb. 1852.

36 Ibid. 31 Jan. 1855

37 *SC local government and taxation in Ireland*, evid. Stokes, para. 3113.

38 Ibid.

39 Rathmines mins. 5 July 1871, DCA, UDC/1/Min 1/4, p. 154.

40 An act to amend and define the borrowing powers of the Rathmines and Rathgar improvement commissioners to enable the commissioners to borrow an additional sum of money and for other purposes: local and personal acts 1892, 55–56 Vict. c. 18.

41 Daly, *Dublin*, pp 161–2.

42 Pembroke mins., 1 Feb. 1892, DCA, UDC/1/Min 2/5, pp 252–3.

43 Ibid., 10 Oct. 1892, pp 302–3, 7 Nov. 1892, pp 309–10: 14 Nov. 1892, pp 312–14.

44 Ibid., 17 Feb. 1902, DCA, UDC/1/Min 2/8, p. 330.

45 Ibid., 27 Mar. 1902, p 342.

46 Ibid., 27 Mar. 1902, p. 342.
47 Ibid., 5 May 1902, pp 355–6.
48 Blackrock mins., 2 Mar. 1893, DLRA, LA/1/8, p. 60.
49 *Dublin Gazette* , 30 Nov. 1849.
50 Rathmines mins. 14 Nov. 1849, DCA, UDC/1/Min 1/1.
51 *The Warder*, 16 Nov. 1850.
52 Ibid., 30 Nov. 1850.
53 Rathmines mins., 20 Dec. 1850, DCA, UDC/1/Min 1/1.
54 Ibid., 5 & 19 May and 2 Jun. 1850.
55 Ibid., 9 Nov. 1853, 7 Dec. 1853 and 21 Dec. 1853, DCA, UDC/1/Min 1/2.
56 Ibid., 4 Jan. 1854.
57 Ibid., 21 Nov. 1861, DCA, UDC/1/Min 1/3 p. 40.
58 Ibid., 18 Jun. 1862, UDC/1/Min 1/3, p. 76.
59 *RC municipal boundaries* 1, evid. John Evans, paras. 2423–2431.
60 An act for extending the Rathmines and Rathgar township so as to include therein the town-
    lands of Cherry Orchard in the parish of St. Nicholas, of Argos, Harold's Cross, Mount
    Jerome, Rathland East, Rathland West, in the parish of St. Catherine in the barony of Upper
    Cross and county of Dublin 1866, 29 & 30 Vict. c. 12.
61 Daly, *Dublin*, p. 206.
62 *IT*, 23 Jan. 1850.
63 *RC municipal boundaries* 1, evidence Thomas Mills, para. 6007.
64 Ibid. paras. 6012–6016.
65 *SC local government and taxation in Ireland*, 1876 (352) x, paras. 2940–2942.
66 Ibid., para. 2942.
67 Rathmines mins., 6 and 20 July and 3 Aug. 1853, DCA, UDC/1/Min 1/2.
68 *RC municipal boundaries* 1, evid. Neville, para. 471.
69 Rathmines mins., 9 Jan. 1861, DCA, UDC/1/Min 1/2.
70 Ibid., 20 Feb. 1861, DCA, UDC/1/Min 1/2.
71 *RC municipal boundaries* 1, evid. John Beveridge, para. 413.
72 *Thom's directory 1872*, p. 1363.
73 Rathmines mins., 1 May 1861, DCA, UDC/1/Min 1/3, p. 1.
74 Ibid., 19 Feb. 1868, DCA, UDC/1/Min 1/3, p. 449.
75 Ibid., 25 Nov. 1857, DCA, UDC/1/Min 1/2.
76 Lyons, *Ireland since the famine* (London, 1971), p. 79; *Thom's directory* (Dublin, 1913), p. 766.
77 Rathmins mins., 15 July 1891, DCA, UDC/1/Min 1/6 p. 352.
78 Ibid., 26 Mar. 1888, DCA, UDC/1/Min 1/6, p. 164.
79 Ibid., p. 165.
80 *Report of the select committee local government and taxation of cities and towns in Ireland*, H.C.
    1878 (352) x, para. 2904.
81 Rathmines mins., 4 Jan. 1888, DCA, UDC/1/Min 1/6, pp 148–9.
82 Ibid., 4 Apr. 1894, DCA, UDC/1/Min 1/7, p. 85 & 2 May 1894, DCA, UDC/1/Min 1/7,
    p. 89.
83 Ibid., 1 Jan. 1896, DCA, UDC/1/Min 1/7, p. 210.
84 Ibid., 5 Jan. 1887, DCA, UDC/1/Min 1/6, p. 83.
85 Ibid., 2 Oct. 1889, p. 246.
86 *RNDL*, 4 Jan. 1896.
87 Ibid.
88 *IB*, 1 Jan. 1896.

89 *RNDL*, 11 Jan. & 7 Mar. 1896.

90 Ibid., 2 & 16 May 1896.

91 Rathmines mins., 15 July 1891, DCA, UDC/1/Min 1/6, p. 352.

92 *RNDL*, 16 May 1896.

93 Rathmines mins., 4 May 1898, DCA, UDC/1/Min 1/7, p. 351.

94 Pembroke mins., 11 Dec. 1916, DCA, UDC/1/Min 2/14, p. 185.

95 *IT*, 25 Mar. 1920.

96 Ibid., 4 Sept. 1912.

97 Rathmines mins. 1 Oct. 1913, DCA, UDC/1/Min 1/7a, pp 400–1.

98 Ibid., p. 401.

99 Ibid., 15 July 1918, DCA, UDC/1/Min 1/9, p. 77.

100 Ibid., 27 May 1921, p. 256.

CHAPTER THREE: HEALTH AND WHOLESOME WATER

1 Rathmines new road committee mins., 7 Oct. 1851, DCA, book 840/C005 (no page number).

2 *SDC*, 13 Oct. 1928.

3 *Irish Builder*, 15 Jun. 1865.

4 *RC municipal boundaries* 1, evid. of Michael Murphy, paras. 3198–3211.

5 Ibid., paras. 3165.

6 Ibid., evid. Mark Bentley and John Evans, paras. 4178–97.

7 Ibid., evid. John Evans para. 2672.

8 Ibid., evid. Evans, paras. 2546–2555.

9 Ibid., evid. Evans, paras. 2556–2558.

10 Joseph V. O'Brien, *Dear dirty Dublin: a city in distress, 1899–1916* (Berkeley & Los Angeles, 1982).

11 *RC municipal boundaries* 1, evid. J.P. Byrne, Dublin councillor, para. 1401.

12 Ibid., evid. Henry Brett, county surveyor of Wicklow, paras. 6460–64.

13 *RFP*, 29 Sep. 1923.

14 Rathmines mins., 8 Mar. 1848, UDC/1/Min 1.

15 Ibid., 23 Aug. 1848.

16 *IT*, 11 Feb. 1850.

17 Rathmines mins., 29 Jan. 1851, UDC/1/Min 1.

18 Ibid., 26 Mar. 1851.

19 *Report of royal commission to inquire into boundaries and municipal areas of cities and towns in Ireland, pt. 2, report: Dublin, Rathmines, Pembroke, Kilmainham, Drumcondra, Clontarf, Kingstown, Blackrock and Dalkey* (Exham commission) H.C., 1881 (2827), l, p.10 (hereafter *RC municipal boundaries* 2).

20 An act to consolidate and amend the acts relating to public health in Ireland, 41 & 42 Vict., c. 52.

21 Ibid., clause 107.

22 Ibid.

23 *Bye-laws made by the urban sanitary authority of the urban sanitary distirct consisting of the Rathmines and Rathgar township in pursuance of the public health (Ireland) act 1878* (Dublin, 1881).

24 Mins. Rathmines public health committee, 26 July 1886, 843 C005.

25 Ibid., 21 Feb. 1887.

26 Rathmines mins., 5 Jan. 1887, UDC/1/Min 1/6, pp 81–2; *Regulations made by the Rathmines and Rathgar commissioners ... under the contagious diseases act 1878 ... and the dairies, cow sheds and milk shops (Ireland) order of August 1878 and the dairies, cow sheds and milk shops (Ireland) order of July 1886* (Dublin, n. d. (1887).

27 Ibid., 23 Aug. 1893, UDC/1/Min 1/7, p. 28.

28 Ibid., 1 Nov. 1893, p. 47.

29 Ibid., 6 Dec. 1893, p. 57.

30 Ibid.

31 Ibid., 4 Oct. 1893, p. 40.

32 Ibid., 3 April 1895, p. 150.

33 *Minutes & reports of the Kingstown commissioners*, 1893, p. 62 (these printed volumes found in NLI have been utilised to obtain material from the reports, not available anywhere else, references to the minutes are to the manuscript volumes in DLRCCA).

34 Ibid.

35 Ibid., 1893, pp 80–2.

36 *Minutes & reports of Kingstown commissioners: report of consulting sanitary officer and medical officer of health*, Feb. 1890, pp 18–20.

37 Rathmines mins., 20 Aug. 1856, UDC/1/Min 1/2.

38 Ibid., 21 Mar. 1860.

39 Ibid., mins. 5 Dec. 1860.

40 Ibid., 1 July 1861, UDC/1/Min 1/3, pp 13–4.

41 Ibid.

42 *RC municipal boundaries* 1, evid. John Evans., para 2443.

43 Rathmines mins., 21 Nov. 1861, UDC/1/Min 1/3, p. 40.

44 Ibid., 23 July 1862, UDC/1/Min 1/3, p. 82 and 6 Aug. 1862, UDC/1/Min 1/3, p. 84.

45 Ibid., 24 Jan. 1866, UDC/1/Min 1/3, p. 317.

46 *RC municipal boundaries* 1, evid. Evans para. 2446.

47 Ibid., para. 6757.

48 Rathmines mins., 17 July 1872, UDC/1/Min 4, p. 205.

49 *RC municipal boundaries* 1, evid. Henry Johnston, paras. 3635–3636.

50 Rathmines water committee mins., 4 Nov. 1873, book 842/C005.

51 *Dublin corporation mins.*, 1882, pp 399–400.

52 Blackrock mins., 27 Dec. 1882, LA/1/4 p. 432.

53 Ibid., 20 Dec. 1882, LA/1/4/ p. 430

54 Richard W. Walsh, 'On wind power and the high level water supply to Dalkey', in *Transactions of the Institution of Civil Engineers of Ireland*, xix (1889), pp 1–19.

55 *Kingstown reports and mins.* 1894, pp 85–6

56 Ibid., 1894 p. 197.

57 Rathmines mins., 6 Nov. 1872, UDC/1/Min 4, p. 220.

58 *FJ*, 10 Nov. 1872.

59 Ibid.

60 Rathmines mins., 4 Dec. 1872, UDC/1/Min 1/4.

61 Ibid., 13 Oct. 1875.

62 Ibid., 24 Oct. 1876, UDC/1/Min 1/4, p. 423.

63 *IB*, 1 Jan. 1877.

64 *RC municipal boundaries* 1, evid. Launcelot Studdert, para. 4490.

65 Ibid., para. 4417.

66 Ibid., para. 4490.

67 Rathmines mins., 14 Mar. 1877, UDC/1/Min 1/4, p. 447.

68 *R.C. municipal boundaries* 1, evid. Mark Bentley, paras. 4110 and 4150.

69 Rathmines mins., 2 April 1877, UDC/1/4, p. 451.

70 Dublin corporation mins. 19 Jun. 1882, pp 221–2.

71 Christopher Moriarty, *Down the Dodder* (Dublin, 1991), p. 44.

72 Rathmines mins., 2 Nov. 1887, UDC/1/Min 1/6, p. 131 & 30 Nov. 1887, UDC/1/Min
    1/6, p. 138.

73 Rathmines mins., 7 Mar. 1888, UDC/1/Min 1/6, p. 161.

74 *RFP*, 22 Sept. 1923.

75 *Kingstown mins & reports* 1896, p.51.

76 *IB*, 15 Mar., 1864.

77 *Report of the royal commissioners appointed to enquire into the sewerage and drainage of the city
    of Dublin, 1880*, H.C. 1880 (18), xxx, mins. of evid. of Thomas Nedley, consulting med. offi-
    cer to Drumcondra. paras. 3097–3103.

78 *RC municipal boundaries* 1, evid. W. Faussett, para. 3657.

79 Rathmines mins., 3 Feb. 1858, UDC/1Min 2.

80 Ibid., 23 Feb. 1871, UDC/1/Min 1/4, pp 132–3.

81 Memorial of citizens of Dublin to lord lieutenant, 1875, NAI, CSORP, 1875, 17121.

82 *The Times*, 20 Mar. 1855, quoted in Stephen Halliday, *The great stink of London: Sir Joseph
    Bazalgatte and the cleansing of the Victorian metropolis* (Stroud, 1999), p. 58.

83 Ibid., pp 62–3.

84 Ibid., pp 164–80

85 Letter of town clerk of Dublin to chief secretary, NAI, CSORP, 1875, 17121.

86 *FJ* ,29 May, 1900.

87 *Kingstown mins & reports*, Feb. 1890, pp 35–37.

88 *IB*, 1 May 1894.

89 Blackrock mins., 8 Jun. 1898, LA/1/10 p. 200.

90 Charles J. O'Sullivan, *The gasmakers; historical perspectives on the Irish gas industry* (Dublin,
    1987).

91 Rathmines mins., 22 May 1848 & 21 May 1851, UDC/1/Min 1.

92 Ibid., 7 Nov. 1854, UDC/1/Min 2.

93 *RC municipal boundaries* 1, evid. Beveridge, para. 432.

94 Petition of Kingstown commissioners against the bill to vest in the Dublin corporation the
    undertaking of the Alliance & Dublin Comsumers' Gas Company, 1873, MS 5201 (NLI).

95 *DB*, 1 Mar. 1864

96 *RC municipal boundaries* 1, evid. Beveridge paras. 307–8.

97 Ibid., evid. Evans, para. 2662.

98 Ibid., evid. Evans. para. 2636–48

99 Ibid., evid. J.R. Ingram paras. 907–15.

100 An act for extending the Rathmines and Rathgar township, so as to include therein the
    adjoining townland of Milltown, in the county of Dublin; for the establishment of a fire
    brigade; and for other purposes 1880, 43 & 44 Vict., c. 108.

101 Mins. Rathmines public health committee, 31 Dec. 1883, Rathmines committee minute book
    843/C005, no page number.

102 Ibid., 22 Nov. 1886.

103 W.N. Hancock, 'Arrangements for putting out fires in Dublin city and the townships of Drumcondra, Clontarf, Kilmainham, Pembroke, Rathmines, Blackrock and Kingstown' in *Journal of Statistical & Social Inquiry Society of Ireland*, viii (Aug. 1882), pp 381–5.

104 *RC municipal boundaries* 1, evid. R. J. Ennis at Kingstown para. 41.

105 *FJ*, 23 Jun. 1900

106 Ibid.

107 *Coall's Kingstown guide* (Kingstown, 1905), p. 9.

108 Blackrock mins.,16 Aug. 1911, LA/1/16 p. 196.

109 Dalkey mins, 14 May, 1904, LA/2/4 p. 358.

110 Trevor Whitehead, *Dublin firefighters* (Dublin, 1970), p. 37.

111 J.A. Hassan, 'The growth and impact of the British water industry in the nineteenth century' in *Economic History Review* , xxxviii (1995), p. 543.

CHAPTER FOUR: THE ROYAL COMMISSION ON BOUNDARIES

1 *RC municipal boundaries*, 1, evid., D.C Heron Q.C. paras 1–5.

2 V.D. Lipman, *Local government areas 1835–1945* (Oxford, 1949), pp 66–7.

3 *RC municipal boundaries* 1, evid., John Beveridge, paras. 71–2.

4 Ibid., evid. Frederick Stokes, para. 2862.

5 Daly, *Dublin*, p.230.

6 *RC Municipal boundaries* 2, p. 2.

7 *Report of the commissioners on local government and taxation of cities and towns in Ireland* (special report by W.P. O'Brien), H.C 1878 xxiii, c. 1965, p. 61.

8 Dublin port and docks bridge act 1876 , 39 & 40 Vict. cap. 85, section 18.

9 *RC municipal boundaries* 2, evid. John Beveridge, para. 344.

10 Ibid., evid. Joseph T. Pim paras. 1041–1045

11 Ibid., evid. John Beveridge, para. 382

12 Ibid., Parke Neville, evid. para. 530

13 Ibid., evid. Beveridge para. 433.

14 Ibid., evid. Parke Neville, para. 549.

15 Ibid., evid. Dr Charles Cameron, para. 843.

16 Ibid., evid. J.P. Byrne, para. 1419.

17 Ibid., evid. Charles Dawson, para. 1499.

18 Ibid., evid. J.P. Byrne, paras. 1343–1344.

19 Ibid., evid. Joseph Todhunter Pim, para. 1018.

20 Ibid., evid. Pim, paras. 1020–1022.

21 Ibid., evid. Stephen N. Elrington, paras. 4317–4318.

22 Ibid., evid. Pim, paras. 1204–1206

23 Ibid., evid. Mark Bentley, paras. 4043–4060.

24 Ibid., evid. Bentley, para. 4079.

25 Ibid., evid. John Saunders, paras. 7560–7561.

26 Ibid., evid. Bentley, para. 4152.

27 Ibid., evid. Bentley, para 4153.

28 Ibid., evid. Bentley, para. 4162.

29 Ibid., para. 4221.

30 Ibid., evid. John Evans, paras. 2792–2795.

31 Ibid., para. 2802.

32 Ibid., evid. Bentley, para. 4136.

33 Ibid., evid. Samuel S. Bolton, para. 2929.

34 Ibid., evid. Evans, paras. 2595–2598.

35 Ibid., evid. Bolton, paras 3172–3190.

36 Ibid., para. 2358.

37 Ibid., evid. Frederick Stokes, paras. 2924–5.

38 Ibid.

39 Ibid., evid. Stokes, para. 6606.

40 Ibid., para. 6612.

41 Ibid., evid. John E. Vernon, para. 6256.

42 Ibid., evid. Vernon, para. 6273.

43 Ibid., evid. B. N. Hynes, para. 5413.

44 Ibid., evid. Vernon, para. 6276.

45 Ibid., evid. Michael Pettit, para. 5242.

46 Blackrock mins., 2 Sept. 1879, DLRCCA, LA/1/4 p. 195.

47 Shorthand writer's report of interview beween representatives of the Pembroke and Rathmines townships and the lord lieutenant re. proposed extension of the municipal boundaries of Dublin, 13 Dec. 1883 (NAI, Pembroke estate papers, 1011/4/42, pp 6–7.

48 *RC municipal boundaries*, 3, report pp ix–x 1881 vol 50.

49 Ibid.

50 Ibid., 4, Belfast evid. Samuel Black, para. 121.

51 Ibid., 2, pp 39–40.

52 Ibid., p.10.

53 Ibid., p. 22.

54 Ibid.

55 Ibid., p. 11

56 V.D. Lipman, *Local government bodies 1834–1945* (Oxford, 1949), pp 66–7.

57 Blackrock mins., 5 Oct. 1881 LA/1/4, p. 336 & 19 Oct. 1881 LA/1/4 p. 342.

58 Shorthand writer's report of interview between township representatives and the lord lieutenant re. proposed extension of the municipal boundaries of Dublin, 13 Dec. 1883 (NAI, Pembroke estate papers, 1011/4/42, pp 6–7).

59 *RC municipal boundaries* 2, evid. John Vernon, para. 4859.

60 Dublin corporation mins., DCA, 21 Jan. 1884, pp 20–1.

61 Daly, *Dublin*, p. 232.

62 Ibid.

63 Ibid., p. 233.

64 Daly, *Dublin* p. 233; Dublin corporation mins. 28 Jun. 1886, pp 160–2.

65 Dublin corporation mins., 27 Oct 1887, p. 274.

66 Charles Dawson, *Greater Dublin; extension of municipal boundaries*, paper read to the Statistical and social inquiry society of Ireland, 1 Feb. 1899 (Dublin, 1899).

67 Dublin corporation mins., 3 Jan. 1898, p. 31.

68 Kingstown mins., 7 Mar. 1898, LA/4/12 p. 377.

69 *Irish Daily Independent*, 14 Apr. 1898.

70 *Hansard parl. debates, 4th. series,* vxi, 6–15 July, 1898, pp 1127–30.

71 Ibid.

CHAPTER FIVE: FROM TOWNSHIP TO URBAN DISTRICT COUNCIL

1   Mins. of joint meeting between Rathmines & Pembroke, 25 Mar. 1892, DCA, UDC/1/Min
    1/6, p. 404.
2   Crossman, *Local government*, p. 93.
3   Dónal A. Murphy, *Blazing tar barrels and standing orders: north Tipperary's first county and dis-
    trict councils 1899–1902* (Nenagh, 1999), p. 66.
4   Blackrock mins., 6 Sept. 1893, DLRA, LA/1/8 p. 143.
5   *RNDL*, 6 Aug., 1898.
6   Rathmines mins., 17 May 1899, DCA, UDC/1/Min 1/7, p. 406.
7   *IT*, 17 Jan. 1902.
8   Ibid.
9   *RNDL*, 9 July, 1904.
10 Ibid., 24 Sept. 1904.
11 Ibid., 22 Oct. 1904.
12 *RNDL*, 25 Jan. 1905.
13 Ibid.
14 Rathmines & Rathgar improvement bill, 1885, 48–49 Vict., c. 151.
15 *RNDL*, 28 May, 1904.
16 Ibid.
17 Ibid.
18 Ibid.
19 *Thom's directory* (Dublin, 1904), p. 1764.
20 *RNDL*, 28 May 1904.
21 Ibid.
22 Ibid.
23 Ibid., 14 Jan., 1904.
24 *IT*, 18 Jan. 1905.
25 *RNDL*, 28 Jan. 1905.
26 Rathmines mins., 12 Nov. 1913, DCA, UDC/1/7a, p. 409.
27 Ibid., 27 Feb. 1917, p. 567.
28 Ibid., 23 Jan. 1914, p. 420.
29 Ibid., 6 May 1914, p. 440.
30 *IB*, 17 Jan. 1908.
31 Ibid.
32 *IT*, 17 Jan. 1911.
33 *IT*, 17 Jan. 1914.
34 Pembroke mins., 14 July 1913, UDC/2/Min. 9, p. 437.
35 Ibid., 11 Aug. 1913, pp 476–7.
36 Ibid., 17 Nov. 1913, DCA, UDC/2/13, p. 33.
37 Pembroke mins., 1 Dec. 1913, p. 41.
38 Blackrock mins., 20 Mar. 1900, DLRA, LA/1/11 pp 74–5.
39 Kingstown mins., 15 Jun. 1914, DLRA, LA/4/18 pp 30–1 & 31 July, 1914, DLRA,
    LA/4/18 pp 44–5.
40 Daly, *Dublin*, p. 235.
41 Dublin corporation reports 1899, vol. 3, pp 211–217.
42 Rathmines mins., 1 Feb. 1899, DCA, UDC/1/Min 1/7 p. 394 & 26 June 1899,
    UDC/1/Min 1/7, p. 412.

43   *IT*, 14 Jun. 1899.
44   *Dublin corporation reports* 1899, vol. 3, pp 214–15.
45   *FJ*, 24 May 1900.
46   Rathmines mins., 16 Nov. 1899, DCA, UDC/1/Min 1/7 p. 431.
47   *FJ*, 29 Jun. 1900
48   *FJ*, 24 May 1900.
49   Anon, *Boundaries or bankruptcy* (n.d. *c.*1900, Dublin), p. 5.
50   Ibid., pp 6–7.
51   Ibid., p. 9.
52   *Boundaries or bankruptcy*, op. cit., pp 10–11.
53   *FJ*, 24 May 1900.
54   Ibid., 24 May 1900.
55   Ibid., 23 Jun. 1900.
56   Ibid., 24 May 1900.
57   Ibid., 24 May 1900.
58   Ibid., 23 June 1900.
59   An act to extend the city of Dublin and for other purposes 63 & 64 Vict. c. 264.
60   DCA, *Dublin corporation reports etc.*, 1900, vol. 3, pp 179–80.
61   Joseph V. O'Brien, *'Dear Dirty Dublin'* (Berkeley), 1982, p. 76.
62   Ibid., p. 96.
63   Rathmines mins., 7 Feb. 1917, DCA, UDC/1/Min1/7a, p. 564 & 7 Mar. 1917, UDC/1/Min 1/7a, p. 571.
64   Ibid., 1 Nov. 1905, pp 133–4.
65   *Dublin Gazette*, 28 Nov. 1879, p. 998.
66   *RNDL*, 20 May 1905.
67   Ibid., 20 May 1905.
68   H.A. Gilligan, *A history of the port of Dublin* (Dublin, second impression, 1989) p. 139; J.W. De Courcy, *The Liffey in Dublin* (Dublin, 1996), p. 128.
69   *RNDL*, 20 May 1905.
70   Pembroke mins., 8 Feb. 1905, DCA, UDC/1/Min 2/9, p. 195.

CHAPTER SIX: CULTIVATING THE CIVIC ARTS

1   Rathmines mins., 9 Aug. 1848, DCA, UDC/1/Min 1/1.
2   J.R. Kellett, *The impact of railways on Victorian cities* (London, 1969).
3   Blackrock mins., 10 May 1865, LA/1/1 p. 142.
4   F.L.M. Thompson, 'The rise of suburbia' in R.J. Morris & Richard Rodger, *The Victorian city: a reader in British urban history, 1820–1914* (London, 1993), p. 156.
5   Rathmines mins., 4 Jan. 1871, UDC/1/Min 1/4, pp 126–7.
6   James Kilroy, *Irish trams* (Omagh, 1996), pp 18–19.
7   Rathmines roads' committee mins, 30 Sept. 1886, book 844/COO5.
8   *Surveyor's report, Kingstown reports and mins.*, 1893, pp 9–11.
9   *Kingstown reports and mins.*, 1893, pp 49–50.
10   Kilroy, op. cit., p. 83.
11   *RNDL*, 4 Jan. 1896.
12   Ibid., 28 Nov. 1896.

13 Ibid., 12 Dec. 1896.

14 An act to empower the Rathmines and Rathgar Improvement Commissioners to purchase and work certain tramways of the Dublin United Tramway Co. and to confer further powers on the commissioners with respect to street widenings, the acquisition of lands, the borrowing of monies and other purposes, 1897, 60 & 61 Vict. c. 114.

15 Pemb. mins., 2 Dec. 1895, UDC/1/Min 2/6, p. 205.

16 Ibid., 13 Nov. 1896, pp 375–6.

17 Ibid., 14 Dec. 1896, UDC/1/Min 2/6, pp 397–8.

18 Fraser, op. cit., p. 92.

19 Quoted in J.B Lyons, *St Michael's Hospital, Dún Laoghaire, 1876–1976* (Dalkey, no date), pp 3–4.

20 Murray Fraser, *John Bull's other homes: state housing and British policy in Ireland, 1883–1922* (Liverpool, 1996), p. 69.

21 Mary Daly, *Dublin: the deposed capital* (Dublin, 1984), p. 281.

22 Ibid., p. 290.

23 Ibid., p. 297.

24 Ibid., p. 72.

25 *RC municipal boundaries* 1, evid. John Evans, paras. 2734 and 2742–44.

26 Pembroke mins. 22 Dec. 1920, UDC/1/Min 2/16, p. 138.

27 Fraser, *John Bull*, pp 79–80.

28 *Dublin Chronicle*, 24 Dec. 1927.

29 Ibid.

30 Ibid.

31 *Kingstown reports and mins.*, 1896. p. 49.

32 Ibid., pp 107 & 109.

33 *IT*, Apr. 1903.

34 Kingstown mins. 16 Mar. 1904, LA/4/14 pp 265–6 and 7 Apr. 1904, LA/4/14 p. 269.

35 Ibid., 15 Mar. 1907, LA/4/16 p. 360.

36 Rathmines mins., 3 Aug. 1887, UDC/1/Min 1/6, p. 117.

37 Ibid., 2 July 1890, p.29.

38 Ibid., 4 Dec. 1889, UDC/1/Min 1/6, pp 258–9 & 1 Apr. 1891, UDC/1/Min 1/6. p. 332.

39 Rathmines mins., 4 Apr. 1894, UDC/1/Min 1/7, p. 83.

40 *RNDL*, 10 Oct. 1896.

41 Rathmines mins., 7 Aug. 1895, UDC/1/Min 1/7, p. 175.

42 Ibid., 2 Dec. 1903, UDC/1/Min 1/7a, p. 70.

43 Jacinta Prunty, *Dublin slums, 1800–1925: a study in urban geography (Dublin, 1998)*, pp 140–1; 284.

44 Ibid., 4 July 1900, UDC/1/Min 1/7, p. 459.

45 Ibid., 2 Dec. 1903, UDC/1/Min 1/7a, p. 70.

46 *RFP*, 17 Mar. 1923.

47 Rathmines mins., 5 Feb. 1930, UDC/1/Min 1/10, p. 206.

48 Rathmines correspondence; letter from William J. Shannon to Seacome Mason, sec., Rathmines council, 24 Jan. 1921, UDC 1/C/385.

49 Ibid., 16 Mar. 1922.

50 Fraser, *John Bull*, p. 280.

51 Rathmines mins., 9 Sept. 1925, UDC/1/Min 1/9, pp 487–8.

52 Ibid., 4 Jan. 1928, UDC/1/Min 1/10, p. 75.

53 Pembroke. mins., 9 May 1927, UDC/2/18, p. 328.

54   Ibid., 16 Apr. 1928, p. 507.

55   Ibid., 14 Jan. 1924, UDC/1//Min 1/17, p.215

56   Ibid., 14 Apr. 1924, p. 216.

57   *IB*, 15 July, 1867.

58   Ibid.

59   John H. Dockrell, 'Blackrock: town hall and baths – some reflections' in *Blackrock Society: proceedings, 1993–4* (Blackrock, 1994). pp 18–33.

60   Legalisation of waterworks act 1893, 56 Vict. c. 22.

61   *RNDL*, 22 Feb. 1896.

62   Ibid., 2 Mar. 1896.

63   *IB*, 15 Oct., 1897.

64   *RNDL*, 20 Nov. 1897.

65   Ibid.

66   *Clontarf's Eye*, no. 7, Apr. 1991, pp 4–8.

67   *DB*, 15 July 1872.

68   Maurice Manning & Moore McDowell, *Electricity supply in Ireland: the history of the ESB* (Dublin, 1985), p.1.

69   Ibid., p. 7.

70   E. Manville, 'Report on the proposed establishment of a municipal electricity generating station in Kingstown', *Kingstown reports and mins.*, 1896, pp 4–10.

71   Rathmines mins., 7 Jun. 1890, UDC/1/Min 1/6, p. 288.

72   Ibid., 2 July 1890, UDC/1/Min 1/6, p. 291 & 6 Mar. 1895, UDC/1/Min 1/7, p. 144.

73   Ibid., Oct. 28 1895, UDC/1/Min 1/7, p. 188.

74   P. Harkin, 'Electricity supply in Dublin, 1880–1930', unpublished paper in ESB library, Dublin, p. 7.

75   Rathmines mins. 5 Sept. 1900, UDC/1/Min 1/7, p. 465.

76   Ibid., 5 Jun. 1901, UDC/1/Min 1/7, p. 493.

77   *Equalisation of rates enquiry*, 1911, table 11, p 452.

78   Rathmines mins., 31 Mar. 1922, UDC/1/Min 1/9 p. 316

79   *Dublin corporation reports*, 1893, vol. ii, pp 647–667.

80   Report of Joseph Berry, surveyor, *Kingstown report & mins*, 1895, pp 4–14.

81   Rathmines mins, 2 Mar. 1904, UDC/1/Min 1/7a, p. 79.

82   H. Norman Leask, 'The destruction of towns' refuse and some of the principles involved in the construction of refuse destructors', in *Transactions of the institution of civil engineers of Ireland*, xxx (1904), pp 63–92.

83   *Equalisation of rates inquiry*, evidence of Pilditch, para. 415.

84   *DB*, 15 Nov. 1862.

85   *IB*, 15 Jun. 1870.

86   Blackrock mins., 2 Aug. 1871, LA/1/2, pp 309–10.

87   Pembroke mins., 27 July 1896, DCA, UDC/1/Min 2/6, p. 319.

88   Ibid., 20 Aug. 1900. UDC/1/Min 2/8, p. 99.

89   Ibid., 9 Dec. 1907, UDC/1/Min 2/10, p. 190.

90   Dalkey mins., 17 July 1895, LA/2/3, p. 527.

91   Legalisation of waterworks act, 1893, 56 Vict. c. 22.

92   Kieran R. Byrne, 'Approaches to technical education in nineteenth century Ireland' in *Technical education: essays dedicated to Michael Clune* (no place, no date, c.1987), pp 17–9.

93   F.S.L. Lyons, *Ireland since the famine* (London, 1971), pp 74–5.

94   Rathmines mins., 1 Jan. 1902, UDC/1/Min 1/7, p. 511.

95 F.S.L. Lyons, *Ireland since the famine* (London, 1971), p. 213.

96 *RNDL*, 16 Sept. 1905.

97 Ibid., 9 Sept. 1905.

98 Charles H. Oldham, *Memorandum of reasons for including modern Irish in the curriculum of the Rathmines school of commerce* (Dublin, 1905).

99 Margaret Ward, *Hanna Sheehy Skeffington, a life* (Cork, 1997), pp 101–3.

100 Rathmines mins., 6 Feb. 1902, UDC/1/Min 1/7, p. 480.

101 Kingstown mins., 29 Jan. 1894, LA/4/11, p. 448.

102 *Kingstown reports and mins.*, 1895, pp 351–2.

103 Ibid., 1899, report of J. Byrne Power, pp 6–7.

104 Ibid.

105 Ibid. pp 56–57.

106 Rathmines mins., 6 Mar. 1907, UDC/1/Min 1/7a, p. 180.

107 W.N. Osborough, *Law and the emergence of modern Dublin* (Dublin, 1996), pp 67–8.

108 Rathmines mins., 7 Jun. 1911, UDC/1/Min 7a, p. 102.

109 *RNDL*, 9 Apr. 1904.

110 Mary Castelyn, *A history of literacy and libraries in Ireland – the long traced pedegree* (Aldershot, 1984); Felicity Devlin, 'Brightening the countryside – the library service in rural Ireland, 1902–35', PhD thesis (NUI, Maynooth, 1990).

111 O'Brien, *Dear dirty Dublin*, pp 57–8.

112 Quoted in *RFP*, 18 Nov. 1922.

113 Legalisation of waterworks act, 1893, 56 & 57 Vict. c. 22.

114 Rathmines mins., 5 July 1911, UDC/1/7a, p. 323.

115 Brendan Grimes, *The Irish Carnegie libraries; a catalogue and architectural history* (Dublin, 1998), pp 96–9.

116 Rathmines mins., 8 Oct. 1913, UDC/1/7a, p. 403.

117 *Irish Independent*, 9 Oct. 1930.

118 *RFP*, 28 Apr. 1923.

119 *RNDL*, 5 Nov. 1904.

120 Ibid., 28 Jan. 1905.

121 Grimes, op. cit., p. 126.

122 Ibid., pp 177–9.

123 Ibid., pp 216–17.

124 Ibid., p. 23.

125 Norman Atkinson, *Irish education; a history of educational institutions* (Dublin, 1969), pp 102–3. Donald H. Akenson, *The Irish education experiment; the national system of education in the nineteenth century* (London, 1970), pp 344–5.

126 *Kingstown reports & mins.*, 1897, pp 40–1.

127 Ibid., 1901 p. 42.

128 Pembroke mins., 9 Mar. 1925, UDC/1/Min 2/17, pp 432–3.

129 Rathmines mins., 7 Nov. 1923, UDC/1/Min 1/9, pp 397–8.

130 Ibid., 3 Dec. 1924, pp 447–8.

131 Ibid., 7 Jan. 1925, pp 447–8.

132 Ibid., 10 June 1895, pp 452–3.

133 Kingstown mins., 6 July 1905, LA/4/15 p. 37.

134 Ibid., 17 Feb. 1908, LA/4/16, pp 22–3.

135 Ibid., 14 Jan. 1907, LA/4/15 p. 310.

136 *RNDL*, 16 Sept. 1905.

137 *Kingstown reports & mins.*, 1899, p. 110.

138 Rathmines mins., 18 Aug. 1908, UDC/1/Min 1/7a, p. 227.

139 Ibid., 5 Jun. 1912, pp 354–5 & 4 Feb. 1914, p. 423.

140 Ibid., 7 Mar. 1923, UDC/1/Min 1/9 p. 361.

141 Hassan, J.A., 'The growth and impact of the British water industry in the nineteenth century' in *Economic History Review* xxxviii, 1995, p. 537.

CHAPTER SEVEN: IN TIME OF INTERNATIONAL AND DOMESTIC WAR

1 Fitzpatrick, David, *Politics and Irish life, 1913–21: provincial experience of war and revolution* (Dublin, 1977), p. 189.

2 Rathmines mins., 2 Sept. 1914, DCA, UDC/1/Min 1/7a, p. 452.

3 Ibid., 4 Nov. 1914, DCA, UDC/1/Min 1/7a, p. 458.

4 Ibid., 20 Aug. 1918, DCA, UDC/1/Min 1/9, p. 85.

5 *IT*, 17 Jan. 1914.

6 Rathmines mins., 2 July 1919, DCA, UDC/1/Min 1/9, p. 128.

7 Ibid., 2, 18 & 23 Jun. 1915, DCA, UDC/1/Min 1/7a, pp 498, 500, 501.

8 Ibid., 5 Jun. 1918, DCA, UDC/1/Min 1/9, p. 71.

9 Ibid., 2 Dec. 1914, DCA, UDC/1Min 1/7a, p. 468.

10 Ibid., 18 Mar. 1915, DCA, UDC/1/Min 1/7a, p. 448.

11 Ibid., 3 Jan. 1917, p. 555.

12 Ibid., 29 Jan. 1917, p. 560.

13 Pembroke mins., 10 Aug. 1914, DCA, UDC/1/Min 2/13, p. 216.

14 Report of J.C. Manly to Pembroke UDC on 1916 Rising in the Pembroke district, DCA, UDC/1/ Min 2/14, p. 80.

15 Kingstown mins., 28 Apr. 1916, LA/4/18, p. 291.

16 Rathmines mins., 7 June 1916, DCA, UDC/1/Min 1/7a, p. 536.

17 Ibid., 1 Nov. 1916, p. 547.

18 Kingstown mins., 1 June 1916. LA/4/18, p. 300.

19 Pembroke mins., 29 May 1916, DCA, UDC/1/Min 2/14, pp 83–4.

20 Rathmines mins., 2 May 1917, DCA, UDC/1/Min 1/9, p. 8; Pembroke mins., 17 Nov. 1916, DCA, UDC/1/Min 2/14, p. 173.

21 Blackrock mins., 3 May 1916, LA/1/18, p. 268.

22 Rathmines mins.; letter from local government board 6 Jun., 1917, DCA, UDC//1/Min 1/9, p. 13.

23 Ibid., 6 June 1917, pp 13–4.

24 Pembroke mins., 7 Mar. 1919, DCA, UDC/1/Min 2/14, p. 212.

25 Rathmines mins., 6 Aug. 1919, DCA, UDC/1/Min 1/9, p. 132.

26 D. Macardle, *The Irish republic* (4th ed., Dublin 1951), pp 325–6.

27 Rathmines mins., 1 Oct. 1919, DCA, UDC/1/Min 1/9, p. 137.

28 Kingstown mins., 13 Oct. 1919, LA/4/19, 326.

29 Macardle, *Irish republic*, p. 326.

30 *To the electors of Blackrock*, Blackrock republican election committee, NLI, ILB, 300, p. 11 (item 44).

31 *IT*, 6 Jan. 1920.

32 Ibid.

33   Mary E. Daly, *The buffer state: the historical roots of the department of the environment* (Dublin, 1997), p. 50.

34   Rathmines mins., 30 Jan. 1920, DCA, UDC/1/Min 1/9, p. 151.

35   *RFP*, 30 Dec., 1922.

36   Hazel P. Smyth, 'Kathleen Lynn, M.D., F.R.C.S.I. (1874–1955)', *Dublin Historical Record*, xxx, no. 2, Mar. 1977.

37   Rathmines mins. 10 June 1920, DCA, UDC/1/Min 1/9, pp 181–4.

38   Ibid., 31 Jan. 1921, pp 225–6.

39   Kingstown mins., 11 Aug. 1902, LA/4/13 p. 428.

40   Kingstown mins., 6 July 1920, LA4/19 pp 467–8.

41   Ibid., 3 May, 1921, LA/4/20, pp 108–10; Pádraig O'Farrell, *Who's who in the Irish war of independence and civil war* (Dublin, 1997), pp 70–71.

42   Arthur Mitchell, *Revolutionary government in Ireland: Dáil Éireann, 1919–22* (Dublin, 1995), p. 158.

43   Tom Garvin, *1922, the birth of Irish democracy* (Dublin, 1996), p. 68.

44   Kingstown mins., 1 Nov. 1921, LA4/20 pp 177–8.

45   Rathmines mins., 1 Sept., 1920, DCA, UDC/1/Min 1/9, p. 200.

46   Blackrock mins., 31 Jan. 1921, LA/1/20, p. 48.

47   David Fitzpatrick, *Politics and Irish life, 1913–1921* (Dublin, 1977), note 31, p. 332.

48   Kingstown mins., 30 Jan. 1920 LA/4/19, p. 367.

49   Ibid., 1 Feb. 1921, LA/4/20, pp 70–1.

50   Ibid., 19 Mar. 1920, LA/4/19, p. 409.

51   Rathmines mins., 14 Sept. 1920, DCA, UDC/1/Min 1/9, p. 205.

52   Kingstown mins., 7 Sept. 1920, LA/4/20 pp 14–15.

53   Kingstown mins., 3 Jan. 1922, LA/4/20, pp 205–6.

54   *RFP*, 11 Nov. 1922.

55   Ibid., 5 May 1923.

56   Rathmines mins. 3 Jan. 1923, DCA, UDC/1/Min 1/p. 335.

57   *RFP*, 28 Apr. 1923.

CHAPTER EIGHT: IN A FREE STATE

1   Rathmines mins., 6 Dec. 1922, DCA, UDC/1/Min 1/9, p. 352.

2   Daly, *The buffer state*, pp 110–11

3   Rathmines mins., 4 July 1928, DCA, UDC/1/Min 1/10, p. 109.

4   *RFP*, 5 Jan. 1924.

5   Ibid., 4 Nov. 1923.

6   *SDC,* 23 May 1925.

7   Rathmines mins., 19 Nov. 1924, DCA, UDC/1/Min 1/9, p. 446.

8   Ibid., 2 Sept. 1925, p. 485.

9   Ibid., 4 Nov. 1925, p. 494.

10   Ibid., 2 Dec. 1925, p. 500.

11   Ibid., 3 Nov. 1926, pp 564–5.

12   Ibid., 7 Oct. 1925, p. 492 & 5 May 1926, p. 534.

13   Ibid., 5 July 1922, p. 329.

14   Ibid., 7 Feb. 1923, p. 360.

15 *SDC*, 10 July 1926.

16 Ibid., 18 Dec. 1926.

17 Ibid., 22 June 1929.

18 Rathmines mins., 20 July 1926, DCA, UDC/1/Min 1/9, p. 547.

19 Ibid., 26 Oct. 1926, p. 559.

20 Ibid., 8 Dec. 1926, p. 573.

21 Rathmines mins., UDC/1/Min 1/10, 24 Mar. 1927, p. 17.

22 Ibid., 22 Mar. 1929, p. 154.

23 Daly, *The buffer state*, p. 119.

24 *Report of the department of local government and public health, 1930–31*, p. 13.

25 Ibid., p. 14.

26 *RFP*, 16 June 1923.

27 Rathmines mins., 2 Jan. 1924, DCA, UDC/1/Min 1/9, p. 406.

28 Daly, *The buffer state*, pp 123–4.

29 Rathmines mins., 4 Feb. 1925, DCA, UDC/1/Min 1/9, p. 456.

30 Report of commission of inquiry (on greater Dublin), R. 32 [IFS], p. 3.

31 Dún Laoghaire mins., 7 Apr. 1925, DLRA, LA/4/21 pp 149–50.

32 Ibid., 15 Jan. 1924, DLRA, LA/4/20 p 447.

33 Blackrock mins., 6 Feb. 1924, DLRA, LA/1/21 pp 121–2.

34 Dún Laoghaire mins., 1 Apr. 1924, DLRA, LA/4/21 pp 4–5.

35 *SDC*, 2 Jan. 1926.

36 *Dublin Chronicle*, 16 Nov. 1929.

37 Rathmines mins., 16 Feb. 1930, DCA, UDC/1/Min 1/10, pp 209–10.

38 Dáil Éireann parliamentary debates, official report 1930, xxxiii, 12 Feb.–21 Mar., pp 930–1.

39 Kingstown mins. 2 Nov. 1916, DLRA, LA/4/18 pp 370–1.

40 *SDC*, 13 Oct. 1928.

41 Rathmines mins., 8 Oct. 1930, DCA, UDC/1/Min 1/10, p. 257.

Commissioners (later councillors) of Rathmines & Rathgar township, 1847–1930*

Adam, James	1906–15	Collis, Robert G.	1856–71
Adye-Curran, John	1901–5	Connor, John	1847–55;
Aitken, William	1872–82		1858–62
Anderson, J.C.	1902–20	Courtenay, Henry	1909–14
Asken, Francis	1860–66	Curtis, Thomas	1892
Askin, Paul	1879; 1888	Daly, George	1920–25
Bailey, W.G.	1914–20	Danford, William	1881
Ball, Edward	1883	Darcy, Patrick B.	1866.
Barry, Henry	1925	Darley, Joseph F.	1867–68
Beater, George P.	1902–20	Dixon, M.K.	1920–25
Beckett, James	1884–90	Dobson, James	1886–89
Benson, Robert	1913–25	Dolan, Terence T.	1847–50;
Bentley, Mark C.	1868–73;		1852–60
	1874–6	Drake, James	1862–65
Bewley, Samuel	1881–85	Drummond, David	1863
Bolton, R.D.	1900–20	Drury, John G.	1883–88
Bolton, Samuel H.	1871	Drury, Thomas	1850–66
Booth, Robert	1894–5;	Dunnill, Thomas	1862–70
	1901–13	Eason, Charles	1876
Boyd, Richard	1882–94	Edmondson, Thomas	1895
Boyd, Samuel P.	1905–14	Ellis, James	1893–99
Brown, Hugh	1861–6	Evans, John H.	1847–74
Browne, Robert	1883–98	Fotterell, Edward	1874–98
Butler, Frederick A.	1886	Ffrench-Mullen,	
Butler, John	1847–55;	Madeleine	1920–27
	1863–76	Fry, John	1862–67
Caldwell, William	1925	Galavan, Edward	1847–57
Carey, William	1875–1900	Gogan, John G.	1927
Carruthers, William W.	1901–20	Greening, Richard S.	1888–1900
Ceannt, Frances	1920–25	Gill, Andrew	1847–55;
Chetwood Crawley, W.J.	1890–93		1857–62
Cockburn, Gilbert	1881	Godley, John	1886–89

* Source: Minutes of Rathmines & Rathgar Township, Dublin City Archives and *Thom's directory*.

Sibthorpe, Thomas S.	1883–90	Thacker, J.W.	1893–4
Slator, John	1912–30	Todd, Henry W.	1862–3
Slator, Samuel	1919–20	Todd, William	1847–55
Smalley, J.J.	1925–7	Tulloch, Jessie M.	1925
Smith, Joseph	1907–20	Turner, David	1915
Smith, Trevor	1895	Wall, Christopher E.	1847–55
Smyth, John A.	1907–20	Ward, Montgomery A.	1873–93
Smyth, P.J.	1899	Ward-Brown, Vere	1889
Spence, William	1904–6	Warren, Samuel	1855–56
Standing, William	1907–14	Watson, G.E.H.	1902–6
Stephens, William R.	1866	Webb, W.F.	1902–5
Stokes, Ambrose W.	1867–72	Whewell, Arthur	1925
Stokes, Frederick	1847–77	Whitney, F.S.	1897
Stringer, John A.	1918–20	Wight, William	1864–73
Sykes, George	1862	Wright, Edward	1853–6
Tallon, Thomas E.	1863–8	Young, Richard	1873–4

Bibliography

PRIMARY SOURCES

I. MANUSCRIPT RECORDS OF DUBLIN CORPORATION & TOWNSHIPS

Dublin City Archives, Pearse St Dublin
Records of Dublin Corporation, corporation minutes 1840–1880, 31 vols., C2/A1/11–41.
Records of Rathmines and Rathgar Commissioners, council minutes 1847–1930, 10 vols., UDC/1/Mins 1/1–10.
Records of Pembroke Commissioners 1863–1930, council minutes 19 vols., UDC/1/Mins 2/1–19.

Dún Laoghaire–Rathdown Archives, County Headquarters, Dún Laoghaire
Archives of the Blackrock Township/Urban District Council, council minutes 1 Sept. 1863–25 August 1933. 24 vols., LA/1/1–24.
Archives of Dalkey Township/Urban District Council, council minutes 17 Aug. 1863–13 Oct. 1930, 7 vols., LA/2/1–7.
Archives of Killiney & Ballybrack Township/Urban District Council, council minutes 4 July 1876–8 Oct. 1930, 8 vols., LA/3/1–8.
Archives of Kingstown/Dún Laoghaire Township/Urban District Council, council mins. 2 Sept. 1834–7 Oct. 1930, 22 vols., LA/4/1–22.

National Archives, Dublin
Pembroke estate papers, accessions 1011, 2011, 97/46.
Persons entitled to vote in Dublin, Rathmines, Rathgar, 1896, MS 1203.
Documents relating to Bohernabreena waterworks, MS 1225–38.

National Library of Ireland
Album presented to Frederick Stokes, 1878, MS 7994
Petition of the commissioners of Kingstown against the Dublin corporation gas bill 1873, MS 5201.

Registry of Deeds, Dublin
Dublin lands register 1708–38, entries relating to Rathmines.

Genealogical Office, Dublin
Heraldic crest & flag granted to Rathmines & Rathgar urban district council 1929.

II. PRINTED RECORDS OF DUBLIN CORPORATION & TOWNSHIPS

Dublin City Archives
Dublin corporation minutes 1881–1930, 50 vols.
Dublin corporation reports etc. 1869–1930, 154 vols.

Regulations made by the Rathmines and Rathgar commissioners ... under the contagious diseases act 1878 ... and the dairies, cow sheds and milk shops (Ireland) order of August 1878 and the dairies, cow sheds and milk shops (Ireland) order of July 1886 (Dublin, n.d. (1887).
Equalisation of rates enquiry, 1911.

National Library of Ireland
Kingstown (later Dún Laoghaire) township reports, minutes, etc. 1888–1930.

III. SELECTED PARLIAMENTARY RECORDS BILLS & ACTS

Public acts
An act to make provision for the lighting, cleansing, and watching of cities, towns corporate, and market towns in Ireland, in certain cases 1828, 9 Geo. IV, c. 82.
Towns' improvement clauses' act 1847, 10 & 11 Vict. c. 34.
An act to make better provision for the paving, lighting, draining, cleansing, supplying with water, and regulation of towns in Ireland 1854, 17 & 18 Vict. c. 103.
An act to afford facilities for the establishment and maintenance of public parks in towns in Ireland 1869, 32 & 33 Vict. c. 28.
An act to consolidate and amend the acts relating to public health in Ireland 1878, 41 & 42 Vict., c. 52.
Electric lighting act 1882, 45 & 46 Vict. c. 56.
An act to amend the law relating to dwellings of the working classes 1885 48 & 49 Vict. c. 72.
Legalisation of waterworks act 1893, 56 Vict. c. 22.
Local government (Dublin) act 1930 [I.F.S. 27/30].
Private acts
An act for paving, watching, lighting, regulating, and otherwise improving the town of Kingstown in the county of Dublin 1834, 4 & 5 William IV, c. 90.
An act for better paving, cleansing, draining, regulating, lighting and improving the district of Rathmines, Mount Pleasant, Ranelagh, Cullenswood, Milltown, Rathgar and Haroldscross and such other portions of the parish of Saint Peter within the barony of Uppercross in the county of Dublin, and for otherwise promoting the health and convience of the inhabitants 1847, 10 & 11 Vict., c. 253.
An act for transferring from the grand jury of the county of Dublin to the commissioners of Kingstown the management of the roads and bridges in the said town, and for better improving the same 1861, 24 & 25 Vict., c. 118.
An act for extending the improvement of the district of Rathmines so as to include therein Rathgar and Sallymount, all in the county of Dublin 1862, 25 & 26 Vict., c. 25.
An act for extending the Rathmines and Rathgar township so as to include therein the townlands of Cherry Orchard in the parish of Saint Nicholas, of Argos, Harold's Cross, Mount Jerome, Rathland East and Rathland West, in the parish of Saint Catherine, all in the barony of Upper Cross and county of Dublin 1866, 29 & 30 Vict., c. 12.
An act for the improvement of the township and district of Dalkey in the barony of Rathdown and county of Dublin 1867, 30 & 31 Vict. c. 134.
An act for the formation and improvement of Clontarf township, comprising the districts of Clontarf, Dollymount and Ballybough in the barony of Coolock and county of Dublin 32 & 33 Vict., c. 85, 1869.

An act for the improvement of Kilmainham in the barony of Upper Cross and county of Dublin 1868, 31 & 32 Vict. c. 110.

Rathmines & Pembroke main drainage act 1877, 40 & 41 Vict. c. 82.

Dublin port and docks bridge act 1876, 39 & 40 Vict. c. 85

Rathmines & Pembroke main drainage act 1877, 40 & 41 Vict., c. 82

An act for extending the Rathmines and Rathgar township, so as to include therein the adjoining townland of Milltown, in the county of Dublin; for the establishment of a fire brigade; and for other purposes 1880 (Milltown extension act), 43 & 44 Vict., c. 108.

An act for the formation and improvement of Drumcondra, Clonliffe and Glasnevin, in the barony of Coolock and county of Dublin; and for other purposes 1878, 41 & 42 Vict. c. 157.

An act to enable the Rathmines and Rathgar improvement commissioners to improve the water supply of the Rathmines and Rathgar township; and for other purposes, 1880, 43 &44 Vict., c. 138.

An act to amend and define the borrowing powers of the Rathmines and Rathgar improvement commissioners to enable the commissioners. to borrow an additional sum of money and for other purposes, local and personal acts 1892, 55 & 56 Vict., c. 18.

An act to extend the city of Dublin and for other purposes 1900, 63 & 64 Vict. c. 264.

Government reports and inquiries

Local government board of Ireland: annual reports 1875–1901.

Royal commission to inquire into municipal corporations (Ireland), pt. 1, H.C. 1835 (23) xxvii, p. 260.

Royal commission to inquire into local government and taxation of towns in Ireland, report and mins. of evidence and supplement, pt 3, Newry, Dublin, Dalkey, Kingstown etc., H.C. 1877 (1787) xl.

Report of the select committee on local government and taxation of cities and towns in Ireland, H.C. 1878 (262) xvi.

Report of the commissioners on local government and taxation of cities and towns in Ireland (special report by W.P. O'Brien), H.C 1878 (1965) xxiii.

Report of the royal commissioners appointed to enquire into the sewerage and drainage of the city of Dublin, H.C., 1880 (18), xxx

Report of royal commission to inquire into boundaries and municipal areas of cities and towns in Ireland, pt. 1, mins of evidence: Dublin, Rathmines, Pembroke, Kilmainham, Drumcondra, Clontarf and also Kingstown, Blackrock and Dalkey (Exham commission) H.C. 1880 (2725) xxx.

Report of royal commission to inquire into boundaries and municipal areas of cities and towns in Ireland, pt. 2, report: Dublin, Rathmines, Pembroke, Kilmainham, Drumcondra, Clontarf, Kingstown, Blackrock and Dalkey (Exham commission) H.C., 1881 (2827), l.

Report of royal commission to inquire into boundaries and municipal areas of cities and towns in Ireland, pt.3, report and evidence, with appendices, relating to towns under the towns improvement act (Ireland) 1854; towns under 9 Geo. 4 c. 82, and town of Carrigfergus; towns under special acts of parliament, and towwns incorporated therewith; towns under the municipal corporation (Ireland) act 1840 (except Cork and Belfast, and special acts relating to the same towns (Exham commission) H.C. 1881 (3089) l.

Report of commission of inquiry on greater Dublin 1926, R. 32 [I.F.S]

Report of the department of local government and public health, 1930–31.

Report of the commissioners on technical education, 1926–27.

Parliamentary debates
Hansard's parliamentary debates, 4th. series.
Dáil Éireann parliamentary debates official report 1930, xxxiii–xxxvi.

IV. OTHER PRINTED WORKS

a. Contemporary pamphlets and books
Anon, *Boundaries or bankruptcy* (n.d. *c.*1900, Dublin).
Anon, *To the electors of Blackrock*, Blackrock republican election committee, NLI, ILB, 300, p. 11 (item 44).
A Ratepayer, *Blackrock township: is it fair?* (Dublin, 1863).
Birmingham, Charles Leo, *Handbook of Irish sanitary law* (Dublin, 1905).
Bye–laws made by the urban sanitary authority of the urban sanitary district consisting of the Rathmines and Rathgar township in pursuance of the public health (Ireland) act 1878 (Dublin, 1881).
Clifford, Frederick, *A history of private bill legislation* (London, 1885–7, 2 vols.).
Coall's Kingstown guide, 1905 (Kingstown, 1905).
Dawson, Charles *Greater Dublin; extension of municipal boundaries, paper read to the Statistical and Social Inquiry Society of Ireland, 1 Feb., 1899* (Dublin, 1899).
Drury, Thomas Chalmers, *Handbook of Irish municipal acts: a compendium of municipal acts in force in borough towns and townships throughout Ireland* (Dublin, 1886).
Dublin Electrical Lighting Syndicate Limited, memorandum and articles of association (Dublin, 1899).
Joyce, Weston St. John, *The neighbourhood of Dublin* (Dublin, 1921).
Muldoon, John & McSweeny, George, *A guide to Irish local government* (Dublin, 1898).
Oldham, Charles Hubert, *Memorandum of reasons for including modern Irish in the curriculum of the Rathmines School of Commerce … written for the information of Sir Horace Plunkett* (Dublin, 1905).
Spencer, Frederick Herbert, *Municipal origins: an account of English private bill legislation relating to local government, 1740–1835, with a chapter on private bill proceedings* (London, 1911).
Thom's directory (Dublin, 1840–1930).
Webb, Sidney James & Webb, Beatrice, *Statutory authorities for special purposes: English local government from the revolution to the municipal corporations act* (London, 1922).

b. Contemporary articles in journals
Hancock, W.N., 'Arrangements for putting out fires in Dublin city and the townships of Drumcondra, Clontarf, Kilmainham, Pembroke, Rathmines, Blackrock and Kingstown' in *Journal of Statisical & Social Inquiry Society of Ireland*, viii (Aug. 1882), pp. 381–5.
Leask, H. Norman, 'The destruction of towns' refuse and some of the principles involved in the construction of refuse destructors', in *Institution of Civil Engineers of Ireland: Transactions*, xxx (1904), pp. 63–92.
Walsh, Richard W., 'On wind power and the high level water supply to Dalkey', in *Institution of Civil Engineers of Ireland: Transactions*, xix (1889), pp. 1–19.

c. Contemporary periodicals and newspapers
Dublin Builder 1859–1867.
Freeman's Journal 1847–1924.

Irish Builder 1867–1930.

Irish Times 1847–1930.

Rathmines Free Press 1895–1907 Nov. 1922–May 1924.

Rathmines News & Dublin Lantern 1895–1907.

South Dublin Chronicle 1925–29; continued as *Dublin Chronicle* 1929–30. *The Warder* 1821–80.

SECONDARY SOURCES

I. BIBLIOGRAPHIES

Martin G.H. & McIntyre Sylvia, *A bibliography of British and Irish municipal history* (Leicester, 1972).

II. BOOKS

Aalen, F.H.A., *The Iveagh Trust: the first hundred years, 1890–1990* (Dublin, 1990).

Aalen, F.H.A. & Kevin Whelan (eds.), *Dublin: from prehistory to present* (Dublin, 1992).

Akenson, Donald H., *The Irish education experiment; the national system of education in the nineteenth century* (London, 1970).

Atkinson, Norman, *Irish education; a history of educational institutions* (Dublin, 1969).

Ball, Francis Elrington, *A history of County Dublin; second part* (Dublin, 1903).

Bannon, Michael J., *A hundred years of Irish planning, vol. 1, The emergence of Irish planning, 1880–1920* (Dublin, 1985).

Bennett, Douglas, *Encyclopaedia of Dublin* (Dublin, 1991).

Best, Geoffrey, *Mid-Victorian Britain, 1851–75* (London, 1971).

Boyle, Lawrence, *Equalisation and the future of local government finance* (Edinburgh & London), 1966.

Brady, Joseph & Anngret Simms (eds.), *Dublin through space and time, c.900–1900* (Dublin, 2001).

Briggs, Asa, *Public opinion and public health in the age of Chadwick* (London, 1946).

— *Victorian cities* (London, 1968).

Burke, Helen, *The people and the poor law in nineteenth century Ireland* (Littlehampton, 1987).

— *The Royal Hospital Donnybrook: a heritage of caring, 1745–1993* (Dublin, 1993).

Burnett, John, *A social history of housing, second edition* (London, 1986). Burton, N.J., *Letter from Harold's Cross, 1850* (reprint Blackrock, 1979).

Butel, P. & L.M. Cullen (eds.), *Cities and merchants: French and Irish perspectives on urban development, 1500–1900* (Dublin, 1986).

Cannadine, David (ed.), *Patricians, power and politics in nineteenth century towns* (Leicester, 1982).

Cannadine, David and David Reed (eds.), *Exploring the urban past: essays in urban history by J.H. Dyos* (Cambridge, 1982).

Carter, Harold, *An introduction to urban historical geography* (London, 1983).

Castelyn, Mary, *A history of literacy and libraries in Ireland – the long traced pedigree* (Aldershot, 1984).

Chadwick, George Fletcher, *The park and the town* (London, 1966).

Clark, Peter & Raymond Gillespie (eds.), *Two capitals: London and Dublin, 1500–1800* (Oxford, 2001).

Clarke, Harold, *Georgian Dublin* (Norwich, 1972).

Clarke, Howard B. (ed.), *Irish cities* (Cork, 1995).

Cosgrave, Dillon, *North Dublin city and its environs* (Dublin, n.d.)

Cosgrove, Art (ed.), *Dublin through the ages* (Dublin, 1988).

Cooke, Jim, Brian Siggins, Jim Boland & Brian Touhy, *The old township of Pembroke, 1863–1930* (Dublin, 1993).

Craig, Maurice, *Dublin, 1660–1860* (Dublin, 1969).

Crawford, John, *St Catherine's parish, Dublin, 1840–1900: portrait of a Church of Ireland community* (Dublin, 1996).

Crossman, Virginia, *Local government in nineteenth-century Ireland* (Belfast, 1994).

Cullen, L.M., *Princes and pirates: the Dublin Chamber of Commerce, 1783–1983* (Dublin, 1983).

Curtis, L.P. Jr., *Coercion and conciliation in Ireland, 1880–92* (Princeton, 1963).

Daly, Mary E., *Dublin, the deposed capital* (Cork, 1984).

— *The buffer state* (Dublin, 1997).

Daly, Mary E., Mona Hearn & Peter Pearson, *Dublin's Victorian houses* (Dublin, 1998).

Dickson, David, *The gorgeous mask: Dublin, 1700–1850* (Dublin, 1987).

Dyos, H.J. & Wolf, *The Victorian city; images and reality* (2 vols., London, 1973).

Farmar, Tony, *Ordinary lives: three generations of Irish middle-class experience, 1907, 1932, 1963* (Dublin, 1991).

Fitzpatrick, David, *Politics and Irish life, 1913–22: provincial experience of war and revolution* (Dublin, 1977).

Fraser, Derek, *Urban politics in Victorian England* (London, 1976).

Fraser, Murray, *John Bull's other homes: state housing and British policy in Ireland, 1883–1922* (Liverpool, 1996).

Gailey, Andrew, *Ireland and the death of kindness: the experience of constructive unionism, 1890–1905* (Cork, 1987).

Garvin, Tom, *1922, the birth of Irish democracy* (Dublin, 1996).

Gilligan, H.A., *A history of the port of Dublin* (Dublin, 1988).

Gledhill, David, *Gas lighting* (Risborough, 1999).

Grimes, Brendan, *The Irish Carnegie libraries: a catalogue and architectural history* (Dublin, 1998).

Haden, Christopher W. & Catherine O'Malley, *The demesne of old Rathmines; an historical survey of Upper Rathmines, Dartry & Milltown* (Dublin, 1988).

Halliday, Stephen, *The great stink of London: Sir Joseph Bazalgatte and the cleansing of the Victorian metropolis* (Stroud, 1999).

Harkness, David & Mary O'Dowd, *The town in Ireland: historical studies xiii* (Belfast, 1981).

Hennock, E.P., *Fit and proper persons: ideal and reality in nineteenth-century urban government* (London, 1973).

Harvey, John, *Dublin: a study in environment* (London, 1949).

Hearn, Mona, *Below stairs; domestic service remembered in Dublin and beyond, 1880–1922* (Dublin, 1993).

Hill, Jacqueline, *From patriots to unionists: Dublin civic politics and Irish protestant patriotism, 1660–1840* (Oxford, 1997).

Hoppen, K. Theodore, *Ireland since 1800; conflict and conformity* (London & New York, 1989).

— *Elections, politics and society in Ireland, 1832–1835* (Oxford, 1984).

Johnson, Stephen, *Johnson's atlas and gazetteer of the railways of Ireland* (Leicester, 1997).

Kellett, J.R., *The impact of railways on Victorian cities* (London, 1969).

Kelly, Deirdre, *Four roads to Dublin, the history of Ranelagh, Rathmines & Leeson street* (Dublin, 1995).

Kennedy, Tom (ed.), *Victorian Dublin* (Dublin, 1980).

Kenny, Colm, *Kilmainham; the history of a settlement older than Dublin* (Dublin, 1995).

Kilroy, James, *Irish trams* (Dublin, 1996).

Lee, J.J., *Ireland 1912–1985: politics & society* (Cambridge, 1989).

— *The modernisation of Irish society, 1848–1918* (Dublin, 1973).

Lincoln, Colm, *Dublin as a work of art* (Dublin, 1992).

Lipman, V. D., *Local government areas, 1834–1945* (Oxford, 1949).

Lyons, F.S.L., *Ireland since the famine* (London, 1971).

Lyons, J.B., *St Michael's hospital, Dún Laoghaire, 1876–1976* (Dalkey, no date).

Mac Giolla Phádraig, Brian, *History of Terenure* (Dublin, 1954).

McDermott, Matthew J., *Dublin's architectural development, 1800–1925* (Dublin, 1988).

McDowell, R.B., *The Irish administration, 1801–1914* (London, 1964).

Mac Lochlainn, Alf, & André Sheehy-Skeffington, *Writers, raconteurs and notable feminists* (Dublin, 1993).

MacManus, Francis (ed.), *The years of the great test, 1926–39* (Cork, 1967).

McManus, Ruth, *Dublin, 1910–1940: shaping the city and suburbs* (Dublin, 2002).

Maguire, W.A., *Belfast* (Keele, 1993).

Mitchell, Arthur, *Revolutionary government in Ireland: Dáil Éireann, 1919–22* (Dublin, 1995).

Moriarty, Christopher, *Down the Dodder* (Dublin, 1991).

Morris, R.J., & Richard Rodger, *The Victorian city; a reader in British urban history, 1820–1914* (London, 1993).

Macardle, Dorothy, *The Irish republic* (4th ed., Dublin, 1951).

Manning, Maurice & Moore McDowell, *Electricity supply in Ireland: the history of the ESB* (Dublin, 1985).

Murphy, Dónal A., *Blazing tar barrels and standing orders: north Tipperary's first county and district councils, 1899–1902* (Nenagh, 1999).

Nolan, William & Anngret Simms (eds.), *Irish towns; a guide to sources* (Dublin, 1998).

O'Brien, J.V., *'Dear dirty Dublin': a city in distress, 1899–1916* (Berkeley, 1982)

O'Donnell, E.E., *The annals of Dublin: fair city* (Dublin, 1987).

O'Farrell, Pádraig, *Who's who in the Irish war of independence and civil war* (Dublin, 1997).

Ó Gráda, Cormac, *Black forty-seven and beyond* (Princeton, 1999).

Ó hÓgartaigh, Margaret, *Dr Kathleen Lynn and maternal medicine in Ireland* (Dublin, n.d. but 2000).

Olson, Donald, J, *The growth of Victorian London* (2nd edition, London, 1979), p. 18).

Open university (no author), *Urban development: the system of control* (Milton Keynes, 1973).

O'Sullivan, Charles J., *The gasmakers; historical perspectives on the Irish gas industry* (Dublin, 1987).

Osborough, W.N., *Law and the emergence of modern Dublin* (Dublin, 1996).

Owen, David, *The government of Victorian London, 1855–87* (London, 1982).

Pearson, Peter, *Dún Laoghaire/Kingstown* (Dublin, 1981).

Prunty, Jacinta, *Dublin slums, 1800–1925: a study in urban geography* (Dublin, 1998).

Rees, Russell, *Ireland, 1905–25: vol 1: text and historiography* (Newtownards, 1998).

Robins, Joseph, *Custom house people* (Dublin, 1993).

Smyth, William J. & Kevin Whelan (eds.), *Common ground, essays on the historical geography of Ireland presented to T. Jones Hughes* (Cork 1988).

Somerville-Large, Peter, *Dublin* (London, 1979).

Stone, Lawrence, *The family, sex and marriage in England, 1500–1800* (London, 1977).

Thompson, F.L.M. (ed.), *The rise of suburbia* (Leicester, 1982).

Vaughan. W.E. (ed.), *A new history of Ireland, vol. vi, Ireland under the union II* (Dublin, 1996).

Ward, Margaret, *Hanna Sheehy-Skeffington, a life* (Cork, 1997).

Webb, Sidney James & Beatrice Webb, *The development of English local government, 1689–1839* (London, 1963).

Whitehead, Trevor, *Dublin fire fighters* (Dublin, 1970).

Williams, Jeremy, *A companion guide to Victorian architecture in Ireland, 1837–1921* (Dublin, 1994).

Young, Ken & Patricia L. Garside, *Metropolitan London: politics and urban change, 1837–1981* (London, 1982).

III. ARTICLES IN BOOKS & JOURNALS

Byrne, Kieran R., 'Approaches to technical education in nineteenth century Ireland' in *Technical education: essays dedicated to Michael Clune* (no place, no date, *c.*1987), pp. 17–19.

Clark, Mary, 'The municipal archives of Dublin', in *Irish Archives Bulletin* ii, 1981, pp. 12–17.

Cullen, Louis M., 'The growth of Dublin, 1600–1900: character and heritage', in F.H.A. Aalen & Kevin Whelan (eds.) *Dublin: from prehistory to present* (Dublin 1992), pp. 254–67.

Dickson, David, 'Second city syndrome: reflections on three Irish cases' in S.J. Connolly (ed.), *Kingdoms united? Great Britain and Ireland since 1500: integraton and diversity* (Dublin, 1999).

Dockrell, John H., 'Blackrock: town hall and baths–some reflections' in *Blackrock Society: Proceedings 1993–4* (Blackrock 1994), pp. 18–33.

Donnelly, Brian, 'An overview of the development of local government in Ireland' in *Irish Archives* iii, no. 2 (new series), Autumn, 1996, pp. 3–20.

Fagan, Patrick, 'The population of Dublin in the eighteenth century with particular reference to the proportions of protestants and catholics' in *Eighteenth-Century Ireland*, vi (1991), pp. 121–56.

Finlayson, G.B., 'The politics of municipal reform' in *English Historical Review* lxxxi, 1966, pp. 673–92.

Fraser, Derek, 'Politics and the Victorian city' in *Urban history yearbook*, 1979, pp. 32–45.

Hassan, J.A., 'The growth and impact of the British water industry in the nienteenth century' in *Economic History Review*, xxxviii (1985), pp. 531–47.

Hill, J.R., 'Artisans, sectarianism and politics in Dublin, 1798–1848' in *Saothar* vii (1981), pp. 12–27.

Hills, Philip, 'Studying the middle class in nineteenth-century Britain' in *Urban history yearbook* 1987, pp. 22–50.

Horner, Arnold, 'The Dublin region, 1880–1982: an overview on its development and planning' in Michael J. Bannon (ed.), *The emergence of Irish planning, 1880–1920* (Dublin, 1995), pp. 36–51.

Horton, C.G., 'Working-class housing companies in Dublin (1870–1939) and their records' in *Irish Archives Bulletin* ii (1981), pp. 26–32.

Kellett, J.R., 'municipal socialism, enterprise and trading in the Victorian city' in *Urban history yearbook* 1978, pp. 36–45.

Kelly, P., 'Drumcondra, Clonliffe and Glasnevin township in James Kelly & U. MacGearailt (eds), *Dublin and Dubliners: essays on the history and literature of Dublin city* (Dublin, 1990), pp. 36–51.

Maguire, Martin, 'A socio–economic analysis of the Dublin protestant working class, 1870–1926' in *Irish Economic and Social History* xx (1993), pp. 35–61.

Martin, J.H., 'The social geography of mid-nineteenth century Dublin' in William J. Smyth & Kevin Whelan (eds.), *Common ground, essays on the historical geography of Ireland presented to T. Jones Hughes* (Cork 1988), pp. 173–88.

Meghen, P.J., 'The administrative work of the grand jury' in *Administration* vi, no. 3 (1958–9), pp. 247–64.

Prunty, Jacinta, 'From city slums to city sprawl: Dublin from 1800 to the present', in Howard B. Clarke (ed.), *Irish Cities* (Cork & Dublin 1995), pp. 109–22.

Thompson, F.L.M. 'The rise of suburbia', in R.J. Morris & Richard Rodger (eds.), *The Victorian city, a reader in British urban history, 1820–1914* (London, 1993), pp. 149–80.

Trainor, Richard, 'Urban elites in Victorian Britain' in *Urban history yearbook* 1985, pp. 1–15.

IV. UNPUBLISHED THESES & PAPERS

Devlin, Felicity, 'Brightening the countryside – the library service in rural Ireland, 1902–35' (PhD thesis, NUI, Maynooth, 1990).

Harkin, P. 'Electricity supply in Dublin 1880–1930' (ESB Library, Dublin).

Hill, Jacqueline, 'The role of Dublin in the Irish national movement, 1840–48' (PhD thesis, University of Leeds, 1973).

Lavin, Anne, 'Leinster Square (with Prince Arthur Terrace, Rathmines, Dublin: an early suburban speculative terraced housing development, 1830–52' (thesis for the degree of master of urban and building conservation, UCD, 1995).

Roundtree, Susan, 'Mountpleasant Square' (thesis for degree of master of urban and building construction, UCD, 1991).

Index